SCALING

ALTRUISM

SCALING

ALTRUISM

A PROVEN PATHWAY
FOR ACCELERATING NONPROFIT
GROWTH AND IMPACT

DONALD SUMMERS

WILEY

For general information on our other products and services or for technical support, please contact our Customer Care Department within the United States at (800) 762-2974, outside the United States at (317) 572-3993 or fax (317) 572-4002.

Wiley also publishes its books in a variety of electronic formats. Some content that appears in print may not be available in electronic formats. For more information about Wiley products, visit our web site at **www.wiley.com**.

Library of Congress Cataloging-in-Publication Data is Available:

ISBN 9781394223459 (Cloth)
ISBN 9781394223466 (ePub)
ISBN 9781394223473 (ePDF)

Cover Design and Image: Wiley

SKY10064713_011224

To Laina, Isabella, and Thomas Lee

Contents

Preface

I grew up very suspicious of businesses. Like so many nonprofit types I would come to admire and support later in life, I abhorred what the big, bad companies were doing to people and the planet, and I spent my time immersed in literature and art. After brief stints as a teacher, I landed in an educational leadership program at graduate school that required classes in management and accounting. I walked into them dreading the content, but after the first class I was smitten. It was fascinating stuff. *This is how the world works,* I thought: *What if we could use these tools for good?*

On graduation, I was able to marry my newfound love for business practice with my altruistic impulses in my next job as a nonprofit fundraiser. Thanks to the power of the business methodology I learned, within three years of graduation, I designed and executed two multimillion-dollar nonprofit fundraising efforts, one at an independent school and another at a large residential community serving adults with cognitive impairments. Another five years overseeing yet another multimillion-dollar fundraising acceleration for the language and literature division at a large research university cemented my belief in the power of business tools for social good. My doctoral research around social sector entrepreneurship indicated how few nonprofits took advantage of the power of basic business tools: financial projections, key performance indicators, and dashboards—the same instruments used to catalyze my success in raising money and accomplishing goals.

It was like discovering a new world of opportunity. But I was simultaneously suspicious and incredulous. Surely I couldn't be the first person to realize the full power of marrying business processes with altruism. Yet there it was: a great gap in the literature.

After almost 10 years of fundraising, I sought new challenges and landed a gig as a CEO of a small charitable foundation, working for a board full of scientists who had all retired wealthy when their companies were acquired. They set up an environmental philanthropy to take an "innovative, systems approach" to environmental challenges. It started out great. After years of hustling for the charitable dollar, I finally landed on the money side. I thought I would be in philanthropy forever.

I lasted about six months. It quickly became clear that the nonprofit grant seekers needed a *lot* more help than the small sums we were doling out could provide. The grant applications described nonprofit programs with exciting, world-changing potential, but the applications often lacked clear goals, sound strategy, clear performance indicators, and a means of sustainable financing. If their missions were summiting mountains, they proposed some courageous and promising new routes up difficult peaks, but their equipment list wasn't much longer than shorts and sandals.

It struck me: *This is a waste of time. These are good people with great ideas who need a lot more than little sums of money doled out after endless hours of grant selection meetings. They need deep guidance on how to structure and scale their programs, many of which appear to have real potential.*

I excitedly pitched my board about how we could use the business tool kit I had been using successfully for years, the same one that had made them all wealthy. To my surprise and disappointment, they were uninterested. As I would later realize, they weren't in it for the impact, despite all the talk of "systems change." It was all just theater. They had made a great deal of money and were following a well-traveled path of setting up a foundation because they needed something to do. They also clearly enjoyed the image and prestige of philanthropy and, frankly, the power trip of deciding who gets money. I wanted to dig in deep with each grantee, unpack the underlying business and organizational constraints, help them fill in the blanks on their program and financial modeling, and then go raise capital. Asking this board to engage in that level of work was like asking retirees on a cruise ship to crack open their accounting ledgers. Interacting with other philanthropies and attending philanthropic conferences, I saw more of the same: the appearance of investing in social impact but little substance—and only a fraction of the necessary capital.

Philanthropy as practiced like this was clearly not for me, so I left and pitched my services as a consultant to two of the grantees. They paid me a couple grand a month to write their business plans and guide them through funding and execution. Just like I had done with my previous organizations, I catalyzed multimillion-dollar growth and delivered social impact that improved the lives of many people around the world, but now I was doing it for more than one organization at a time.

Success was intoxicating. I worked hard on developing the methodology with moderate levels of success. And then I had the Treehouse engagement, where we landed a moonshot in the world of social services, creating a level of social and financial acceleration that few thought possible. It was yet another confirmation that I was on to something truly important: the secret to unlocking the untapped potential of the entire social sector.

It made me overconfident. I was not dissimilar to insufferable tech founders who sold their first start-up to Google and thought they could do no wrong. Fortunately, my hubris didn't last. I got ejected from client engagements like a virus because I didn't listen enough or spend enough time aligning decision makers. I also chose clients without being careful about first making sure they possessed growth mindsets and risk tolerance.

For about five years, I produced decent results and even some very strong outcomes, but I also kept failing for reasons that were only clear in hindsight. I would paddle along in my little methodological rowboat, smash into a hidden rock, and sink right to the bottom. Finally, after multiple sinkings and hole-patchings, my arrogance gave way to humility. And the humility made me a much better consultant, better able to empathize with my clients. Failure motivated me to improve the process further. It took years of trial and error, the help of supportive colleagues, and the input of hundreds of nonprofit executives and board members, but I eventually landed on a comprehensive, step-by-step process that consistently accelerated nonprofit growth and impact.

Today, I have calluses on my butt from all the swift kicks I've earned. When I observe in the pages that follow that getting things right takes time and lots of perseverance, I speak from experience. The Japanese call this continuous pursuit of improvement *kaizen*. (I don't have any tattoos, but were I to get one, I'd get a kaizen tattoo.)

The boutique consulting firm I founded to deliver this methodology, Altruist Partners, works today with a small set of ambitious clients around the United States and internationally. We have also set up a nonprofit arm, the Altruist Nonprofit Accelerator, to teach the methodology to cohorts of nonprofits, and this book serves as the backbone of the curriculum. Early deployments in nonprofits around the world are encouraging.

In the spirit of kaizen, the methodology presented in this book isn't perfect. It was improved by the review of so many wise and generous experts, and I am confident I will get much more constructive feedback now that it is all in book form. I will be very happy if this book attracts critique and advice from those who don't agree or have better ideas.

Delivering an effective management system that enables widespread improvements across the nonprofit sector is my dream. If this work represents only marginal progress or serves to support superior efforts elsewhere, I will still die happy. Therefore, please forgive gaps or mistakes. Write to me at **donald@altruistpartners.com** with your ideas. I'll do my best to read and respond to everyone.

And before we begin: While this book may offer any number of blunt critiques about the current state of nonprofit performance, I am truly grateful to live in a world with so many fellow altruists. Thank you for all the good work you currently do to help make the world a better place.

Acknowledgments

For three decades I've had the privilege of working alongside smart, generous, and talented people: nonprofit professionals, directors, executives, volunteers, funders, government and corporate partners, and advisors, academics, and advocates of every stripe. Their wisdom fueled this book, and their work to make the world a better place continues to inspire and motivate me.

To the dozens of social impact leaders who provided their feedback on early drafts, thank you. Particular thanks go to Janis Avery, the incredible founder and now retired CEO of Treehouse, for her courage, skill, and partnership and for her generosity in allowing me to share the story of our work together; to Akhtar Badshah, for his guidance and support; to my colleagues at Altruist Partners, especially Ian Hanna, who helped develop and refine this methodology; to BrightRay Publishing, who helped me produce my first draft; to my publication team at Wiley, including Brian Neill and Deborah Schindlar, who have supported the book's final maturation and development; and to my editor, Angela Morrison, whose sensibility, judgment, and advice have improved this text immensely.

Introduction

Every man must decide whether he will walk in the light of creative altruism or in the darkness of destructive selfishness.

—Martin Luther King, Jr.

In 2013, Ken Stern, the former CEO of National Public Radio, wrote *With Charity for All*,[1] an exhaustively researched, evidence-filled, and incredibly shocking account of how the nonprofit sector is pervasively dysfunctional and filled with organizations that routinely fail to deliver on promises. Whether one agrees with Stern or not, it is clear that the nonprofit sector has at least an image problem: according to the Better Business Bureau, only one in five Americans trust charities to use their donations well.[2] This mistrust may be a driver behind a collapse in charitable donations from small donors, individuals who make up 98% of all nonprofit supporters. In 2021, fewer than half of American households gave to charity, down from two-thirds only a decade ago.[3]

Like the rest of society, the charitable organization landscape in the United States and elsewhere is a story of *haves* and *have-nots*. While giving collapses among the middle class, wealthy donors and foundations continue to donate record levels to universities, hospitals, and other large nonprofits, a class of organizations that share the same tax status as their smaller brethren but are run with the sophistication of major corporations. Approximately 95% of the nonprofit sector

---

[1] Ken Stern, *With Charity for All: Why Charities Are Failing and a Better Way to Give* (New York: Doubleday, 2013).
[2] "**Give.org** Donor Trust Report 2022: Five-Year Review of Trust and Giving Attitudes," **Give.org**, BBB Wise Giving Alliance, **https://www.give.org/docs/default-source/donor-trust-library/donor_trust_report_2022_five_year_review.pdf**.
[3] "Fundraising and the Generosity Crisis," *The Chronicle of Philanthropy*, **https://www.philanthropy.com/package/fundraising-and-the-generosity-crisis**.

is composed of small organizations with average budgets of about $500,000. The remaining 5%, or about 35,000 total, are often large and complex organizations that have far more in common with Microsoft than a neighborhood soup kitchen. Many operate on a global scale and are our most significant engines for social good. For example, American nonprofit universities, both public and private, consistently lead the world in educational rankings. While US higher education's success is by no means assured, they are, comparatively speaking, mostly well-managed organizations that deliver beneficial products and services at scale.

For example, the University of Washington in Seattle raises approximately $2 million in private gifts and grants every day of the year. It earns billions more in contracts with corporations and the federal government. Pay and benefits are excellent, the facilities are world-class, and the university churns out more patents than almost every other research university in the world. Steve Olswang, the university's former vice provost, explains: "Make no mistake. The University of Washington is a business. We are in the business of education and discovery."

On the other end of the spectrum is the 95% of nonprofits, over 1 million organizations in total, that survive on budgets under $5 million a year, with the average budget holding steady at just under $500,000.[4] These include homeless service agencies, community clinics, tutoring programs, arts and theater groups, animal shelters, conservation organizations, human rights advocacy groups, environmental sustainability advocates, and tens of thousands of other types that form so much of our social fabric. Most are financially threadbare, chasing grants, begging for dollars, and existing in or near the zone of insolvency.[5] Few can meet more than a small fraction of the demand.

Figure I.1 illustrates that large nonprofits such as hospitals and universities, while few in number, command over 85% of the resources in the nonprofit sector.

---

[4]Urban Institute, "Nonprofit Sector in Brief," 2019, **https://nccs.urban.org/ publication/nonprofit-sector-brief-2019#size.**
[5]See Ron Mattocks, *The Zone of Insolvency: How Nonprofits Avoid Hidden Liabilities and Build Financial Strength* (New York: John Wiley & Sons, 2008).

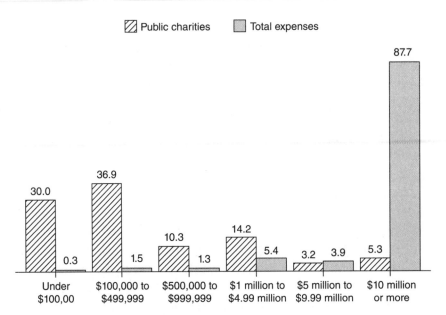

FIGURE I.1   Nonprofit Sector Resource Distribution.[6]

There is relatively little examination of why so many nonprofits remain so small. William Foster and Gail Fine's article in the *Stanford Social Innovation Review*, "How Nonprofits Get Really Big,"[7] provides one explanation, citing a complex financial landscape where few nonprofits have figured out how to grow their revenue. The authors target what they see as the major challenge: sustainable, scalable revenue. Leslie Crutchfield and Heather McLeod Grant's *Forces for Good*[8] examines a set of high-growth nonprofits and attempts to distill from them a set of effective organizational scaling strategies. While an important set of strategies emerges, the book leaves it to executives to figure out how to formulate, finance, and execute them.

[6]Urban Institute, National Center for Charitable Statistics, Core Files (Public Charities, 2016).
[7]William Foster and Gail Fine, "How Nonprofits Get Really Big," *Stanford Social Innovation Review*, **https://ssir.org/articles/entry/how_nonprofits_get_really_big**.
[8]Leslie R. Crutchfield and Heather McLeod Grant, *Forces for Good: The Six Practices of High-Impact Nonprofits* (New York: John Wiley & Sons, 2007).

For-profit business executives wishing to expand their organizations and generate more profit enjoy access to a massive education, support, and funding ecosystem. Around the world there are hundreds of MBA programs, incubators, and accelerators; scores of mentoring programs and entrepreneurial support and coaching organizations; an extensive literature filled with well-established guidance; a large, expert service industry of consultants and business solutions providers; and an enormous and sophisticated capital marketplace filled with banks and investors of every stripe.

By contrast, nonprofit executives seeking to expand their organizations to deliver greater levels of social impact face a much more austere landscape, one with significant gaps in entrepreneurial, management, and financial training; a comparatively sparse and incomplete literature; relatively thin supporting organizational and professional service resources; and a fractured funding marketplace with a complex, confusing variety of gifts, grants, contracts, and loans sourced from millions of individuals, tens of thousands of corporations and foundations, and hundreds of local, state, and federal agencies.

While running any type of organization is difficult, life as a nonprofit executive is therefore particularly hard, and there is little debate that, for all but the largest, most wealthy nonprofits such as hospitals and universities, social impact suffers as a result. Staff are underpaid and overworked; technology is often underutilized; and underinvestment in program measurement, evaluation, and improvement is common. For example, the National Council of Nonprofits reports that 40% of nonprofits surveyed in 2023 responded that they have a quarter to a third of their staff positions currently unfilled, with most citing low salary as the barrier. Nearly 50% have a service waiting list more than a month long.[9]

When noted management expert Michael Porter observed, "Philanthropy is decades behind business in applying rigorous thinking to the use of money,"[10] he identified one part of a much bigger

---

[9]National Council of Nonprofits, "Nonprofit Workforce Shortages: A Crisis That Affects Everyone," 2023, **https://www.councilofnonprofits.org/reports/ nonprofit-workforce-shortages-crisis-affects-everyone**.

[10]"The Business of Giving," Special Report, *The Economist*, February 2, 2006, **https:// www.economist.com/special-report/2006/02/25/the-business-of-giving**.

truth: the nonprofit sector is decades behind the for-profit sector in the rigorous use of organizational growth methodology. There remains a significant gap in the literature for current and future nonprofit leaders around how to lead a small to midsized nonprofit to continuous annual growth and impact.

This book is aimed at this gap. It presents a comprehensive nonprofit management system, the *Altruist Impact and Growth Methodology,* proven to catalyze significant acceleration in organizational revenue, performance, and impact for nonprofits under $50 million in annual revenue, or over 95% of nonprofits operating today.[11] It is based on two decades of continuous development, a comprehensive review of the for- and nonprofit management literature, and thousands of hours of partnership with hundreds of nonprofit executives and board members in diverse fields. It attempts to provide a comprehensive acceleration platform in a step-by-step sequence for accelerating organizational impact and growth, one that organizations can follow independently and at their own pace. It is aimed at the following audiences: nonprofit executives and board members, public and private funders, and graduate students.

- *Nonprofit executives and board members* find a practice guide with tools, templates, and implementation guidance to catalyze sustained annual growth in organizational revenue and social impact.
- *Public and private funders* discover new insights for assessing nonprofit performance and supporting scalable social impact efforts.
- *Graduate students* learn effective social change leadership practices not found in graduate programs.

There are seven phases to this methodology. Each chapter focuses on a particular phase, breaking it down into a series of organizational development steps called *practices*. In total there are about fifty practices across all seven phases. After the purpose and benefit of each practice is explored, implementation steps follow, supplemented with exercises, templates, case studies, anecdotes, metrics, protocols, and

---

[11]"The Nonprofit Sector in Brief," Urban Institute, 2019, **https://nccs.urban.org/ publication/nonprofit-sector-brief-2019#size**.

talking points to help changemakers embed the practices into their day-to-day operations. Technical terms are italicized on first use, explained in context, and defined in the glossary.

In addition, a supplementary tool kit of templates, examples, and additional resources is available on this book's companion website, **www.altruistaccelerator.org**. Users will find electronic versions of all the tools and templates provided here such as business plan templates, organizational charts, financial projection, and scorecard models. There is also a selection of real-world examples we have developed with our clients, ones they have used to successfully grow their revenue and impact.

If applied with fidelity and discipline, the methodology promises to catalyze accelerated organizational performance and resolve barriers keeping smaller nonprofits understaffed, underpaid, and trapped in survival mode. However, implementation is difficult. Nothing about growing any type of organization is easy, as any entrepreneur will attest. The journey requires courage, optimism, grit, discipline, urgency, and focus.

The gravity and magnitude of today's social challenges create enormous opportunities for nonprofits to harness the power of entrepreneurial growth practices so they can solve social problems, not just tinker at the margins. Success creates profound advances in social, economic, human, and ecosystem benefits, as the success stories below indicate.

Success Stories

In over one hundred deployments with nonprofits of all types, the methodology outlined in this book has catalyzed a sustained median annual impact and revenue growth rate of 25%. Examples of the methodology's track record with a diverse set of organizations include the following:

- A human services organization set a goal to double high school graduation rates for foster children in a major metropolitan area. It tried for two years but didn't move the needle on graduation rates.

Then it applied this system and, over the next five years, tripled its annual revenue, increased the numbers of foster youth it served from hundreds to thousands, and doubled foster youth graduation rates, increasing them from a baseline of 40% to 80% for the entire population in a major metropolitan area. The organization's program model is now being followed by educational support programs and government agencies nationally.

- An educational philanthropy delivering financial support for low-income public school students wanted to break through annual service levels that were flat year over year. After deploying this system, student service levels accelerated from 25,000 to over 350,000. The organization is today on track to providing educational needs such as calculators, student activity cards, extracurricular supplies, glasses, and other assistance for every low-income student in the state.

- A global reforestation organization grew its annual budget from $19 million to over $40 million and achieved a 10x program acceleration to reach the milestone of 1 billion trees planted, creating the world's largest and most efficient ecosystem rehabilitation program and establishing a model for hundreds of similar efforts.

- In 18 months, a three-person, $250,000 environmental advocacy organization running a small corporate responsibility pledge transformed into a $1.5 million, 20-person operation that delivered a global ISO 14001 certification in partnership with hundreds of companies such as Samsung, LG, Bloomberg, and Capital One. The certification catalyzed sweeping changes in a global $20 billion recycling industry and significant reductions in hazardous waste dumping around the world. Public awareness milestones included an award-winning *60 Minutes* episode viewed by over 30 million and front-page articles on major media outlets worldwide.

- A social services agency providing food, shelter, clothing, and educational support for low-income families had been a pillar of its community for over a century, but it continuously struggled to make its annual budget and served only a fraction of its potential service audience. By year 2 of deploying the impact and growth methodology, the organization had doubled its budget and service audience and tripled them by year 3. It is now co-locating its programs in the region's public schools and is on track to serve every vulnerable child and family in its service area.

- An educational start-up launched a clinical training program to teach doctors how to talk to families about terminal illness, growing the work from an NIH-funded grant project into a multimillion-dollar organization reaching tens of thousands of clinicians nationwide.

- A social services start-up enabled individuals to make direct charitable gifts to early-stage, scalable agricultural innovations in developing countries through a rigorous process borrowed from finance.

- The nation's oldest PBS affiliate pivoted from consistent 5% annual losses in membership to a 10% increase and a concomitant 20% increase in charitable gift revenue in the first year of deployment. A similarly positioned NPR station increased its previously static advertising revenue 30%, improved charitable gift receipts 20%, and secured the first million-dollar charitable gift in the organization's history.

- A global NGO operating on multiple continents within a complex membership network of governments, major corporations, other industry bodies, and peer NGOs currently is executing the first planning and execution cycle and has already reversed a years-long decline in membership numbers, generating their first $1.5 million in unrestricted funding.

These examples, all from the past 15 years, follow the example created by a small number of exceptionally high-growth, high-performing nonprofit start-ups from the 1980s and 1990s that achieved national scale. Well-known examples include Teach for America (**teachforamerica.org**), City Year (**cityyear.org**), and KIPP (**kipp .org**). Another less well known example is EducationSuperHighway (**educationsuperhighway.org**), founded in 2012, which has successfully closed the digital divide for millions of low-income households. An early-stage organization that appears poised to achieve similar levels of success is Housing Connector (**housingconnector.com**), a start-up founded in 2019 in Seattle. They use logistics and technology expertise to house thousands of homeless individuals at an efficiency and effectiveness that leads the social sector, all after only a few years of operation. Asked to explain why he is so successful when so many organizations in the homelessness space struggle to deliver more than marginal impact, founder and CEO Shkëlqim Kelmendi says, "We are strong at execution."[12]

What does that mean, to be strong at execution? While the vast majority of small to midsize nonprofits struggle for survival and deliver marginal levels of impact, what explains the breakout success of these positive outliers? A small set of funders recognize that these success stories share a common playbook that can be installed in other organizations. While practiced by a diverse array of organizations and funders, the set of organizational acceleration principles and practices behind all of these success stories is remarkably similar. As the opening line of *Anna Karenina* states, "All happy families are alike. All unhappy families are unhappy in their own way." The methodology of this book attempts to document our success playbook and provide a step-by-step process any nonprofit can execute.

Whom This Book Is For

As their organizations struggle to perform, some nonprofit leaders adopt a defensive posture that asserts outsiders are illegitimate critics: "We are a unique organizational type with unique challenges. People who tell us we need to run like a business have no idea." This is the *myth of uniqueness*, an assertion that a nonprofit is a fundamentally different type of organization, a mysterious animal that outsiders, especially business types, cannot appreciate or understand. Normal organizational practices don't apply; business planning is impossible because the nonprofit is subject to forces beyond its control; clear outcome measures are impossible because social impact is too hard to measure; growth is impossible because nonprofits have no control over external funding from foundations, government agencies, and

---

[12]Personal interview, September 12, 2022.

capricious rich people. This myth is used as a smokescreen to confuse business-minded board members and deflect funders seeking transparency and accountability.

This book is written for nonprofit executives, board members, and social impact leaders who believe that success and scale for nonprofits are possible and that the myth of uniqueness is just that—a myth.

While additional attitudes and mindsets are detailed in Chapter 2, "Align," we've found the following six characteristics of leaders that are fundamental to the pursuit and application of the practices outlined in this book:

- *Courage:* They are unafraid of change and take measured risks, understanding that failure is an ingredient of success and that there is more merit in setting a scary goal and failing than never stepping outside comfort zones.
- *Optimism:* They believe in their work and have or are working to get evidence that they have a best-of-field solution that can solve a major problem.
- *Grit:* They understand that growth and performance are hard. They expect to fail repeatedly and demonstrate resilience when they do.
- *Urgency:* Talk is not a deliverable. Meetings are short. They are biased toward action and experiment, not analysis and reflection. There are no social impact tourists on the board or staff.
- *Discipline:* They plan the work and then work the plan. They are analytical and base decisions on data. They don't chase shiny objects and invent a program to fit a grant opportunity.
- *Focus:* They pick a goal, define strategies, and then stay focused on the small handful of metrics that measure the execution of the strategy. They don't create new programs on a whim. They don't boil the ocean. They are trying to solve one specific, hard problem.

Successful entrepreneurs are far from the brilliant know-it-alls portrayed in popular media. They are most often remarkably humble and have achieved success from tenacity and continuous learning and improving. Jim Collins describes these successful entrepreneurs as *Level 5 leaders:*

> *Level 5 leaders display a powerful mixture of personal humility and indomitable will. They're incredibly ambitious, but their ambition is first and foremost for the cause, for the organization and its purpose, not themselves. While Level 5 leaders can come in many personality packages, they are often self-effacing, quiet, reserved, and even shy.*[13]

CEOs must not be the only ones with these attitudes. They can only succeed with close partnership and support from boards; a high-performing executive team; and well-curated, compensated, and supported staff and volunteers.

How to Use This Book

Fifth graders learn about *PEMDAS*, which is the *order of operations* for completing a math equation. Do the work in parentheses first, then exponents, then multiplication and division, and finally addition and subtraction. Accurate calculation alone isn't enough. Do correct calculations in the wrong order and you get the wrong answer.

Apply the tools in this book out of sequence and you dramatically reduce the odds of success. We've realized over decades of practice that accelerating social impact demands that an order of operations be carefully followed. Untold tens of thousands of nonprofit leaders are mired in a game of whac-a-mole, all because they aren't aware of the correct order of operations. They hire fundraising experts but don't realize that their fundraising will struggle to gain traction until they can show funders their strategy is informed by evidence. Huge sums and many hours are spent building teams, only to have efforts eroded by turnover because of low pay. So many efforts spent on board development and activation are wasted because of information overload,

---

[13]Jim Collins, "Level 5 Leadership," **https://www.jimcollins.com/concepts/level-five-leadership.html**.

poor recruitment practices, and weak job descriptions. Pick a typical nonprofit and there is usually any number of critical enabling factors that aren't recognized as foundational.

The practices presented in this book are therefore clearly sequenced. The success of each depends on organization-wide embrace of the one before it. While adopting each practice will yield benefits even if pursued by themselves, maximum increases in organizational performance and acceleration demand that all get executed in sequence, a process that we've found takes between 6 and 18 months, depending on organizational size and complexity.

In addition to the sequence, there is the underlying robustness of this methodology. It demands a level of commitment and determination not dissimilar to what is required to successfully complete a diet and exercise program. Following the practices in this book will likely require significant behavioral change for everyone in an organization. This will need a champion, or even better, a team of champions (ideally the board of directors) to evangelize these practices and then hold themselves and everyone else accountable to ensure they are adopted and followed. So prepare for change and hard work. The likelihood of accelerated impact and growth is maximized if leaders adopt the practices in the sequence provided here and *refuse to quit.*

One final note before we launch into the methodology: there are about two dozen templates illustrated throughout the book, for business plans, scorecards, database protocols, and the like. Since these would be difficult and time consuming to reproduce from scratch, we offer downloadable versions on the book's companion website (**www .altruistaccelerator.org**), along with helpful other resources and real-world examples of business plans, fundraising strategy, scorecards, and more. Each chapter ends with a list of these resources.

CHAPTER 1

Assess

You must never confuse faith that you will prevail in the end—which you can never afford to lose—with the discipline to confront the most brutal facts of your current reality, whatever they might be.

—Jim Collins, "The Stockdale Paradox," from *Good to Great*

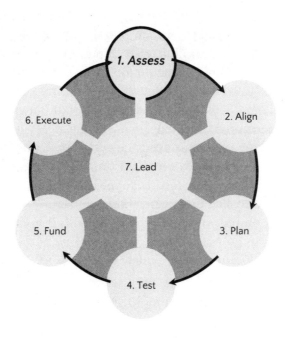

LEARNING OBJECTIVES

By the end of this chapter, you will be able to:

- Understand the value performance benchmarking can bring to your organization;
- Identify the organizational assets and capabilities essential for driving organizational growth and impact; and
- Apply performance benchmarks to your organization to establish a shared understanding among board members and executives around organizational strengths and opportunities for development.

Experienced leaders understand that, before beginning any organizational change effort, there should be a shared understanding of what needs changing—and what doesn't. Therefore, they commonly engage in performance benchmarking exercises, such as SWOT analysis. First developed in the 1960s, traditional SWOT analysis (strengths, weaknesses, opportunities, and threats)[1] is a simple, self-explanatory model that examines where the organization is and is not functioning well, what the growth potential is, and what risks might be encountered. While it is probably better than jumping into planning without any preparation at all, as practiced in the nonprofit sector, we have found that it and other nonprofit benchmarking exercises tend to result in long documents filled with abstract findings, leaving leaders in doubt about what planning should address. So we built our own nonprofit performance benchmarking model to provide leaders with a punch list of what is working and what needs development. After hundreds of deployments and thousands of incremental improvements, we landed on a set of critical success factors that appear to be the most influential when it comes to scaling up organizational impact.

Let's linger on the word *scale* for a moment. It is the crux of this entire book. I can go out in my backyard and plant a tree and make a marginal contribution to the climate crisis. But we need to reforest

---

[1]Mike Morrison, "History of the SWOT Analysis," RapidBI, **https://www.rapidbi.com/history-of-the-swot-analysis/**.

about 10,000 hectares (24,700 acres) a day for an entire decade to recover the forests lost since the industrial revolution. The point is this: marginal impact is relatively easy. Scaling up that impact is very difficult—but urgently needed.

Therefore, to guide discussion among boards and executive teams on the most critical issues to organizational growth, essential *must-haves* for delivering increasing levels of impact year after year, consult the list below, consider the key questions, and discuss them openly among board members and staff. After this performance benchmarking chapter, subsequent chapters offer a step-by-step planning and execution model that will help leaders leverage strengths and fill identified gaps.

Before delivering our assessment framework, examine the first of many short Treehouse Case Studies presented throughout this book to land the practices within a specific organizational context. Treehouse's performance assessment was informed by many of the same benchmarks outlined in this chapter.

Case Study: Treehouse's Performance Assessment

In 2012, Treehouse was already one of Seattle's most admired human service agencies. For most of its 25-year history, it provided clothing, resources, and educational support for children and youth in foster care to help them succeed in school. After more than two decades of hard work, leadership realized that providing material assistance did little to change what remained troubling educational outcomes for the population, with only 40% of youth in foster care graduating from high school, less than half the rate of their peers. Treehouse's CEO, Janis Avery, was eager to shift from doing good to moving the needle. "No more congratulating ourselves for trying. We have to do better. Their lives depend on it."

So, after extensive deliberation, Treehouse set an audacious goal: deliver interventions to ensure all foster children in King County would graduate at the same rate as their peers with a plan for their future by 2017. This would mean expanding services to hundreds of schools over 26 separate districts and doubling graduation rates for over one thousand youth from 40% to 80%. As no documented interventions had improved graduation rates more than a few percentage points, and the organization was presently only delivering educational support to approximately 200 youth in a few districts, the goal's ambition was met with skepticism and even criticism, even from executives in other nonprofits. It seemed too unrealistic when so many other richly funded efforts run by respected leaders had failed.

The organization brought in top subject matter experts to design pilot programs to deliver interventions that would demonstrably improve graduation rates. However, after two years of efforts and hundreds of thousands of dollars in expenditures, the skeptics appeared to be right. "We put in a huge effort and spent tons of money, and then when we measured our results, we found out that we barely made a dent in the problem. We moved our desired outcomes a maybe percentage point or two," Janis observed.

While many leaders would have written off the effort as a worthwhile experiment and moved on, Janis doubled down. Following the organizational value statements, which included the phrase "fierce optimism," Janis hired another consulting team[2] to assess the organization's performance and deliver a set of recommendations to the executive team and board for improving the graduation program outcomes. A summary of the organizational performance assessment findings are as follows:

- Treehouse's programs to provide enrichment (scholarships, summer camps) and material support (clothing, school supplies) to foster youth are efficient and effective and are reaching all the children in greater Seattle and many across the state.
- The organization had made smart investments in financial and development software, adequate technology, and positioned its staff to be mobile and connected via a pro bono consulting relationship with Deloitte.
- Treehouse's educational programs—the focus of its audacious goal— were beset with performance barriers:
  - Greater than 30% annual turnover in educational program staff and unit-level leadership.
  - Lack of program clarity and confusing, ambiguous program terminology: services were siloed among a statewide "advocacy" program, King County educational services, and an "enrichment" program that all required lengthy explanation to separate conceptually.

---

[2]The author was the project lead on this consulting engagement.

- ○ Inconsistent program structure and service delivery: each educational program staff person delivered any number of assorted supports and services to children in their care, all without measurable outcomes.
- ○ The program's "logic model" had consumed many months of staff and consulting time, but there was still no clear view of the program strategy or architecture across multiple, competing, lengthy plans in draft form.
- ○ Over 20 pages of data was collected at the service delivery point for each youth, but there was no process for analysis; long debates about how to use data to inform the program model produced no clear next steps.
- Over time, the organization had accumulated multiple management layers: the org chart articulated eight distinct management hierarchies among a total of 75 staff.
- The organization relied on a high-cost, low-return transactional event fundraising model. Talented and hard-working marketing and fundraising staff achieved remarkable success with the many fundraising events it ran and had built up considerable awareness. However, donor attrition rates exceeded 50%, and fundraising cost-per-dollar was increasing, already nearly $0.37 (best practice is < $0.15).
- The donor database listed over 750 individuals who had given over $1,000 to the organization but who had not received personal relationship-building contacts for subsequent gifts. Such a large population of potential major donors who had never been personally approached for a larger investment was a clear indication of the substantial opportunity cost of their current fundraising model.
- The board was supportive and engaged, but significant numbers expressed concern at the lack of clarity around the educational program model and governance reporting.

The board, CEO, and staff had fostered and maintained a healthy culture of open, clinical inquiry. Every member of the team, from directors to front-line staff, were well aware of these challenges, discussing them openly and continuously. They had no trouble confronting brutal reality: they did it every day. None of the problems were due to organizational incompetence or lack of effort. They were all interpreted as the expected challenges of a maturing organization attempting innovative programming. However, leadership and staff knew these performance deficits needed to be fixed, and fast, were they to make any progress toward their hugely audacious goal. Everyone knew the clock was ticking.

While it can be uncomfortable talking about performance challenges, take solace in the fact that even a high-performing, well-regarded nonprofit such as Treehouse faces significant performance challenges. Every organization has challenges, but instead of sweeping them under the rug and projecting a false sense that everything is fine, Janis's attitude was this: "We can't win if we hide the ball." Her courageous transparency was supported by strong leaders on the board such as John Enslein, a pioneering employee at Microsoft who helped build the first version of Windows; attorneys Alexandra Brookshire and Juli Farris; and Tim Davis, a principal at Deloitte. Like Janis and others, their grit and resilience, paired with diverse executive skills and judgment, propelled the organization to confront and solve these assessment findings. A capable executive team had already led the organization through the work of setting a challenging, time-bound goal, creating the focus and urgency necessary to address the underlying barriers.

The findings made it clear that Treehouse needed to radically shift both its service and revenue model to achieve its ambitious goals. We are optimistic that all nonprofit leaders can gain valuable insights by measuring their performance against this same set of benchmarks. We start you on this path with the first practice of this book.

Assess Practice 1.1: Benchmark against Robust Performance Standards

We categorize the important drivers of nonprofit performance into four buckets: people, programs, plans and policies, and finance, with each bucket containing about a dozen elements. Each appears below along with questions for group discussion.

This assessment is rigorous. When our firm delivers it, we give scores for each driver, aggregate all the scores, and come up with a number from 1 to 100, where meeting all the standards is a 100 and none of them a zero. We find most organizations fall between 25 and 50. Deficits should not result in finger-pointing or embarrassment but rather as immediate opportunities to make improvements that together will enable the organization to deliver more positive social impact. It can inform a critical self-assessment by boards, executive teams, and staff. The most common outcome is the realization by leaders that they have a lot of work to do. This is what management expert Jim Collins calls "confronting brutal reality."

Make no mistake: this is *not* a comprehensive list of everything an organization must do to succeed. It attempts to capture and assess only the *most important* performance capabilities, leaving out other still important pieces to keep the process relatively concise, focused, and manageable. Performance benchmarks are categorized under the four managerial domains—people, programs, plans and policy, and finance—to make it easier to grasp the total picture. Each domain contains subcategories with three additional variables that are measured by collecting data. For example, in the "people" domain, we consider five subcategories: staff, board, CEO, volunteers, and fundraisers. For each of these subcategories, we score what we consider are the three most important performance variables. For example, in the "people" category and "staff" sub-category, we measure (1) staff pay, (2) turnover, and (3) morale. Each variable is scored based on our data collection, and a resulting measure is produced that gives a subcategory level score. These subcategory scores are then aggregated to deliver an organization-wide performance index that ranges from 0 to 100, with 0 meaning the organization has zero capability and 100 meaning everything is running perfectly.

While we won't go into details around the scoring methodology here, I mention it because, having run this benchmarking exercise well over one hundred times, we've found most nonprofits score between 25 and 50 out of a total possible score of 100, with occasional negative outliers in the teens and positive outliers in 60s and 70s. These results over the past 15 years allow us to conclude that (1) most nonprofits are missing critical drivers of growth and impact and (2) while doing it right is hard, the most tenacious organizations can fill most of their gaps in a period of 9–12 months to catalyze a substantial acceleration of organizational revenue, development, and social impact. We often rescore our clients annually to establish trend data, and when organizations stay focused on these measures and improve their performance around each, organizational growth and impact follow.

Below are our scoring categories, subcategories, and component variables. Instead of providing the complex scoring rubric, which would be onerous to reproduce, for each performance benchmark, we provide instead questions for discussion among boards and executive staff to enable productive, focused discussions around what is most important to consider on the organization's journey to make the world a better place.

Finally, note that this performance assessment contains a number of technical terms and acronyms such as SROI and KPIs. The notes in each category provide a brief explanation, and subsequent chapters explore these very important concepts in careful detail. Consult the Glossary for other terms that may be unfamiliar.

People

Staff (Pay, Turnover, Morale)

- **Pay:** Competitive pay and benefits are a must for organizations that want to build high-performing teams. Martyrdom should never be a feature of your human resources strategy. We measure compensation benchmarks compared to similarly sized *for-profit* organizations and measure the gaps in percentage terms.

  Question: Can you compete for top talent with private sector companies? (Do you believe that this is an impossibility, or are you curious about how it might be accomplished?)

- **Turnover:** High rates of turnover may indicate dysfunctional leadership. However, in restructurings, there is often intentional turnover, so consider a running average of the previous three years. Barring unique circumstances, we look for turnover from 5% to 10% at most. Numbers higher than this should be intentional.

  Question: Do you measure your annual turnover and diagnose the reasons behind unnaturally high staff departures?

(continued)

- **Morale:** We ask all board, staff, and volunteers to anonymously state their level of agreement with the statement "I feel empowered to do my best, most meaningful work."

    Question: Do you collect anonymous measures of staff morale and solicit staff input on how to improve it?

Board (Network, Expertise, Priority)

- **Network:** Access to philanthropic, earned, and borrowed capital is a critical characteristic of nonprofit board members. While boards of course need diversity, which we consider in other elements of our analysis, we hone in on access to capital and look for board members who have one-degree access to individuals with at least $1 million in liquid assets (accredited investors).

    Question: How many of your board members have one-degree connections with wealthy individuals? (And what is their willingness to engage these relationships in your mission?)

- **Expertise:** We look for board members with successful senior executive or C-suite experience at enterprises with over $50 million in annual revenue. We've found that too many nonprofits are governed only by subject matter experts and grassroots-level volunteers, so they lack essential management wisdom and expertise in law, accounting, finance, human resources, operations, and information technology, which are critical for robust oversight and governance.

    Question: How many of your board members have held profit-and-loss responsibility and led successful efforts to grow companies? Do you possess deep expertise in each of the expertise domains critical for robust board functioning?

- **Priority:** We measure board member engagement on how much they agree with the following statement: "This organization is my #1 cause, and I give it top priority for my charitable dollars, time, and leadership energy and skills." Social impact tourists have no place on nonprofit boards. The number one job of the board chair is to ensure that each member is 100% committed.

(continued)

Question: Are your board members deeply committed to your mission, or are they more like tourists who present the appearance, but not the substance, of engagement?

CEO (Growth, Speed, Ambition)

- **Growth:** The first thing we look for in CEOs is growth experience. Have they led growing organizations before? Few have. Most non-profit CEOs are subject matter experts in the programming of the nonprofit and have precious few business or leadership skills and experience. If the CEO does not have a consistent track record of catalyzing growth levels of 20% or more, coaching, mentorships, additional executives who possess this experience, and a strong entrepreneurial presence on the board are all essential.

  Question: Who in the C-suite has successfully grown companies before? (Also: How many MBAs are on the executive team or board?)

- **Speed:** The CEO must be biased toward action and experiment, not analysis and reflection. A frozen, risk-averse CEO crushes growth potential. Documents, survey data, and interviews are used to ascertain the CEO's speed and agility. For example, we look for strong agreement with the statement "Our organization makes decisions quickly, and then we take prompt actions. We are not tentative, and we avoid debating the same things over and over."

  Question: Where do you and other organization members fall on the action versus reflection and discussion spectrum?

- **Ambition:** The final component of our CEO analysis is a "Go big or go home" attitude. Effective CEOs set ambitious goals and continually measure the organization's progress against them.

  Question: Does your organization measure its progress around solving the entirety of a social problem, or are you tentatively nibbling around the edges?

Fundraisers (Efficiency, Experience, Breadth)

- **Efficiency:** Most nonprofits are stuck in survival mode because of high-cost, low-return fundraising strategies. The profitability

(continued)

of the fundraising effort is assessed by measuring the marginal expense of each dollar raised, or cost per dollar (CPD). Mature fundraising enterprises raising large investments will typically have a CPD in the range from $0.10 to $0.15. Efforts that lean on transaction-based strategies such as fundraising events or grants will have far higher costs (and lower returns): we frequently encounter CPDs above $0.50. (Sometimes a higher CPD is necessary in the early stages of any revenue generation because of the need to make leading investments in new staff and infrastructure.) To find out where you fall, measure the *full cost* of your fundraising effort: all the staff time, salaries, operational costs, etc. Compare that to how much money is generated and compute the quotient to arrive at a CPD.

Question: Unless you are in the first 12 to 18 months of an expertly designed effort to build in the teams and infrastructure to launch a major new revenue initiative, are you spending more than 25 cents to raise a dollar?

- **Experience:** As soon as a fundraiser establishes a successful track record, their market value skyrockets. The most successful and experienced are quite well compensated, with salaries that start well above $250,000 and climb rapidly after that. However high their salary, they raise it many times over for the wealthy organizations that can afford them. Mindful that fundraising talent quickly migrates up the pay scale, wise leaders at smaller organizations don't hesitate to budget generously for these positions. That extra $50,000 needed to attract and retain top talent is one of the smartest investments smaller organizations can make (if they know how to judge between the players and the pretenders, which can be hard).

   Question: Are you paying for top performers to produce world-class results, or are you stuck with marginally effective (or totally ineffective) staff who can produce the appearance of fundraising activity but not the results?

- **Breadth:** The best fundraisers do a lot more than write grants. They understand the full range of gift, grant, contract, earned, and

(continued)

invested revenue from individuals, foundations, corporations, and government agencies. They may have experience with impact capital, for-profit subsidiaries, licensing campaigns, and other more exotic ventures. Top professionals are really gifted entrepreneurs, interested more in impact than equity.

Question: Are you missing critical expertise needed to drive your growth? Who in your organization is aware of the many ways nonprofits can be financed? How do you know you are not overlooking five or six ways you could be making millions of dollars every year?

Volunteers (Recruitment, Support, Turnover)

- **Recruitment:** Nonprofits enjoy access to what appears to be a free labor pool: volunteers. But working with volunteers brings big hidden costs, and because these costs aren't recognized or funded, volunteers are frequently mismanaged and under-resourced, and they often do more harm than good. When identifying volunteer needs, you must establish a documented volunteer recruitment strategy with metrics, goals for volunteer roles, numbers of volunteers needed, and the volunteer program's rationale.

  Question: Do you fully leverage the power of a free volunteer labor pool and identify the optimal numbers needed?

- **Support:** Volunteers can be so important and valuable and are so often under-appreciated and supported. Two additional variables beyond recruitment should be considered: support and turnover. Look for the following: (1) a limit on the number of volunteers supported per staff; (2) ongoing solicitation of performance feedback from volunteers; and (3) clear volunteer roles, expectations, and performance accountability.

  Question: Do you adequately support and supervise volunteers after they join, to the point of off-boarding volunteers who are not effective or committed?

- **Turnover:** Most volunteers leave an organization in frustration because they are not well supported, and turnover is one possible indicator of their satisfaction. Volunteer turnover rates should correlate with that of all staff.

  Question: Do you measure and seek to improve volunteer loyalty?

Programs

Quality (SROI, KPIs, Perception)

- **Social return on investment (SROI):** Businesses produce profit. If they are successful, they spend money to produce even more money, generating a return on investment (ROI). ROI is the most fundamental measure of business performance. The same principle applies to nonprofits, but instead of producing dollars, the nonprofit produces social impact, which the organization can express along economic, social, environmental, and even moral dimensions. Look for robust measurement of the exact financial *and* nonfinancial benefits the organization delivers.

  Question: Can you identify each of the following dimensions of SROI? (1) Who or what you change; (2) both economic and non-economic benefits of these changes; (3) independent, third-party evidence of these changes; (4) the resulting changes in context of the size of the entire problem you are addressing; and (5) other influences on this problem.

- **Key performance indicators (KPIs):** Look for the existence of organization-wide KPIs, a set of no more than five to seven aggregate metrics that measure the effectiveness of the organization's strategy and its overall progress toward its goals.

  Question: Do you measure your impact with a small set of performance measures that evaluate (1) program quality, (2) program scale, and (3) efficiency, and are these measures collected and reported biweekly by staff, monthly by leadership, and quarterly by the board?

- **Perception:** Internal confidence in the mission is a critical and often hidden driver of performance, so you should measure your organization's agreement with the statement "We can prove we are the best at what we do. We are the leader in our field."

  Question: Do all your staff and board members believe that you are the highest-quality provider of your type of program and service?

Scale (Goal, Milestones, Resources)

- **Goal:** High-performing organizations set ambitious, clear, accountable goals and continuously measure their progress toward them.

(continued)

Question: Do you (1) set a goal toward solving a problem, (2) measure progress against complete success, (3) take risks to accelerate growth, and (4) act with urgency?

- **Milestones:** Effective organizations identify and track incremental progress points, called *milestones*, toward their overall goal, breaking up the larger goal into component pieces that together establish a sequential road map to success.

  Question: Have you identified a small set of the most important progress points along your journey toward your goal, and do you track your progress toward them at least quarterly, reporting progress to all internal and external audiences?

- **Resources:** Too many nonprofits believe they are supposed to work in an environment starved of resources, a cultural assumption that prizes martyrdom and frugality over the adequate funding and support of staff, infrastructure, and operations.

  Question: Ask your board and staff if they agree with the following statement: "We have all the talent and resources we need to do our best work and fulfill our full promise and potential."

Leverage (Network, Value, Learning)

- **Network:** Nonprofits capture "leverage" when they achieve a multiplier effect on their impact or growth efforts through partnerships. Most nonprofits say they have lots of partners, but few are anything more than informal relationships. The best organizations establish true working partnerships with an explicit, documented, mutually beneficial exchange of value.

  Question: Do we continuously scan for possible nonprofit, corporate, and government partners that can extend, deepen, or complement our work?

- **Value:** Too many so-called partnerships in the nonprofit space are really little more than informal working relationships or casual exchanges of information. Effective partnerships are robust and measurable and transparently deliver added value.

  Question: (1) Do we have clear, compelling data that shows the clear value of our partnerships; (2) do we evaluate partnerships for efficiency and effectiveness, seeking to continually improve; and

(continued)

(3) do we transparently, accurately report on the performance and value-add of our partnerships to internal and external audiences?

- **Learning:** Capturing feedback from external stakeholders in a transparent, accountable way during planning formulation is a powerful way to leverage the best minds in a network. Doing this brings the concomitant benefit of cultivation for future investment and stronger relationships. Organizations should measure their process for capturing feedback on draft, high-level plans and initiatives with external audiences before launching them.

  Question: Do you share your program plans and initiatives with stakeholders in your nonprofit, corporate, government, and funder environment to solicit and incorporate their feedback before you launch them?

Plans and Policy

Business Plan (Architecture, Updates, Focus)

- **Architecture:** Look for all the elements that make organizational plans "investment grade"—that is, they would impress the most discerning audiences and serve as the basis not just for program execution but for fundraising, governance, and other key activities. You should seek a clear, emotion-free explanation of what the organization does, how it does it, and how resources are deployed to achieve a specific, ambitious, measurable goal. There are many pieces to a business plan, and they all must be presented in a clear, concise document (no more than 10–15 pages).

  Question: Does your organizational plan explain (1) the problem you are solving, proof you can solve it, and what success looks like; (2) your milestones and key performance indicators; (3) a clearly articulated program strategy; (4) the size of your addressable audience and how you compare to other actors in your space; (5) your financial strategy; (6) a detailed, multiyear staffing and financial projection; (7) organizational risks and how they will be identified and managed; and (8) the talent of the team you have assembled to execute?

(continued)

- **Updates:** Business plans are dynamic documents continuously revised by all managers and leaders to align the organization's work both internally and externally. Business plans should be developed and used according to these guidelines:
  1. The plan is shared with all staff at least annually and feedback is incorporated.
  2. The board provides written feedback and updates annually.
  3. The plan is continuously shared as a draft with funders and partners.
  4. Partner feedback influences the plan.
  5. The CEO manages the live copy and ensures it is kept current to reflect an evolving and improving organization.

     Question: Does our planning process include these elements and characteristics?

- **Focus:** Many nonprofits are caught in a well-meaning attempt to solve more problems than they have resources to support. Leaders often invent new initiatives in pursuit of funding opportunities before they have made adequate progress on existing programs, or they find it hard to say no to an emotionally compelling issue that nonetheless results in mission creep.

     Question: Is our program model a focused investment of our time, energy, and resources on a clearly defined problem, or are we chasing new initiatives and starting new programs without adequately investing in what we are already doing?

Operations (Infrastructure, Alignment, Clarity)

- **Infrastructure:** Because nonprofits often struggle with fundraising, attempt to do too many things, or operate under the cultural assumption they are supposed to suffer in an environment starved of resources, they underinvest in operational infrastructure that is critical to success. Look for the following elements:
  1. Best-practice human resources processes and policies;
  2. A robust technology plan;
  3. Physical plant condition and operations aligned with business goals;

(continued)

4. Data collection that is robust, efficient, and well directed; and

5. Speedy organizational processes and execution.

Question: Do we adequately invest in our organizational infrastructure and resources?

- **Alignment:** Another dimension of trying to do too many things or not having enough focus is the existence of programs and efforts that lack a strategic coherence to each other. Look for "fugitive" or legacy programs that exist because of funding or inertia, not because of their value to advance a focused mission.

    Question: Is there a clear rationale behind every piece of our program and service offering, or are there outdated or misaligned elements that exist because of inertia, funder support, or other non-mission-related reasons?

- **Clarity:** Every volunteer, staff, and board member should know their job clearly and why it contributes to organization-wide success.

    Question: Do we have clear, accountable job descriptions for all staff, board members, volunteers, and partners in our organization, and do we hold people accountable to them?

Social Responsibility (DEI, Sustainability, Integration)

- **Diversity, equity, and Inclusion (DEI):** DEI efforts often produce little more than lip-service and check-the-box exercises. Organizations should measure the following dimensions of a strong, functional DEI stance:

    1. The organization has a comprehensive DEI policy.

    2. Staff and board engage in activities that advance DEI at least quarterly.

    3. The organization has clear, measurable DEI goals and measures progress toward them.

    4. Staff and board composition reflect the diversity of the population being served.

    Question: How does our DEI activity compare to these robust standards?

(continued)

- **Sustainability:** All nonprofits—and every other type of organization—have an ethical duty to improve their environmental sustainability. Doing so drives employee engagement, efficiency, and effectiveness. Like DEI, this management dimension is typically addressed with actions oriented toward appearance, not substance. Organizations should measure the following dimensions of a strong, functional sustainability stance:

  1. The organization has a comprehensive sustainability policy.

  2. Staff and board engage in regularly scheduled activities that advance sustainability.

  3. The organization has clear, measurable sustainability goals and measures progress toward them.

  4. The organization has net zero climate impact. All financial reserves are invested in socially responsible funds and investments.

     Question: Do we invest in sustainability or are we taking it for granted?

Finance

Framework (Controls, Reporting, Clarity)

- **Controls:** Robust financial controls are mission critical for any organization. Your organization should examine the following elements, and **if even one is missing, you should take immediate corrective action**. This is the only aspect of the organizational assessment where you must act immediately.

  1. Has a past audit revealed any concerns? (In accounting-speak, are there any unresolved material weaknesses or significant deficiencies in the most recent management letter?) Is the board treasurer a CPA, or does the organization regularly consult with one to monitor and improve financial controls?

  2. Are there clear documents and robust processes on financial controls with at least two members of the staff executive team conducting oversight?

(continued)

3. Does each board meeting review the most recent balance sheet, statement of operations, budget versus actual, and 12-month, month-over-month cash flow projection?

   Question: Do we conform to these standards? If not, are we prepared to take immediate corrective action?

- **Reporting:** High-performing nonprofits go well beyond pie charts in annual reports and provide the following:
  1. Itemized budget projections are provided to donors and partners.
  2. The balance sheet, budget, and statement of operations are accurate, easy to read, and accessible to anyone who asks.

     Question: Do we possess the capabilities, time, and resources to provide this level of transparency and accountability?

- **Clarity:** Internal financial accountability is important as well. Measure your organizational members' responses to the following statement: "I understand the current financial health of my organization and can get clear, accurate answers to any questions I have about it."

  Question: Do we believe that all staff members and volunteers deserve transparent reporting about the organization's financing?

Health (Cash, Forecast, Transparency)

- **Cash:** Prudent nonprofit leaders ensure they hold at least six months of operating cash in their reserve fund. Any less and the organization risks insolvency.

  Question: If we hold fewer than six months' operating cash in reserve, do we have a plan to get there?

- **Forecast:** The highest-performing nonprofits project their budget—at an itemized level—at least three years into the future to show what growth looks like in financial terms. This makes the budget cycle easier, gives current and prospective donors confidence, and brings multiple other benefits.

  Question: Do we possess the focus, capability, and forward vision to produce a detailed, year-over-year financial projection that goes out at least three years?

(continued)

- **Transparency:** Every staff person should understand the current financial state of the organization. Donors, volunteers, and members of the public should be given accurate, detailed financial statements. The organization should clearly show who gives it money and how they give it.

  Question: Do we go above and beyond when it comes to transparency, or are you obscuring, or even hiding, information about how you make money and spend it?

Revenue (Strategy, Metrics, Awareness)

- **Strategy:** Most nonprofits are stuck in survival mode because of poor fundraising strategy. Look for the following:
  1. Best-practice relationship-based appeals to individuals;
  2. Corporations solicited based on co-branding, sponsorship leverage, and affinity programs;
  3. Foundations solicited for seed funding; production outsourced unless grant revenue exceeds $1 million per year;
  4. Agency funding supported with professional staff;
  5. Full scope of earned revenue activities researched and tested.

  Question: Are we stuck chasing small amounts of money with ineffective, uninformed fundraising strategies because that's all we know how to do, or are we willing and eager to look beyond typical survival strategies to learn higher-ROI approaches?

- **Metrics:** Fundraising strategies are meaningless without continuous and focused measurement. Look for the following fundraising activity:
  1. Relationship activity with donors is tracked by stage and compared to goals.
  2. The number of donor contacts is regularly collected and reported.
  3. A 12-month forecast is tracked and updated monthly.
  4. Clear data collection and reporting on important fundraising performance measures such as annual loyalty, median gift size, number of gifts, largest gift, and others (see Chapter 5: "Fund" for a list of fundraising metrics).

(continued)

> *Question: Do we accurately, robustly measure our fundraising performance using metrics such as these, or are we more "hope, pray, and wait for the end of the year to see how we did"?*
>
> - **Awareness:** Measure board and staff responses to the following statement: "We understand the very best ways to raise money from individuals, foundations, corporations, government agencies, and earned income." Comparing this measure with what you actually see indicates whether or not the organization is confusing its opinion with knowledge.
>
> *Question: Do we have access to the small number of proven nonprofit fundraising experts who have a demonstrated track record of generating millions of dollars in all the revenue domains available to us, or are we confusing confidence in our own opinion with knowledge?*

What to Do about All the Gaps

This assessment methodology sets a high bar, and for good reasons. Only high-performance organizations can deliver the social impact at scale that the world desperately needs. To solve problems, versus nibbling at the edges, courageous nonprofit leaders must first confront the brutal reality of where their organization sits along all these essential dimensions of performance.

The good news is that, while this is a high bar, it is possible to achieve all of these standards. We know because we have helped many organizations do it. It can take months of sustained effort, often up to a year, but we have seen many organizations struggling with chronic performance deficits follow this methodology and transform themselves into high-growth, high-impact enterprises.

The best pathway to addressing performance gaps is to follow the development process outlined in the following chapters. If done with tenacity and fidelity, embedding every practice before proceeding to the next one, organizations will close many, if not most, of the performance gaps surfaced by this assessment.

To support leaders in the pursuit of this intensive course of organizational development, this book is supplemented by additional tools and resources available on the book's companion website, **www .altruistaccelerator.org**. For each chapter, it provides examples, templates, and additional references and guides that are all oriented toward practical execution of the practices presented here. For organizations that would like more support, the accelerator offers a cohort-based program to guide organizations with a 12-week development course. Consider joining one if the book proves useful. Growth and impact are hard, and the journey is made somewhat easier with the wisdom and support of peers.

Additional Resources

Go to **www.altruistaccelerator.org** for samples of organizational assessments from a variety of nonprofits (all anonymized).

CHAPTER 2

Align

It is the long history of humankind (and animal kind, too) that those who learned to collaborate and improvise most effectively have prevailed.

—Charles Darwin

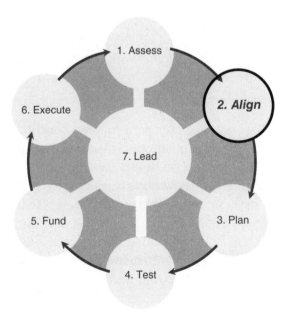

LEARNING OBJECTIVES

By the end of this chapter, you will be able to:

- Identify the attitudes, concepts, and decisions that boards, executive teams, and staff must agree upon *before* attempting to create a plan for organizational growth and impact;
- Recognize how word choice and language can differentiate your organization and identify it as compelling, effective, and entrepreneurial;
- Craft concise, compelling, and actionable mission and vision statements;
- Write a value proposition;
- Derive a *big, hairy, audacious goal* (BHAG) from a vision statement;
- Differentiate between your organization's growth strategy and its impact strategy;
- Identify year 1 initiatives;
- Choose an initial set of key performance indicators to measure the execution of your organization's impact and growth strategy; and
- Create a one-page business framework to provide boards and teams with a clear and concise format for generating consensus.

Leaders who have studied the performance benchmarks in Chapter 1 with their staff and board and given serious consideration to that series of hard, detailed questions have hopefully generated new awareness about their organization's performance gaps and perhaps identified one or more areas that need development. While these benchmarks are presented as a list, the process of closing performance gaps is very different from just ticking through a task list. Performance improvement demands a comprehensive process of planning, testing, finance, and execution that, if followed according to the design presented in this and subsequent chapters, will naturally result in the closure of many, if not most, performance gaps. In other words, don't use the benchmarks as a task list. They are there to raise awareness, not generate a task punch list. Follow the next step presented in this chapter: generating consensus and alignment around a small set of statements, decisions, and measures that will serve as the initial framework for a business plan.

Before we begin, let's explore another type of case study, what we will call *dysfunction junctions,* anonymized snapshots of nonprofit organizations that operate without leaders who are aware of all the necessary elements that support organizational performance and impact. They are presented not to mock or disparage but to illustrate a few of the many fatal organizational problems that occur when leaders are ignorant of important organizational management practices.

Dysfunction Junction

It was 2005, and the City of Portland had just announced a bold effort to end homelessness, calling it a "public emergency" and allocating $10 million to fund the creation of a plan provisionally entitled "Portland's 10-Year Plan to Eradicate Homelessness." To run the effort, the mayor appointed James Square, a recently retired senior partner at one of the city's largest law firms.

Square spent the first 18 months of the citywide effort consulting with various stakeholder groups: nonprofit service providers, business associations, neighborhood groups, hospitals, affordable housing coalitions, corporate leaders, and private philanthropies. At the end of the year, Square released a 247-page document that described the root cause of homelessness as a lack of affordable housing. It proposed the building of 50,000 units of new affordable housing over the next decade.

At a private meeting with Square, I asked him the following question: "Jim, thanks for all your hard work on this document. You have staked out a bold vision to build badly needed affordable housing. I only have one question: The plan doesn't say how we are going to pay for it all. How will we?"

"I don't know," Jim replied. "I'm a lawyer, not a finance guy."

Good planning is critical to success. But organizational planning is a complex space, with a seemingly endless set of confusing approaches, tools, and concepts. Many leaders produce documents with the word *plan* somewhere in the title, but 99% of these documents have significant gaps that leave essential questions and decisions unanswered.

Robust organizational planning is a very specific and specialized discipline. Few organizations possess staff with the capability to produce disciplined, actionable plans, and the professional consulting class that nonprofits can typically afford is perhaps only marginally more capable. As most leaders know, even high-priced consultants are fond of delivering long, complex documents and fancy slide shows that look impressive but end up accomplishing little because there is little thought given to the practical steps of paying for everything and then actually getting started.

Even when organizations know exactly what robust, compelling, and actionable plans must contain, decisions often require generating consensus among various organizational stakeholders that they spend many months—and even years—attempting to bring everyone together. By the time they arrive at a document, the world is a different place. Not only do social impact plans need to be good, but they need to get done quickly and then put into action. This chapter provides a clear path forward that breaks up this difficult challenge into digestible concepts, decisions, and steps. Take things one step at a time. Make sure that decision makers understand the particular item under consideration, exactly what the planning standards and requirements are, and how to articulate and present the decision in a concise, actionable format free of buzzwords and empty slogans.

This chapter breaks up this difficult challenge into digestible concepts, decisions, and steps. It is the first of two planning steps in this methodology. Follow the practices and exercises here to establish a high-level consensus among the board and executive team to produce a business plan framework. This 1-page document is then expanded on in the next chapter to create a more detailed (but still concise, about 10 to 15 pages) business plan that is drafted by the CEO and the executive team. Breaking things up into these two steps makes planning easier and keeps the board closely involved in the big decisions but also keeps them insulated from the more time consuming details, ones that are the responsibility of staff.

The practices in this chapter are challenging. To help organizations learn and embed them, companion one-time exercises are included to help land some of the practice concepts through activity and shared discussion. Remember, a practice represents a set of principles, behaviors, and choices the organization must permanently own and sustain. An exercise is a one-time activity meant to catalyze an understanding of what the practice means. Exercises bring people together around an activity that will hopefully help embed the practice as a permanent organizational capability.

We begin this journey with a warm-up exercise to surface the often unspoken reality that many organizations spend their days working very hard on any number of programs and initiatives, all with great variance in understanding around the overarching organizational goal and how these programs and initiatives are connected to the goal. If key decision makers have different understandings of the organization's goal and means to achieve it—again, a surprisingly common situation—this exercise will identify this barrier and set the stage for resolving it.

Note that, as the align practices presented in this chapter involve building consensus, there are a larger number of exercises than in other chapters. Complete each exercise in a group setting with all appropriate decision makers and stakeholders actively participating. Taking the time to ensure everyone is engaged may make the difference between a successful planning effort and an unsuccessful one.

Align Exercise 2.a: Do We Really Understand Our Goal and Strategy?

At the next board and executive team meetings, hand everyone a single, medium-sized Post-it note and pencil and say, "Let's do a short exercise to see if we share the same understanding of our goal and strategy. Without consulting anyone or anything, just off the top of your head, write down bullet points that capture your best understanding of (1) our goal and (2) our strategy. As this should only take a minute or two, respond immediately. We will put our notes up on the wall and see how our answers line up."

The results should provide immediate insight into the work necessary to foster the deep alignment required for articulating an actionable plan of action. Teams that are aligned will give roughly the same short answers from memory. But getting everyone to recall short, accurate answers isn't easy: we all live in the age of information overload, our attention has been monetized, hundreds of businesses fight for our attention every hour of every day, and decision fatigue and response fatigue are endemic.[1] So people show up and do their jobs on autopilot without truly internalizing the work. Research shows that only 15% of employees know their organization's goals, only 5% understand strategy, 60% of organizations don't link budgets to strategy, and 85% of executive teams spend less than one hour a month discussing how they will achieve their goals.[2] *Disorganization* is a more accurate term for how people work together: if organizations were soccer teams, only half the necessary players would be on the field, with most players wearing headphones, absorbed in their smartphones. Two or three would be arguing about where the goal is and what the score is, with very little in the way of passing and forward progress.

This state of disconnection, disengagement, and distraction is one of the reasons most businesses are mediocre at best and very few nonprofits deliver needed levels of social impact. It's the age-old challenge of trying to get human beings to work together as disciplined teams. And it appears to be getting harder in today's environment of constant distraction and information overload. In this era of limited attention spans, getting people to answer an email is hard enough, so building an effective team executing in alignment around a challenging goal seems daunting indeed. However, there is a way forward: after getting the team to confront brutal reality and commit to doing something about it, leaders can generate focus and alignment one deliberate, careful step at a time, following a sequential, cumulative pathway that ratchets

[1]See Tim Wu's *The Attention Merchants* (New York: Vintage Books, 2017), an important work that explains how our attention spans are constantly under attack.
[2]Franklin Covey, "Discipline 1: Focus on the Wildly Important," Course: The 4 Disciplines of Execution, **https://www.franklincovey.com/the-4-disciplines/discipline-1-wildy-important/**.

the organization's functioning forward bit by bit toward a clear finish line. How can leaders do this? By following the practices below.

While they are rigorous and challenging, organizations can take each practice at their own pace. Transformation doesn't happen all at once. We recommend a process that's borrowed from the world of health care: a *low-dose, high-frequency* approach. Instead of long, boring meetings and expensive, exhausting planning retreats, convene all-hands practice meetings, 30 minutes only, twice every week, to work through each of the practices below. Keep it disciplined: everyone must show up on time, phones down, paying attention and focusing on the task at hand. How do you eat an elephant? One piece at a time.

Align Practice 2.1: Establish a Growth Mindset

Start with honest discussions to see if your organization can develop a *growth mindset*. The following preliminary exercise will uncover leadership's potential to imagine, and then begin, an entrepreneurial journey.

Align Exercise 2.b: What Would We Do with Tons of Money?

"Imagine that we got a call from the Gates Foundation. They said they love our mission and will give us any amount of money we need. All we have to do is tell them what we will spend the money on. Each of us needs to make a list. Please take a few minutes and write down everything you think we need to spend the money on. Anything at all. You have three minutes. Go!"

Most members of an organization are so weighted with the difficulty of just getting by that an invitation to think and dream can be hard to accept and even harder to articulate. Typical answers to this exercise reveal that dreams of growth and success are usually modest: get a new copier; move into a new office; hire those two program staff positions. Rare is the response to establish teams of well-paid staff in offices in every major city, to serve the entire target audience, or to create an endowment that will fund it all in perpetuity.

Responses give insight into the depth of the challenge the organization faces from transitioning from a subsistence to a success mindset. If the hypothetical funding allocations do not go beyond the mundane, explore the responses and discuss openly what they reveal about mindsets, attitudes, and cultural constraints toward growth.

Multiple exercises may be necessary to spur imaginations. The following exercise can be conducted as a follow-up to align exercise 2.b. Delivered together, they can be useful starting points in establishing a growth mindset.

Align Exercise 2.c: Resistance to Growth

Share the following hypothetical case study with your teams and discuss the questions that follow.

A human services agency has been hard at work for 20 years delivering after-school support and services to low-income youth in their city. Their service audience has grown from a few dozen to over 400, and they have compiled positive evidence that programs are beneficial: increased educational achievement and reduced engagement with the justice system. As they enter a new fiscal year, they explore the potential for expanding their service numbers by an incremental amount, depending on how the economy is doing, what they think they can raise from their fundraising events, and what they are told by the government agency staff who fund one of their programs. They are understandably focused on keeping the lights on and helping the kids they are presently serving. The idea of rapid growth has never been discussed.

At the organization's annual retreat, the only time of the year the organization brings teams together to plan programming, a guest speaker, a social impact expert, has caused a stir. Toward the end of the retreat activity, the consultant asked the board and staff members the following question: "How many youth in your service area need your help? How many are you not helping?" One of the program staff familiar with the census figures responded, "There are approximately 10,000 youth from low-income families who live in our current service area."

The consultant replied, "Thank you. Now, if you knew there was a way to grow your funding and scale your services to serve all 10,000 youth in, say, the next five to seven years, would you be willing to explore it?"

There was only a muted response to this question, and several people in the group looked visibly uncomfortable. The retreat discussion moved on to different topics and concluded. Soon afterward, several staff sent angry emails to the CEO: "I'm tired of these so-called experts telling us we aren't doing enough. They have no idea what it's like. We are doing good work already!"

Questions to discuss as a group:

1. *If you are the CEO, how do you respond to those angry emails?*

2. *What would we say to the consultant if this was our retreat and we were asked the same question? How do we react?*

The pathway to defining a clear and concrete vision for ultimate success is a litmus test to determine if an organization is ready for growth. Instead of looking at last year's budget to see what next year's will be, budgets and plans should be based on an ambitious vision. Aspirational growth does not necessarily mean scaling up services to serve the entire world. A vision of success may be to serve everyone in a single neighborhood. After that, the organization can think about two neighborhoods. Pace and ambition will vary, as long as organizational leadership lets stretch goals drive planning. The rule to follow here is ironclad: Let plans determine budgets; do not let incremental budgets constrain plans. This rule applies only if participants have a growth mindset that gives them the freedom to imagine what a fully funded and resourced organization might look like.

Some may respond with defensiveness and even anger to any implication the organization is not doing enough. Fear, risk aversion, the myth of uniqueness, and other constraints can make any discussion of accelerated growth seem not only fanciful but threatening and even personally insulting. If this is the reaction of the CEO or a majority or vocal minority of board members, it is unlikely this methodology will take hold until there is one of two changes: (1) a personal change on behalf of decision makers to set aside mental constraints and follow a growth pathway or (2) a change in leadership altogether. Both the CEO and the board chair must be aligned on a growth mindset, and then they must ensure that the rest of the team shares their view. This is not to suggest the organization plunge headlong into a growth-at-all-costs endeavor: Chapter 4 will outline how the risks of change and growth are articulated and managed, so even the prudent and cautious team members have an important place in the planning process (as long as they don't forestall the possibility of growth at the outset).

Others will react with curiosity and a willingness to explore what aspirational growth looks like. Getting started requires inspiration, optimism, and a leap of faith, and it's up to both the CEO and chair to inspire this big thinking, see it articulated in an actionable plan, and executed with focus and discipline.

Figure 2.1 illustrates the differences between a mindset that is stuck in the past and a growth mindset that is focused on a successful future. Leaders of an organization need to identify anyone on the board or staff who lines up in the stuck column and carefully consider how they influence organizational planning and execution. Leaders and managers with stuck mindsets are often there for any number of personal or historical reasons, and getting them unstuck, while not impossible, often entails a great deal of work. In short, boards of directors must ensure the CEO has a growth mindset, and CEOs need to ensure that all key managers and staff share the same outlook.

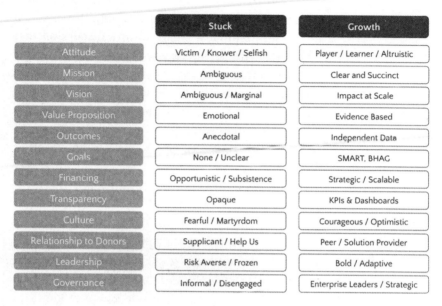

	Stuck	Growth
Attitude	Victim / Knower / Selfish	Player / Learner / Altruistic
Mission	Ambiguous	Clear and Succinct
Vision	Ambiguous / Marginal	Impact at Scale
Value Proposition	Emotional	Evidence Based
Outcomes	Anecdotal	Independent Data
Goals	None / Unclear	SMART, BHAG
Financing	Opportunistic / Subsistence	Strategic / Scalable
Transparency	Opaque	KPIs & Dashboards
Culture	Fearful / Martyrdom	Courageous / Optimistic
Relationship to Donors	Supplicant / Help Us	Peer / Solution Provider
Leadership	Risk Averse / Frozen	Bold / Adaptive
Governance	Informal / Disengaged	Enterprise Leaders / Strategic

FIGURE 2.1   Stuck Versus Growth Mindset.

Align Practice 2.2: Choose Powerful Language

With the criticality of a growth mindset established, it becomes necessary to bring people together around a new set of norms that create and support powerful, high-functioning teams. The first set of norms relates to language and the word choices an organization makes. For starters, recall the disturbing statistic presented at the beginning of the book—only one in five Americans trust charities to use their donations well. If for no other reason besides optics, it is wise to avoid using terms popular with organizations people mistrust. This book's methodology very intentionally introduces terms borrowed from the private sector, ones used less often in the social sector.

Consider the differences between the terms *charity* and *social impact enterprise*. They can both describe a 501(c) corporation, but *charity* evokes a world of soup kitchens and martyrdom for the public good, while *social impact enterprise* (SIE) implies a value-centered organization that uses sophisticated management practices. Even if the latter term is unfamiliar, it invites curiosity and discussion, not rapid stereotyping. The acronym *SIE* is used throughout this book's methodology to refer not only to ambitious nonprofits but also to social enterprises, B-Corps, Public Benefit Corporations, LC3s, and other corporate constructions that prioritize people and planet, not just profit. While they are not tax-exempt and don't typically solicit gifts and grants, most of the practices apply well to these other corporate types.

To explore another example in more depth, consider the most common word in nonprofit fundraising: *gift*. While the term *charitable gift* carries important legal contexts, avoid the term unless legally necessary (such as in a donation acknowledgment letter or endowment contract). *Gift* describes something given without payment, with no expectation of return: a problematic word choice for funds given to a nonprofit, implying the nonprofit deserves the money and will do nothing in return. *Donors* (another problematic term) make a contribution to a charity *expecting* that the donation will be used for a good cause. Indeed, charities loudly proclaim the need they are working on, but then ask for gifts, thereby creating a dynamic in which they take and offer nothing in return. This is the dysfunctional state characterizing too many nonprofits: consuming money with little to show for it—hence the lack of trust among donors and their extraordinarily low rates (below 50%) of ever giving the charity a second gift.

Instead, use the term *charitable investment*, or *investment* for short, to bring the listener into a different, more powerful frame: "We don't seek gifts. We seek investments, not for a financial return, but for a clear and measurable social outcome. We treat our donors not as people who give us gifts but more like stockholders who make an investment in us and expect results." Choosing powerful language differentiates the organization as one thinking about effectiveness and impact and separates it from a space filled with organizations that barely survive, let alone succeed.

More importantly, the terminology shift shown in Figure 2.2 provides new traction points to build teamwork and a supportive culture;

Charity	Social Impact Enterprise
Gift	Charitable Investment
Donor	Charitable Investor
Strategic Plan	Business Plan
Theory of Change	Strategy
Executive Director	CEO
Trustee	Director
Development	Investment & Partnerships
Charity	Impact Enterprise
Need	Opportunity

FIGURE 2.2   Charity Versus SIE Frameworks.

recruit and retain the most talented board members; partner with major corporations; and engage with the most sophisticated, high-net-worth individuals.

Align Practice 2.3: Create Compelling, Actionable Mission and Vision Statements

Traditionally, organizational planning starts with mission and vision statements. Too often, these are long, ambiguous, jargon-filled paragraphs that take forever to write and that no one can remember. As there is rarely consensus behind them, or their length and ambiguity were the only way consensus could be created, they become performative exercises that leave individuals carrying forward with their own unique conceptions of purpose and success, destroying teamwork and organizational potential.

Move past the difficulty of aligning around specific, actionable statements by first defining exactly what the terms mean. The word *mission* is ambiguous. Make it clear by adding the definition "We are solving this problem in this way." By starting with the problem being solved, the organization distinguishes itself from one that is merely "working on" a challenge. It is fundamentally a courageous stance. The mission (and vision) demonstrates this courage.

The next challenge is to describe what success looks like in clear, succinct, measurable terms: the *vision* statement. Similarly, enhance the word *vision* with "This is what complete success looks like in specific terms." Follow these additional rules for writing strong, actionable mission and vision statements:

- Make them short and memorable: 15–20 words at most. (Test to see if staff and board can remember them after a few minutes. Practice this repeatedly until everyone can.)
- Avoid words that are more than 12 letters or four syllables.
- Choose language that is clear, concrete, and compelling.
- Avoid buzzwords and jargon.

The CEO writes the first draft and revises it via feedback from one individual at a time, starting with the executive team and the most important members of the board. Avoid group wordsmithing. With individual conferences complete, the CEO can then conduct final tune-up sessions to capture group buy-in, keeping in mind that these statements need only be 80% adequate. They, along with everything else, will be continually improved via action and experiment, not dialogue and reflection.

Consider the following mission statements from organizations working at local, state, and global scales:

1. Bellevue LifeSpring fosters stability and self-sufficiency for Bellevue's families by providing food, clothing, educational support, and emergency assistance.
2. Treehouse delivers evidence-based support for foster youth that enables them to graduate high school and launch successfully into adulthood.

3. The Global Coffee Platform promotes farmer prosperity, improved well-being, and environmental sustainability.

Vision statements follow this same concise format. However, as they involve describing a future state, as opposed to what the organization is doing now, they are harder to write. There will be varying opinions around what success looks like, and there will be different appetites for risk. If that is the case, consider another exercise to build consensus.

Align Exercise 2.d: Writing Our Success Story

Assign the following short writing task to everyone in the organization, board and staff. Give them one day to give their answers: "It's five years from now, and we have achieved our most spectacular aspirations of success. The *Wall Street Journal* (or famous publication of your choice) is writing an article about us. Imagine what the article says and give a short response to each of the following questions.

- What's the headline?
- What are two highlights of our success and innovation?
- How did we accelerate our impact?
- What two issues do we still have to address?
- What's the outlook for our future?

Compile the responses in a table for comparison, and put the table in front of the CEO and board chair. Then consider these points of analysis:

- Are we ambitious or playing it safe?
- Are we all giving similar answers, or is there a significant variety in our responses?
- Can we put the headlines together into a goal?
- Do the "how did we accelerate" answers have anything in common? If our goal is *what we will achieve,* our strategy is *how we will get there.* Any themes or patterns?

The CEO comes up with an initial draft, builds consensus and specificity with the executive team, and then gets the board to review, comment, and approve. The pathway to this alignment among and between board and staff tremendously varies from organization to organization, and it all depends on personalities, skills, experience, ambition, and character of those involved. If there are many strong personalities with varying visions of success and different opinions on how to get there, consulting expertise may be helpful.

Align Exercise 2.d will build momentum to overcome alignment challenges. First, the courageous pursuit of a shared definition of success can inspire morale and teamwork. Second, this pursuit invites everyone into the planning conversation instead of treating them as functionaries: everyone is in the kitchen, not on the menu. Staff and volunteers are far more likely to support what they have a hand in creating. Third, this reduces perceived pressure and risk of articulating such a specific goal with the following approach: "Look, this is just a draft. High performing organizations set ambitious goals, not delusional ones. It's okay to think big and set a specific, accountable goal. We will tune this up in the coming weeks and months, talk with our major supporters and stakeholders, and make sure our vision has support before we launch. For now, we need to move with urgency and not let the perfect become the enemy of the good."

The following are the same mission statements presented earlier, with each followed by exemplary vision statements:

1. **Mission:** Bellevue LifeSpring fosters stability and self-sufficiency for Bellevue's families by providing food, clothing, educational support, and emergency assistance.

    Vision: All students in Bellevue can focus on their education because their basic needs are being met.

2. **Mission:** Treehouse delivers evidence-based support for foster youth that enables them to graduate high school and launch successfully into adulthood.

    Vision: All foster youth in our state receive individualized support that helps them graduate high school and plan for their future education, employment, and housing.

3. **Mission:** The Global Coffee Platform promotes farmer prosperity, improved well-being, and environmental sustainability.
   Vision: A thriving and sustainable coffee sector.

Align Practice 2.4: Define the Organization's Value Proposition

With mission and vision statements drafted, leadership continues to the next align practice: crafting a concise, compelling *value proposition*. This is a short statement of organizational ability to achieve the vision along with evidence, known as *proof points*, that the organization is capable of achieving it. If the venture is new or the organization is a start-up, evidence may not exist, in which case it is suitable to provide the next best thing, which is a credible, research-based program design and a short, clear pathway to test it and collect evidence at the pilot level.[3]

Nonprofits may encounter cultural or individual barriers that interpret value propositions as rude or boastful. The deep legacy of humility will spur doubts: "Aren't good nonprofits humble? We shouldn't boast about why we are the best at what we do, right? We might offend someone!" While humility is individually laudable, organizationally it is counterproductive. If an organization isn't the best at what it does, why is it asking for money, time, and attention if there is another, more capable organization? It's not enough to discuss a need and tell heartwarming stories. If the challenge is urgent, partners and funders are impatient to understand why a particular organization is the best solution.

Furthermore, articulating convincing proof points demands organizational tenacity and patience to test programs at the pilot level and build the evidence basis that they work. It's easy to be distracted by the whirlwind of daily organizational concerns, but building up

---

[3]A popular tool for developing value propositions is the Value Proposition Canvas, a free tool by Strategyzer (**strategyzer.com/canvas**).

independent, third-party validation that programs actually work—and conveying this proof in a sentence or two—is an essential foundation if an organization wishes to attract more funding, partnerships, and other resources.

The next part of the Treehouse case study offers a value proposition that aligns with Treehouse's mission and vision. As value propositions must contain at least one or two proof points, these will run longer than 25 words; 50 is usually sufficient.

Case Study: Treehouse Mission, Vision, and Value Proposition

- **Mission:** Treehouse delivers evidence-based support for foster youth that enables them to graduate high school and launch successfully into adulthood.
- **Vision:** All foster youth in our state receive individualized support that helps them graduate high school and plan for their future education, employment, and housing.
- **Value proposition**: 85% of foster youth we serve graduate high school, compared to a baseline of 40% for all foster youth. Our annual program expenditure of $6,500 per youth saves our community over $1 million per youth in reduced future public expense.

Align Practice 2.5: Pick a BHAG

One of many useful terms Jim Collins introduced in his seminal works on organizational performance is *BHAG: big, hairy, audacious goal*. A BHAG takes the vision further by targeting a specific amount of change to be delivered by a specific date in the form *X to Y by Z*: here is our specific impact now, and here is where it will be by this date. Collins refers to BHAGs as "the clear finish line so an organization can know when it has achieved the goal[;] . . . it reaches out and grabs people in the gut . . . [with] little or no explanation."[4] BHAGs focus internal teams and engage external stakeholders as the formula provides built-in accountability.

As we saw in the growth mindset exercises (align exercises 2.2 and 2.3), entering into any discussion about ambitious changes will likely prompt objections. "What if we don't succeed? We will look bad!" Manage these fears by asserting the following: First, a BHAG is a promise, not a guarantee. No one will be punished if the organization doesn't achieve the goal. Furthermore, the most important people, and the ones with the most resources, are only attracted to organizations with audacious goals—to them, organizations look bad without audacious goals.

Second, the testing process outlined in Chapter 5 will calibrate the BHAG with key decision makers and centers of influence. The strongest BHAGs have been tested with not just funders, but with key stakeholders from other nonprofits, appropriate government agencies, and from the business and philanthropic communities. (Doing so begins a process of building alignment toward a *collective impact* model, one touched upon further below.)

Third, identify major risks and how they will be monitored and managed. What are all the ways the organization could fail to achieve the BHAG? Write them all down, categorize them, and discuss contingencies. Articulating these risks shows external audiences the organization possesses the foresight and prudence to manage the audacity inherent in the goal. Jim Collins observes that successful leaders pursue BHAGs with *productive paranoia*, continuously scanning for threats and failure points that could confound progress. Further guidelines on risk identification and management are offered in Chapters 3 and 4.

Finally, and most importantly, almost every nonprofit mission is relatively simple to convert into a BHAG: Identify everyone in the current service audience the organization is not serving and then set a path of accelerated growth and impact to reach them all. When that is done, expand or deepen the service area.

---

[4]Jim Collins, "BHAG," **https://www.jimcollins.com/concepts/bhag.html**.

Reaching the goal may or may not happen. The courage and optimism to make the attempt are all that is necessary at this stage. For a shining example of how courageous leadership sets a BHAG, see the next part of the Treehouse case study below.

Case Study: Treehouse's BHAG

By 2012, Treehouse had already spent 25 years helping foster children with material assistance and educational support. Its goal was to "give foster children a childhood and future." While this is a wonderful sentiment, it is impossible to measure. While proud of the organization's work she had founded, the CEO, Janis Avery, was ambitious to solve core challenges facing foster youth, not just nibble around the edges. She committed her organization to courageously articulating a BHAG in the form of X to Y by Z goal: *By 2017, all foster children in our region will graduate high school at the rate of their peers.* This was a fiercely optimistic and audacious statement. First, the organization had tried to move graduation rates in the past and had failed to move them even a percentage point or two. This goal demanded that graduation rates for approximately 2,000 foster youth increase by over 100%, from a baseline of 40% to over 80%. There was no other effort that had identifiably moved graduation rates for this most challenged of populations either. Given the magnitude of the proposed goal, Janis received no small share of criticism from other social sector leaders who considered the goal not audacious but impossible. Like all bold leadership teams, Janice and her team forged ahead. *Whether you think you can or think you can't, you are probably right.* Janice, her executive team, and her board came together around this BHAG by themselves, building on their courage and fierce optimism.

Align Practice 2.6: Define Impact and Growth Strategy

At this stage of the align phase, there is a clear, actionable mission; an aspirational vision of success; a compelling value proposition and evidence-based proof points; and a BHAG that sharpens the vision in a specific *X to Y by Z* format. These are all fairly discrete, easily understood concepts.

Next is a far more complex and widely misunderstood concept: strategy. The literature on strategy is complex and centered on thinkers such as Michael Porter, whose five forces analysis[5] provides useful direction for business executives.[6] Because most discussions of strategy are written from a lens of fierce business competition, like Porter's, they overlook elements unique to the nonprofit sector, such as the gains that can be made with partnerships with other nonprofits or collaboration with government agencies, corporations, and funders.

While strategy resists easy definition, the following attempt is hopefully acceptable to all but the most persnickety management theorists: If the mission is the problem being solved, the vision is what ultimate success looks like; if the BHAG is the next ambitious organizational target, then strategy is *how* the organization is going to achieve the target. Strategy describes a complete set of clearly defined choices and behaviors that define the organization's complete formula or system for achieving success.

While strategy is widely misunderstood in the private sector, the social sector often jettisons the term completely, using niche language instead, such as *theory of change* and *logic model*. The first term is acceptable for start-ups: any "theory of change" isn't theory if it works. The second term is redundant. One certainly hopes any organization addressing a social challenge would inherently use a logical approach, versus, say, an irrational or magical one. Forced to invent a unique term, *change model* or *impact model* would be preferable. None of these specialized terms are wise to use, however. Niche language only creates barriers to engaging with other actors, such as corporations, individuals, and government agencies, that nonprofits typically need to partner with to be effective. Sector-specific language creates barriers for building trust and exchanging ideas.

----

[5] "Porter's 5 Forces Explained and How to Use the Model," Investopedia, updated October 30, 2023, **https://www.investopedia.com/terms/p/porter.asp**.
[6] Michael E. Porter, "What Is Strategy?" *Harvard Business Review*, November–December 1996, **https://hbr.org/1996/11/what-is-strategy**.

Stick with the term *strategy*, and do a modest amount of additional reading to understand what it means. While we define *strategy* as "the full set of choices and behaviors that define how a nonprofit will achieve its BHAG" and offer a useful working example with the Treehouse case study, there are many facets to the term, and it would take a separate book to give the subject proper treatment. Instead, in addition to the outline and examples presented here, consider a few additional references. The concept of strategy is at least three thousand years old in written form, first defined in still one of the best books on the subject, Sun Tzu's fifth-century BC masterpiece *The Art of War*, in which the author advises leaders of the necessity of detailed planning, complete knowledge of the landscape, self-knowledge, and other guidance still very relevant today. For contemporary definitions of organizational strategy, take a look at the following short, clear articles. While written for private sector audiences, they provide clear and helpful explanations of what strategy is:

- "Many Strategies Fail Because They're Not Strategies" (**https:// hbr.org/2017/11/many-strategies-fail-because-theyre-not-actually-strategies**);
- "Your Strategic Plans Probably Aren't Strategic or Even Plans" (**https://hbr.org/2018/04/your-strategic-plans-probably-arent-strategic-or-even-plans**).

While these basic ideas will get teams started on strategy formulation, experienced leaders recognize that effective strategy takes time. It is often an unpredictable journey of discovery and iteration. Strategy is always uncertain in the early stages, and it is not until deeper into execution that leaders will know if it is working. Therefore, cast strategies in clay, not concrete—they evolve as execution yields new discoveries and lessons learned. This is one of many reasons that this book's methodology is a circle, one that symbolizes continuous development and improvement.

With an initial idea of what strategy is—and is not—leaders can then begin the challenging task of defining it for their organization. Make a complex and challenging undertaking somewhat easier by distinguishing between two types of organizational strategy and working on them one at a time. The first kind of strategy is related to how the organization will deliver a program or intervention at the individual or unit level of service. This we will call *impact* strategy. The second kind is the strategy related to delivering more and more of that particular intervention or service to all the people or things who need it. This we will call *growth* strategy.

Impact Strategy

Impact strategy is a summary of what an organization does to make desired change happen at the most granular level of service. Whatever or whomever the organization serves or supports, impact strategy summarizes the actions and choices that deliver an improvement or solve a problem. If the starting condition or problem is X, and Y is the state after the successful social intervention and solution is delivered, defining impact strategy means summarizing the major steps and ingredients of the recipe of how the organization interacts with X to make Y happen. No long academic arguments—just bullet points with as few words as possible. What are the collective choices and behaviors necessary to change X to Y, and how are they effective? This is impact strategy: the best possible recipe for solving a particular problem. We will explore Treehouse's impact strategy to illustrate this concept.

Case Study: Treehouse's Impact Strategy

The Treehouse assessment included this observation about their impact strategy:

- The program's *logic model* had received significant attention from multiple staff and much time and work had been expended, but there was still no clear view of what the program's strategy or architecture was, and the only legacy of this effort were multiple, competing, lengthy plans in draft form.

This is a common problem with impact strategy formulation. Even though there was a clear BHAG, the organization got stuck because of a common cultural assumption that good strategy is complicated. A string of prominent consultants and a program director with a PhD had delivered a 22-page-long evaluation model. Everyone discussed the information overload problem, but the answer—keep it simple!—was culturally alien. People were socialized to think that complex problems need complex answers. Multiple iterations of the same complex solution weren't going anywhere, but there was no model pointing in a different direction.

The strategy discussion in the business literature is clear. Strategy isn't actionable unless it is clear, concise, and measurable. "Let's start over. If we want to impact graduation rates, what are the main drivers? If graduation rates are the cause, what are the effects of that cause?" It didn't take long to discover the four major drivers of successful graduation: good school attendance (fewer than a handful of unexcused absences), good behavior (no severe disciplinary events), grades at C or above, and positive psychosocial development. The first three are easy to measure, so we developed a clear and parsimonious strategy:

1. Partner with the school district to get real-time data on foster youth attendance, behavior, and coursework;

2. Develop a system to flash a red light any time a student has a graduation risk indicator: an unexcused absence, a disciplinary event at school, or a grade below a C;

3. Hire educational coordinators to manage a portfolio of no more than 30 students each, so that they would have time to get to know each youth and deliver them student-centric, evidence-based interventions addressed at whatever issue caused the risk flag, interventions sourced from the entire community to make it an efficient, collective effort.

This program strategy created new organizational needs: a new data system and a revamp of the HR strategy to ensure the hiring and training supported this new lean and disciplined approach. Everything was discussed and boiled down to bullet points, which are offered below. Good strategic development results not in long documents or fancy diagrams but bullet points that people can hear once or twice and remember:

- Focus on ABC+ for each youth (attendance, behavior, coursework, and P/S development).

- Get the data sharing agreements with the districts and build a new IT system to provide actionable, real-time data.
- Hire, train, and support educational coordinators to deliver youth-centered interventions within 24 hours of a risk indicator to a cohort small enough they can build trust and deliver student-centered solutions.

This impact strategy didn't appear overnight. It took weeks of consultation, development, and refinement. Notably, this organization had previously spent years working on its program strategy and ended up in a muddle. What was the key difference? Focus and simplicity. Even though no one knew the outcome, the focus was kept on the best available research that could be tested and revised quickly—in a matter of months, not years.

Another aspect of this and any good impact strategy is *collective impact*, which means combining forces with peer SIEs, government, corporations, and philanthropy. Strategy and resources are aligned until an entire community is working together, often via a coordinating body called a *backbone organization*. While a compelling theory, it is difficult to implement as it requires high levels of agreement on process and mutual trust among diverse groups (its formal difficulty leads more skeptical observers to call it *collective impasse*). What is typically most successful is an incremental approach that builds trust and confidence at a manageable pace that can, over months and years, eventually capture the most important assets and efforts in a given service geography.

One note of caution: The term *strategic partnership* in the social sector is ideally meant to convey this type of collaboration, when organizations combine resources to create a multiplier effect. In the Treehouse example, there were authentic strategic partnerships with other nonprofits, which provided educational support for youth such as tutoring or counseling; with government agencies responsible for foster youth, which explored how to advance more supportive policies; and with corporations, which provided funding, volunteers, and technical assistance. For example, Deloitte built the data system *pro bono*, an important contribution to success. These collaborations were *strategic* in that they were selectively, intentionally designed and chosen to create both efficiency and effectiveness.

Growth Strategy

Growth strategy explains how the organization will harness all the necessary resources to get the impact where and when it is needed. For example, once Treehouse had defined an efficient, effective model for helping a single foster youth, it had to figure out how to help *all of them* in their service area.

Growth strategy can be frightening. Many nonprofits shy away from articulating a growth strategy because, first of all, it is hard to imagine growth when most organizations struggle to survive. Stuck mindsets, pessimism, lack of awareness and experience about raising money, or simply the fear of looking bad if the goal isn't achieved— these are some of the many leadership barriers preventing even organizations with a strong impact strategy from charting a companion growth strategy.

Savvy nonprofits with growth mindsets understand that articulating an ambitious growth strategy helps build confidence that the goal is achievable. High-performing organizations set *audacious* goals, not *safe* ones, and they have a strategy that explains how they can be achieved. They aren't afraid of failure: they recognize it as an opportunity to learn and improve.

Like many small nonprofits, Treehouse's growth was very slow. It took 25 years to build up to $6 million in revenue, money raised the hard way through grants, auctions, and mail and digital solicitation. The growth strategy for Treehouse was to (1) transition away from the high-cost, low-return, hard-to-scale event-based fundraising model and (2) invest in a lower-cost, higher return, more scalable strategy focusing on major investments from individuals and corporations. With proven success, the organization could then (3) secure permanent state funding to help it scale further.

When formulating a growth strategy, it is smart to recall align practice 2.2: "Choose Powerful Language." For example, consider the common nonprofit revenue strategy called *major gifts*, which is soliciting five-, six-, and often seven-figure philanthropic contributions primarily from individuals. These are solicited by *development directors*. Instead, we recommend the term *charitable investment* to signal that the organization will be using funding effectively. Likewise, call fundraisers *investment and partnership officers* (IPOs), a title that frames their work more accurately and specifically.

It is worth noting that not every high-impact social impact organization needs to have an aggressive growth strategy. Many organizations can deliver wide-reaching solutions via existing networks. For example, if the impact strategy is a certification program that creates benefits for companies, it can be delivered through a preexisting global network of auditors and accreditation bodies. The nonprofit need only fund the certification model and associated marketing costs—the infrastructure for dissemination of the solution is already in place. For another example, an organization that seeks to reduce high rates of recidivism can develop a set of evidence-based rehabilitation practices for incarcerated populations that could conceivably be scaled up by departments of correction. Nonprofits can conceive of themselves as research and development labs for government or other networks, privately funding and testing ideas that, if they work, can be then publicly funded.

One highly effective social impact leader conceives of growth strategy as reshaping the current systems that are already working at scale. Jeff Walker, chair of the board of directors of New Impact, the highly successful venture philanthropy mentioned in the Introduction, says, "I am focused on showing NGOs [nongovernmental organizations] they don't have to scale themselves but can be great innovators and then scale through working with many stakeholders through system level change assisted by system catalysts who help coordinate that change. We have lots of success with that strategy." New Impact's approach has catalyzed significant social impact and should be closely studied by change leaders especially other philanthropies.

We can see this approach materialize in Treehouse's journey from onerous, subsistence-level funding efforts to a more effective growth strategy.

Case Study: Treehouse's Growth Strategy

Treehouse was founded by social workers. For 25 years, they raised money like most other grassroots nonprofits: *pack donors in a hotel ballroom once a year, wine and dine them, tell them stories of heartbreaking need and heart-warming success, and then ask them for gifts.* This strategy delivered slow but steady growth. The talented marketing and fundraising staff and consistent messaging had built the revenue to approximately $6 million over 25 years of sustained effort. As the Treehouse findings indicated, over 700 people in their donor database had written checks for $1,000 or more at their annual fundraising event.

The organization was understandably reluctant to change its fundraising strategy, holding to an understandable bird-in-hand mindset. Yet there was obvious goodwill and tremendous untapped investment in the database. As the organization had already reacted well to the short, sharp shock delivered around impact strategy, I tried the same thing to catalyze better growth strategy.

I met with the board's executive committee and made the following bold proclamation: "Ever hear the story about how, in the 1932 World Series against the Cubs, Babe Ruth got up to the plate, pointed to the outfield, and then crushed the next pitch 500 feet into the centerfield bleachers? This is known as calling the shot. Your untapped fundraising potential is so clear, I can call the shot. Follow my advice, exactly, about how to staff and execute a major investment strategy, and we will double revenue in the next 12 months and then sustain years of strong and continuous revenue growth, beating anything you've done historically. I'll tear up my business license if this doesn't work."

The untapped potential was that obvious. The team was coachable, talented, and dedicated, and everyone signed on. We hired three new officers to pursue larger charitable investments from individuals and corporations and made a host of other infrastructure and staffing moves. In the next 12 months, we raised approximately $6 million in new funding and quickly grew the annual budget to over $10 million annually, with each successive year seeing an additional 10% to 20% growth.

One interaction with a major investor prospect demonstrated the utility of the business plan we had developed and why that needs such focus before beginning the fundraising. A board member presented the Treehouse business plan to executives at AT&T, a corporation that had previously donated $25,000. They said, "We've never seen a charity show us a business plan this strong." Six months later they invested $1 million.

Align Exercise 2.e: Drafting Impact and Growth Strategy

Ask the CEO, board, and executive staff to write down their best ideas for organizational impact and growth strategies as a series of bullet points, restricting the length of response to an index card or Post-it note. Is there consensus? Do the answers reflect a maturation of thinking and focus compared to the results from the align exercise 2.a? As elsewhere, don't let the perfect be the enemy of the good. Building consensus around strategy demands interactive, iterative process demanding tenacity, the input of the entire executive team and board, and as many credible third-party experts as practical.

Align Practice 2.7: Draft Year 1 Initiatives

With progress on strategy, the next focus is articulating what major actions the organization will take in the next year to implement the strategy. These we will call *year 1 initiatives*: the most immediate and important steps on the journey to the BHAG. While strategy is a continuous guide to organizational choices and behavior, year 1 initiatives are the things being built or created to execute the strategy. Consider a simple hypothetical: An organization has a mission to build a house. The vision is to build an affordable, beautiful, 2,000-square-foot Tudor bungalow using sustainability principles. The impact strategy is to use recycled building materials, local architects and labor, passive solar, and permaculture design for the yard. The growth strategy is to showcase the build on YouTube, build traffic, and capture sponsor revenue. In this scenario, the year 1 initiatives might be "Hire architect; source building materials; launch YouTube channel." Year 1 initiatives are a specific type of progress point that planners call *milestones*. Other longer-term milestones for this example might include site preparation, drawings completed, foundation poured, roof construction, and so forth.

Breaking down a social impact enterprise's planning elements to this level of clarity and simplicity takes time. Organizations may find it impossible because they have chased too many grants, launched too many discrete initiatives, and overshot organizational capacity because it is seductively easy to launch a program, only later to discover that executing it well is much harder. These are common challenges. If the organization lacks focus, the board chair and CEO must be aligned in creating the focus. Unless there is strong leadership to ensure goals and resources are aligned, the organization is unlikely to accomplish much.

Year 1 initiatives around growth typically involve building the sales and marketing team and infrastructure. Examples range from "Hire chief investment and partnerships officer" to "Bring in knowledge management specialists to untangle and automate our database and CRM process" to "Convert our fundraising events to donor building trust and stewardship events only." We can see what Treehouse landed on below.

Case Study: Treehouse's Year 1 Initiatives

- Build a new data system.
- Hire three new investment and partnership officers.
- Revise the educational coordinator hiring and training process.
- Build a dashboard to assess the delivery of interventions within 24 hours of a risk indicator.

Align Practice 2.8: Create Key Performance Indicators

Early in my consulting career I had the good fortune of attending a meeting of top executives at Bloomberg, a famously well-managed company that was considering a partnership with one of my clients. As I sat in the luxurious meeting room, the executives kept using an unfamiliar acronym. "What's the KPI?" someone would ask. "What are the trends?" Another would ask, "Well, who owns that KPI?"

As I soon learned, a *key performance indicator* is a supremely important management tool for organizations. As the Treehouse example shows, information is abundant and cheap, but attention and focus are scarce and expensive. Therefore, leaders of high-performing organizations learn to focus attention on a small, carefully designed set of measures that, if the design is good, provide quick, accurate insights into how well the organization is executing on its strategy.

Plans are not worth the paper they are printed on until measures of execution via a small set of KPIs are consistently collected, analyzed, and used to improve execution. KPIs come in two flavors: *leading* and *lagging*. A *lagging indicator* is the desired outcome, the ending results: impact created, dollars raised, and so forth. In Treehouse's case, they had one major lagging KPI: aggregated graduation rates for the population of foster youth engaged in their programs. They put a circle around every youth they served, measured the percentage of how many graduated high school, and compared it to the baseline. The baseline graduation rate for foster youth, due to so many disadvantages and the trauma of the foster care system, was about 40%, and everything they did was focused on moving that number up until it hit at least 85%, which was the average rate for all students in the region.

Focus on lagging indicators is achieved when everyone in the organization writes down the same answer when quizzed about how success is measured. Only then is it time to identify the second flavor of KPIs, known as *leading indicators*: the activities performed today to create the outcomes that are desired tomorrow. They are evidence-based practices, the causes that are most likely to create the desired results. Treehouse's leading indicators were the percentage of child-centered interventions delivered within 24 hours of a risk indicator around attendance, behavior, and coursework, along with proactive exercises to foster healthy psychosocial development. The leads were summarized in a simple, memorable term—*ABC Plus*—announced in planning meetings to build internal awareness that, to move graduation rates tomorrow, staff needed to take action today to resolve barriers to getting to school, staying out of trouble, and doing well in classes.

Figuring out the lagging indicator is the easier of the two. What is the desired quantitatively measurable outcome? "Empowering community members" doesn't work. Of course, that's hard to measure: it doesn't mean anything specific. When someone says, "Social impact is hard to measure," they are very likely saying, "I haven't thought hard enough about my outcome or how to get there." Therefore, start with the specific desired outcome that is measurable by numbers. If there is any real difficulty figuring out those lagging indicators, return to align practice 2.1 and repeat them until there is focus on a specific goal. "Percentage of increase in registered voters in our community" is a better lagging indicator.

When there is a crisp, numerical lagging indicator, do the research, talk to the experts, and figure out the best ways to produce that outcome. What are the most proven practices to register voters? A clear understanding of the impact strategy is essential. If the strategy is a door-to-door campaign that seeks to target unregistered voters, a good leading metric might be "Number of face-to-face conversations with unregistered voters." Do the research, be crystal clear about the strategy, and break the strategy down into lead and lags.

Organizations that are primed to perform have taken the time to get everyone laser-focused on their goal, their strategy, and the set of KPIs they will measure to see if everything is working, and a robust summary can fit on a single page. However, developing leading and lagging indicators, the keys to successfully executing strategy, may take time, so be prepared for hard thinking.

Strive to match these characteristics of effective KPIs:[7]

Sparse	The fewer KPIs, the better.
Drillable	Users can drill into detail.
Simple	Users understand the KPI.
Actionable	Users know how to affect outcomes.
Owned	Every KPI connects to one directly responsible individual (DRI).
Referenced	Users can view origins and context.
Correlated	KPIs drive desired outcomes.
Balanced	KPIs consist of both financial and nonfinancial metrics.
Aligned	KPIs don't undermine each other.
Validated	Workers can't circumvent the KPIs.

Align Practice 2.9: Create a Planning Framework

With a growth mindset established and board and staff input on each of the align practices in this chapter, the next step is to consolidate all responses within a one-page *planning framework,* a document that will serve to generate consensus on important elements to be expanded on later in a complete business plan. The planning framework is an

---

[7]Adapted from W.W. Eckerson, "Performance Management Strategies," *Business Intelligence Journal* (2009), 14(1), 24–27.

important milestone toward a full business plan and will make the production of this latter document much easier.

The planning framework provides a vehicle to generate consensus in a manner that is focused and concise. The process of articulating the short statements the framework requires will likely bring up cultural or personality-based barriers that must be addressed and resolved. The CEO must proceed with two minds: (1) to build consensus and articulate clear, concrete responses to these align practices, and (2) to identify and resolve cultural and personality barriers that confound this process. The CEO must be intentional about creating change and managing the change process, to bring people along and ensure the new direction sticks. The term *change management* encapsulates the science for making that happen, an entire field of organizational process, which, like all others, is overstuffed with too much information and little indication of what works and what doesn't. Chapter 7: "Lead" will provide useful leadership and governance practices that will help the CEO and board leadership over the inevitable friction that change creates.

Planning Framework Templates

A planning framework template is shown in Figure 2.3. Treehouse's planning framework is shown in Figure 2.4.

With this planning framework template filled in, leadership can then assess if the document provides enough clarity on direction to proceed to the next chapter, which will discuss expanding the planning framework into a full business plan. Remember, don't let the perfect be the enemy of the good: always stop at an 80% confidence and consensus level and maintain a bias toward action and experiment, not analysis and reflection.

BHAG: Your organization's highest ambition stated as a quantifiable objective.

Mission

This is what we do.

Vision

This is what success looks like for us in aspirational terms.

Values

- Here are our values and org culture in concrete terms.

Value Prop & Proof Points

Why we are better, faster, and/or cheaper than current solutions
Proof point #1
Proof point #2
Proof Point #3

Impact & Growth Strategy

- **Strategy 1** a set of choices/positioning that we are making to achieve our goals.
- **Strategy 2** another set of choices
- **Strategy 3** a third set of choices that we are making to achieve our goals. Together, these strategies hang together in a coherent way.

Year 1 Imperatives

1. Driving Initiative
   - Details
2. Driving Initiative
   - Details
3. Driving Initiative
   - Details

Sample Metrics (choose 5–10 total)

Financial	Stakeholder	Organizational	Impact
Annual growth	New members	Compensation	Social return on investment
Unit cost	Retention & satisfaction	Turnover	Sustainable development goal context
Months of cash on hand	Partnership value	Governance engagement	% of problem solved
Budget v. actual	Engagement	Employee morale	Evidence for practice
Profit margin		Use of data	
Cost per dollar raised		Learning & development	

FIGURE 2.3 Planning Framework Template.

Treehouse BHAG: *By 2017, all foster children in King County will graduate high school at the rate of their peers*

Mission

Treehouse delivers evidence-based support for foster youth that enables them to graduate high school and launch successfully into adulthood.

Vision

All foster youth in our state receive individualized support that helps them graduate high school and plan for their future education, employment, and housing.

Values

- Fierce optimism
- Deep commitment to racial and social equity
- Focused and driven by data

Value Prop & Proof Points

The foster youth we serve graduate at 85%, compared to a baseline of 40% for all foster youth. Our total annual program expenditure of $6,500 per youth saves our community over $1 million per youth in reduced future public expense.

Impact & Growth Strategy

1. Focus on ABC+ for each youth
2. Hire, train, and support educational coordinators to deliver youth-centered interventions within 24 hours of a risk indicator
3. Build the IT system to fuel a dashboard that provides actionable, real-time data.
4. Transition from event-based to relationship-based fundraising

Year 1 Imperatives

1. Build an executive dashboard and review it monthly to continuously improve
2. Hire three new investment & partnership officers
3. Inventory community-sourced ABC+interventions
4. Revamp educational coordinator job description and training provides actionable, real-time data.

Core Metrics (leading + lagging; 6–8 total)

Financial	Stakeholder	Organizational	Impact
Annual growth	School partnership evaluation	Compensation	Graduation rates
Months of cash on hand	Impact partner contribution and responsiveness	Morale	ABC plus
Budget v. actual		Turnover	% of foster youth engaged in service area
Cost per dollar raised		Governance engagement	
Cost per youth served			

FIGURE 2.4 Treehouse's Planning Framework.

Additional Resources

See **www.altruistaccelerator.org** for tools and examples.

Tools

- Vision Development Tool
- Operating Environment Map
- One-Page Business Framework Template

Examples

- Sample One-Page Business Frameworks
- Additional Sample Mission, Vision, and Goal Statements

CHAPTER 3

Plan

Give me six hours to chop down a tree and I will spend the first four sharpening the ax.

—Abraham Lincoln

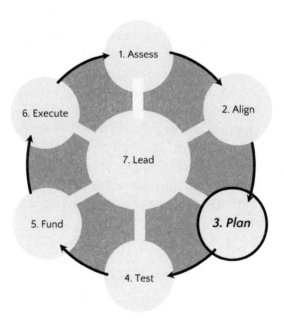

LEARNING OBJECTIVES

By the end of this chapter, you will be able to:

- Identify and apply the 15 essential elements of a robust business plan; and
- Articulate your own organization's expression of each element in a manner that builds consensus and teamwork among board and staff members.

Without a robust business plan that clearly articulates board- and staff-wide consensus on all matters of organizational importance, an organization is actually a *disorganization*, with individuals left to follow their own guesses and instincts about what to do. Very few of the many hundreds of nonprofit plans we have reviewed contain all the elements necessary. When these gaps are filled, organizations are ready to accelerate their growth and impact.

The fact that most nonprofit plans are missing essential information is neither the fault of the practitioners nor a disparagement of their skills or intellect. Writing a concise plan that covers all issues of organizational importance is hard. An even bigger obstacle is the lack of awareness and understanding among nonprofit leaders of what, exactly, should be in a business plan and how they are properly written and developed. Poor training, cultural barriers, organizational myths, and other constraining forces contribute to this stiff challenge. As a result, most nonprofit planning efforts result in a state of ambiguity and paralysis, not unlike the state of affairs described in the following fictionalized case.

Dysfunction Junction

> *The Chicago Youth Alliance (CYA) was founded in 1992 by a group of community activists alarmed by the nearly 1,000 murders committed in the city the previous year. The Reverend Abigail Jones, the organization's charismatic founding CEO, brought together a group of volunteers, activists, educators, and*

*elected officials to "identify our community's at-risk youth and
provide them with services and support to help build a safe and
healthy community." Funded by church groups, small grants,
and fundraising event revenue from an auction and raffle, the
organization added programs and services over the years. By
2022, CYA had grown to 10 staff and $1.5 million in annual
revenue. It operated over 15 individual programs and provided
services to nearly 5,000 area youth via after-school programs
and evening programs in area churches.*

*The future of CYA was far from certain. Halfway through
the 2022 fiscal year, Reverend Jones was diagnosed with a serious medical condition, and doctors prescribed home rest and a
long series of medical treatment. She tendered her resignation
to her three-member board of directors, who met in emergency
session to appoint an interim executive director until a permanent hire could be found. The board hired Shauna Jackson, a
respected nonprofit consultant in the city, to guide it through
this transition.*

*At the following board meeting, Jackson began the meet-
ing with a disturbing announcement: "This organization is in
crisis," she said. "First, we have fewer than thirty days of cash
in our reserve fund. If we don't get even one of the grants we are
counting on, we will have to let staff go. Second, we are running over one dozen separate programs, and we are overwork-
ing our low-paid staff and demanding they generate outcomes
for far more programs than they can manage. High rates of
turnover and staff vacancies mean we can't deliver the services
we promise to funders. I've looked at our last three years of
grant applications: each one proposes what is practically a new
initiative with separate promises that were negotiated separately
with each funder. There is not enough funding to complete
any of them. We say we serve over five thousand youth, but all
but seventy-five of them are one-time interactions in our after-
school services. We lack the process and technology to track the
individuals we serve. The bottom line is this: we are offering the
appearance of community support and intervention but not
the substance. Our programs have not impacted our local rates*

of murder, incarceration, or unemployment. We are selling an illusion of services, not the real thing."

"This organization has been doing fine work!" yelled Jacob Bell, the board vice chair. He had been with the organization since its founding and was a close friend of Reverend Jones. "I don't believe what I am hearing. Reverend Jones has been one of our city's most valued leaders for decades, and we continue to be a pillar of faith and support for our young people today! So many people love her."

"Wait, let's hear her out," the board chair responded. "Shauna, what should we do?"

"Thank you," Shauna replied. "First, we need to face the fact we do not have a plan. Our fundraising events only generate a modest fraction above what it costs to produce them, so we have been chasing grant dollars and proposing new initiatives, all without a plan to guide our execution. The right thing to do is meet with all our funders and share the true state of affairs to see if we can renegotiate our agreements and buy us time to restructure. We need a plan."

The planning process outlined in this chapter takes time and focus. Too many small- to midsize nonprofits are so marginally staffed and financed, they can do little more than lurch from crisis to crisis and try to make payroll. For organizations in this state, there are typically two options: If there are valuable programs worth saving, they can either hand over their programs to another nonprofit, or they can try to secure at least six to nine months of operating funding to hire a turnaround specialist—if one can be found. Most often, they grind to a halt when the charismatic founder leaves or retires.

For the tens of thousands of more stable small- to mid-sized organizations with ambitious leadership and enough resources, there is hope and help. For those who have generated the initial consensus described in Chapter 2, the planning process below will build out the one-page framework into a world-class business plan.

Leaders ready to produce a world-class organizational plan should remember align practice 2.2: "Choose Powerful Language." Start by calling your document a *business plan* instead of a *strategic plan*. The way they are typically produced, most "strategic" plans are neither strategic nor credible. Perhaps we have been overexposed to the problem, but we have found so many badly written documents masquerading under the term *strategic* plan that we believe the term itself is tainted by poor practice. Furthermore, it is a savvy decision for nonprofits to embrace the term *business* to distinguish them from the dysfunction junctions.

Business plan is a widely accepted and well-defined norm for structuring and presenting an organizational road map. Many social sector leaders chafe at being told they need to "run like a business," and they are understandably suspicious of tools that come out of the white, male-dominated business world, and particularly ones that trash the planet and exploit people. But the framework is amoral, not immoral. The business planning model is nonetheless the best way to organize teams and raise money. Consider the fact that, in the United States today, the number one source of wealth is business ownership. Wealthy people are likely familiar with business terminology and process. While there are any number of funders who give away money to inflate their egos, exercise power, stoke emotions, or serve any other number of perverse incentives, we have found that the majority of funders appreciate the clarity and concision of the model described here.

Apart from optics and credibility with funders, there are many other reasons to develop a business plan. Think of them as Swiss army knives with many functions and benefits. They provide:

1. An actionable road map for staff giving everyone new clarity on job purpose and direction;

2. Key insights for new hires on the organization and compelling reasons to join;

3. Improved direction for how boards can better fulfill their duties as directors and fiduciaries;

4. Compelling reasons for partners and stakeholders to participate;

5. A library of core messages to drive successful marketing and communication;

6. Powerful fuel for fundraising; and

7. A dynamic platform for continuous improvement.

Done well, business plans are edited each year, not reinvented.

One Internet search will yield many business plan templates, all with various components and structures. There are many "experts" who encourage nonprofits to create documents called "theory of change" and "logic models," but as we have seen firsthand many times over the past two decades, these sector-specific approaches only generate ambiguity when it comes to finance, staffing, execution, risk, and other critical planning elements. The most concise and robust models are, as elsewhere, designed for for-profits. To make the discipline of the for-profit planning models applicable to the social space, we provide a synthesized model here.

Plan Practice 3.1: Follow Good Process

Keep the following good process pointers in mind throughout the planning process:

- Do not try to start a business plan from scratch. Start with the exercises 2.a through 2.e in Chapter 2: "Align" to generate the necessary consensus on high-level decisions.
- With the align practices accomplished, the CEO directs the process of building out the general framework into a full plan. The plan should not be written by committee. The CEO is the chief planner and should either write the document herself or closely oversee either staff or consultants to help.
- Short and simple is superior to long and complex. Ensure the person drafting the business plan is a gifted writer, unpretentious and concise. The point is clarity, concision, and ease of reading. Avoid hype and "sales-y" language. Be plain spoken. Delete adjectives.
- Use numbers, facts, and research as evidence.
- Don't let the perfect be the enemy of the good. High-caliber plans often demand dozens of iterations. It might take 2 or 3 revisions or 20 or 30. This is a dynamic document, and it evolves on an unpredictable path.
- Get the plan to 80% complete and follow the guide in Chapter 4: "Test" to improve it via a consultation process.

- Skip fancy formatting and pretty pictures. Business plans should not look like brochures. These documents are always drafts to be improved as the organization learns and evolves. The biggest barrier for CEOs is trying to create it solo. While the CEO or a close colleague should write it, revision is a group exercise. Chapter 4: "Test" provides additional insight here.

- One of the hardest parts is presenting all the business plan elements in a document no longer than 10 or 15 pages. People rarely read long documents, especially staff and board members. Take the time to make it short.

- Finally, remember that even the most carefully constructed plan will get many things wrong. It needs testing and then at least a year of implementation and revision before traction builds. Good business plans take three months to create, another three to test, and at least a full year of funding and execution before they begin to really solidify.

Plan Practice 3.2: Develop a Clear Problem Statement

Business plans get right to the point in the opening sentences with crisp, clear, concise language that describes the problem in the world that needs to be fixed. Use descriptive statistics and best available research to describe the cost of the problem in multiple dimensions: human, social, moral, economic, and environmental. Keep it under 250 words. Consider the example below from Treehouse.

Case Study: Treehouse's Problem Statement

Youth entering foster care face tremendous challenges. The abuse and neglect that lead to removal from their birth home have a lasting impact on children's social and emotional well-being. Entering foster care itself often means a change in schools, time out of school, and a loss of support for their education. There are 1,500 kids in foster care in King County on any given day; every year, 600 more youth face a crisis in parenting. Just over a third of these children will graduate from high school on time (Washington State Institute for Public Policy 2009). Fewer than 2% of alumni of foster care complete four-year degrees (Casey Family Programs 2005). Even those who work to reverse these outcomes face challenges of their own, including challenged schools, scarce public resources, and a support landscape that is complex and gap ridden. Studies demonstrate the long-term impact that inadequate education has on the lives of foster youth: nearly one-fourth of foster care alumni will experience homelessness as adults; 80% of foster care alumni aged 19–20 live below the poverty line, and one-third rely on public assistance (Washington State Institute for Public Policy 2008). The median income of former foster youth in their mid-20s is $8,000 (Chapin Hall Center for Children 2004).

Plan Practice 3.3: Describe the Solution

What does success look like? Different people care about different things, so describe not just the social justice or moral benefits but the economic and/or environmental ones. Perhaps the proposed impact corresponds to one or more of the United Nations Social Development Goals. End this section with the vision statement—a critical element that was covered in Chapter 2.

Case Study: Treehouse's Solution Statement

There is a large—and growing—body of research that tells us that kids are much more likely to graduate from high school when they attend class regularly, are not removed from their classroom for behavioral disruptions, and don't fall behind on accumulating course credits (Casey Family Programs

2005; Chapin Hall Center for Children 2004). We also know from both research and practice that foster kids succeed more often when they have a positive academic mindset, have a plan for their future, and are engaged in a meaningful extracurricular activity (Washington State Institute for Public Policy 2009; University of Chicago Consortium on Chicago School Research 2009). Therefore, Treehouse is targeting its efforts to keep the youth we serve on track in these areas—attendance, behavior, course completion, mindset, planning, and extracurricular engagement.

In order to achieve a sea change in graduation rates for foster youth in King County, we know we need to serve every student in foster care through middle and high school. Beginning with the expected graduation class of 2017—this year's eighth graders—Treehouse will scale its services to meet this need. Students will be brought on track to graduate and kept on track with targeted support and services.

Plan Practice 3.4: Refine the Value Proposition

As *New York Times*'s Nicholas Kristoff observes, "Any brand of tooth-paste is peddled with far more sophistication than the life-saving work of aid groups."[1]

The missions of social impact enterprises are often far more important and compelling than the consumer goods that attract our attention every day, but we don't know about them or why they are important because social sector leaders are socialized not to proclaim their own value. There's a time and place to be quiet, humble, and self-effacing— but not when leading a social impact enterprise.[2] Use this section to define why the organization is the best solution to the problem and include evidence—that is, proof points—that the organization is capable of solving the problem.

[1]Nicholas Kristoff, "Would You Let This Girl Drown?" *New York Times*, July 9, 2009, **https://www.nytimes.com/2009/07/09/opinion/09kristof.html**.
[2]One organization investing enormous sums in marketing is St. Judes. While we do not applaud guilt-inducing pictures of bald children fighting cancer, this organization's marketing budget has earned it billions. For another organization that's an exemplar of successful nonprofit marketing, see charity: water (**https://charitywater.org**).

Like the hard work aligning decision makers around a BHAG, the work creating a value proposition should be largely completed in Chapter 2. Even so, it is worthwhile to spend additional time to refine the value proposition until it is concise, clear and compelling.

If early-stage organizations don't have evidence yet, they can say they are following the best available research or running best-in-field pilot studies to find the optimal solution. There's always a value proposition.

Case Study: Treehouse's Value Proposition

Treehouse is entering its 25th year and is nationally recognized for its commitment to serving our most vulnerable youth. With fierce optimism, Treehouse is investing in the lives of these young people who have faced a crisis in parenting. By securing the opportunities they equally deserve, we are helping them build their lives and prosper in a society where all of our children are wanted and needed. Preparation for this initiative included a complete restructuring of Treehouse programs and staffing to create a lean, flexible, and data-driven social enterprise; a commitment to working in focused partnerships with agencies with shared goals; and development of an agency infrastructure that will allow the scaling necessary to serve every middle and high school youth in foster care in King County.

Attentive readers recognize that this value proposition is missing proof points. When the Treehouse plan was written in 2012, the organization had zero evidence its proposed interventions would work. In fact, previous efforts at boosting graduation rates had failed. The value proposition for Treehouse presented as an example in Chapter 2 was only possible years later when the programs had become very successful.

New programs and initiatives will thus lack proof points, so work with the evidence at hand: if there are no proof points, lean on best research or analogues. Limit the risk of failure by starting small and generating the necessary proof points before attempting to grow (often called a "crawl, walk, run" approach). The quality and clarity of the business plan can compensate for their absence, along with well-prepared and knowledgeable staff who present the plan and make it clear, as was the case with Treehouse, that it was an early-stage effort yet to generate the results. The organization had also built up tremendous good will and earned credibility for its previous work, so in this case, the absence of compelling proof points was not fatal.

Plan Practice 3.5: Explain Who Is on the Team

When private sector organizations raise money, the first thing they emphasize is not their product but *who is running the organization.* Introduce people to leadership with brief bios of the board and executive team. Highlight their expertise and professional experience and explain that these are proven industry professionals that deserve trust. As elsewhere, keep it short and simple.

Take note: Is this team world class? Sophisticated investors always look first at the team and then at the business model. Jim Collins calls this "First Who—get the right people on the bus—Then What."[3] The best plan and strategy won't get executed well without great people doing the executing.

Plan Practice 3.6: Refine the BHAG

If the organization has done the hard work of aligning board and staff according to the practices in Chapter 2: "Align," picking a BHAG should be relatively simple. Trying to write a business plan from scratch, without first taking this and the other incremental steps described earlier,

---

[3]Jim Collins, *Good to Great* (New York: Random House, 2001). **https://www.jim collins.com/articles**.

is extremely difficult. How does one eat a (metaphorical) elephant? One bite at a time. A BHAG can be scary—that's why it is called *audacious*—and the big challenge is keeping everyone focused on the task and not getting overwhelmed by all the other elements.

An organization should have only one BHAG—an ambitious, long-term outcome, not output, that aligns every member of the team around one unified vision. A succinct, understandable goal is essential to ensuring everyone understands the organization's objectives and how they will be achieved. To survive, too many nonprofits, even large ones, chase opportunities and bow to funder demands to define objectives. Whether called a BHAG, North Star, or other term, setting a focused goal is as much about what the organization will *not* do as much as it will do. In a 2011 *Forbes* interview, Steve Jobs shared one of his secrets for success:

> *People think focus means saying yes to the thing you've got to focus on. But that's not what it means at all. It means saying no to the hundred other good ideas that there are. You have to pick carefully. I'm actually as proud of the things we haven't done as the things I have done. Innovation is saying "no" to 1,000 things.*[4]

A BHAG is expressed in the form of X to Y by Z, making it very clear what the organization will achieve, and by what time. As Jim Collins writes, "The best BHAGs require both building for the long term and a relentless sense of urgency: What do we need to do today, with monomaniacal focus, and tomorrow, and the next day, to defy the probabilities and ultimately achieve our BHAG?"[5]

Apart from ignorance of the concept, the number one reason nonprofits fail to set a BHAG is fear. BHAGs are inherently bold and offer clear accountability. Leaders fear looking bad if they fail. What these leaders don't understand is that failure is normal. The necessity to be brave, learn from mistakes, and try again is basic life advice

---

[4]Carmine Gallo, "Steve Jobs: Get Rid of the Crappy Stuff," *Forbes*, May 16, 2016, **https://www.forbes.com/sites/carminegallo/2011/05/16/steve-jobs-get-rid-of-the-crappy-stuff**.
[5]Jim Collins, "BHAG," **https://www.jimcollins.com/concepts/bhag.html**.

any good parent gives their children. What these fearful leaders don't recognize is that the absence of a clear, accountable, aspirational goal broadcasts their fear and aversion to sophisticated audiences with the most power and wealth to help them. If an organization is working on solving an important social problem and doesn't have a BHAG, the smart money is quietly noting leadership's lack of courage and accountability.

In 2012, despite the failure of all its previous efforts to improve foster youth graduation rates, Janis Avery and her board articulated a remarkable BHAG (underlined in the case study below), one that would ultimately reshape the future of tens of thousands of vulnerable young people in Washington State and beyond. To the present day, we remain delighted with the courage that Treehouse leadership expressed with their BHAG.

Case Study: Treehouse's BHAG

Despite these obstacles, Treehouse is committed to ensuring that foster kids succeed. With fierce optimism, Treehouse will invest in the lives of these young people who have faced a crisis in parenting. *Because of Treehouse, foster youth in King County will graduate at the same rate as their peers with a plan for their future by 2017.*

At the time this BHAG was released in 2012, it inspired no small amount of vocal derision and skepticism from "experts" in the social sector. They are very quiet today as the Treehouse model expands across the United States.

Plan Practice 3.7: Describe Your Market

The market section in the business plan explains how the organization will identify, inform, and engage the many audience types necessary for success. *Market* is a basic business term to define a given population or geography. It could be a local community, city, state, region, or particular type of individual everywhere. A good business plan contains numerical descriptions of current or proposed market(s) with statistics that demonstrate understanding of the space in which the organization operates.

Start by describing the total number of people or things in the addressable audience that need changing or support. How many people are there in the service area? How many trees need saving? How many historic buildings need restoration? Is the scale a neighborhood, a town, a city, a region, a country, or the entire world, or the cosmos?

Next, describe the other organizations that are influential in the market, those with which the organization is competing or collaborating. Inform the reader about the landscape, the key actors in it, and how the organization compares to them.

A business world tool that may be helpful to succinctly describe how one organization compares to the rest of the alternatives in a given space is the *features comparison table* (see Figure 3.1). This table lays out organizational features or benefits in rows and benefits in columns and shows how they compare to other organizations.

	Benefit 1	Benefit 2	Benefit 3	Benefit 4	Benefit 5
Us	✓	✓	✓	✓	✓
Other 1	✓	✓		✓	
Other 2	✓		✓		✓
Other 3	✓			✓	

FIGURE 3.1 Sample Features Comparison Format.

These tables emphasize the value proposition by highlighting important features others don't have. Alternatively, they can present a collaborative context, showing how partnerships extend organizational reach and/or capability, so either competition or partnership could be the basis for a features comparison.

The Treehouse example below describes the "market" for Treehouse, which is the number of foster youth in its immediate service area. It also makes the important point that there are no alternatives—thus there is no need for a features comparison. Finally, it describes how Treehouse will grow its services to help every foster youth.

Case Study: Treehouse's Market

No one else is addressing the graduation crisis among foster youth in our community. Treehouse is committed to ensuring that foster kids succeed. There are 1,500 kids in foster care in King County distributed among 144 different high schools in 26 unique school districts. Almost every school has at least one foster youth, ranging from 1 to 20 in smaller rural high schools and more in urban settings. However, in order to achieve a sea change in graduation rates for foster youth in King County, we know we need to serve every student in foster care in middle schools as well. Beginning with the expected graduation class of 2017—this year's eighth graders, approximately 175 youth—Treehouse will scale its services to meet this need. Students will be brought on track to graduate and kept on track with targeted support and services. Five years from now, this group will graduate from high school at the same rate as their peers with a plan for their future.

Plan Practice 3.8: Refine Impact and Growth Strategies

With the initial drafts of the impact and growth strategies outlined in the planning framework, now is the time to develop them further in the business plan. The strategy section of the business plan is typically the hardest section to make clear, short, and simple. Start with an internal team and then incorporate the feedback of board members and trusted outside experts. Ask, "Is this clear and easy to understand? Is this credible? Are we leaving anything out? Are we confusing strategy with goals, initiatives, or anything else?"

Remember that strategy is an evolutionary process. In Chapter 4: "Test," we will review how to solicit and capture feedback on strategy and other elements of the business plan, so keep things in draft form. In Chapter 6: "Execute," we will describe how to use key performance indicators to test and refine both types of strategy. Work hard to be as specific as possible up front, but expect constant testing and refinement, especially in the first year of execution. Marry your goal, but date your strategy.

A strategy's success is wholly dependent on the specificity of the vision and how many dedicated people are ready to work together on it. Avoid easy platitudes such as "Engage the community" or "Empower our youth." These are slogans, not strategies.

The most effective strategies have four characteristics:

1. **Focused:** The strategy has few components. Three is the magic number.
2. **Simple:** The strategy is easy to explain, specific, and even memorable.
3. **Scalable:** The strategy will work with 1,000, and then 10,000, and then 100,000 people.
4. **Measurable:** The strategy has a clear, measurable cause and effect. Measure the cause first to ensure delivery, and then measure the effect. These are your leading and lagging indicators.

It's a near constant refrain in the social sector: measuring social impact is hard. But here's the truth that few people recognize or confront: anyone who complains that measuring social impact is hard is really admitting they don't have a clear strategy.

It's useful to return to the Treehouse strategy, which illustrates these characteristics so well: ABC+. It's focused, easy to describe, memorable, and scalable. It even rolls off the tongue.

Formulating strategy demands subject matter expertise, leadership, experience, curiosity, and most of all, tenacity. There is no way of getting around the hard work of doing the reading, consulting with experts and stakeholders (especially a representative sample of the proposed service audience), and grinding out the refinement, testing, and measurement. It bears repetition that, if they can be found, entrepreneurs with a successful track record and subject matter expertise are also excellent resources on strategy. So are leaders of other high-performing organizations. One of the many enjoyable things about working in the social sector is that the best organizations are willing to share what works. They know that we are all in this together.

The case study below is taken verbatim from the original Treehouse business plan in 2012. While long overdue, this model is finally getting the national attention it deserves.[6]

Case Study: Treehouse's Strategy

Our solution to the high school graduation crisis for foster youth combines the nationally recognized and research-based Check & Connect model with Treehouse's experience and expertise working with foster kids and within the child welfare system. Every aspect is designed to drive improvement in our areas of focus: attendance, behavior, course completion, mindset, planning, and extracurricular engagement.

Each youth we serve is at the center of our services. Every student has a Treehouse education specialist whose primary goal is to keep education a salient issue for foster students and their caregivers. The education specialist works with students throughout their education and follows them from school to school. The education specialist is trained to serve as a hub for coordinating the efforts of school staff, extracurricular activity providers, community partners, and volunteers, keeping services focused on research-based factors for driving high school graduation.

---

[6]The Seattle Times editorial board, "Treehouse, a WA Success with Foster Youth Education, Gets D.C.'s Attention," *Seattle Times*, December 14, 2022, **https://www.seattletimes.com/opinion/editorials/a-wa-success-with-foster-youth-education-gets-d-c-s-attention/**.

This collective work surrounds each youth with critical resources, each of which has a role in helping the student achieve success:

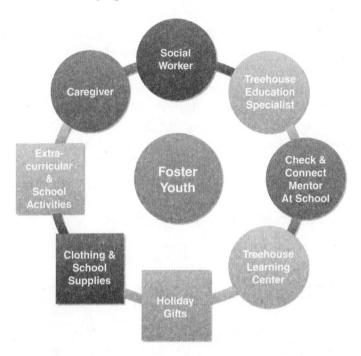

We pair a paid, in-school mentor with the Treehouse education specialist to ensure that attendance, behavior, and course data are continuously monitored for risk indicators: an unexcused absence, a disciplinary event, or a grade below C. When the education specialist identifies a risk, they take immediate action to provide targeted support to improve performance.

This pairing maximizes the efficiency of our education specialists, who serve a mobile and dispersed youth population. Education specialists also engage youth in the process of developing a plan to reach high school graduation milestones and to identify their post-graduation goals—whether it is college, a career, or service. Furthermore, specialists are trained to include coaching in their meetings with youth to help them see themselves as learners who can achieve their goals through their efforts, which is often a more important indicator of academic and career success than measures of intelligence.

Plan Practice 3.9: Define Growth Milestones

Milestones are exactly what they sound like: the most important progress points on the journey to the BHAG. One of the easiest and most memorable ways to articulate milestones is within a "crawl, walk, run" framework:

- **Crawl:** Demonstration programs are rolled out at the pilot level. Core staff are hired, technology issues are resolved, and evidence for leading indicators is established.
- **Walk:** Proof points for the value proposition are established, along with scalable impact strategy development and concomitant growth strategy formulation. Governance and team capability are developed.
- **Run:** Organizational growth and impact strategies are up and running. Ambitious pursuit of growth capital and refinement of the revenue model drive programs to scale at 25% a year. More partners, money, and new strategies accelerate growth even further. There is a credible pathway to solving the entire problem.

Use quarters or years to estimate how long it will take to get to each one. If there isn't certainty, take an educated guess. Put them together in a format similar to the Treehouse example shown below: a fair degree of specificity for year 1, with things moving into softer focus the farther out the horizon. This approach maintains flexibility while presenting a superior, longer-term horizon than the typical one-year format, demonstrating insight and imagination. This layout is always a draft and should be revised each year with experimentation and discoveries.

1. Crawl Phase (2023)
   - Q1: Hire marketing and fundraising staff;
   - Q2: Launch recruitment campaign;

- Q3: Train and deploy first volunteer cohort; and
- Q4: Publish evaluations and refine strategy in preparation for further scale.

2. Walk Phase (2024–2025)
- 2024: Expand to second major metropolitan area;
- 2025: Achieve projected impact metrics for >10,000 people served.

3. Run Phase (2026+)
- Create licensing structure and launch national affiliate model;
- Roll out national advertising campaign; and
- Increase annual budget to >$50 million.

As elsewhere, there will always be tension between the specificity demanded by business planning and the uncertainty of the person drafting the plans. If the person tasked with writing the plan won't write anything down without 100% certainty or is anxious about what other people will think if the document turns out to be flawed, reassign the task to someone more comfortable producing drafts that will be revised as the organization learns more.

Case Study: Treehouse's Milestones

During the 2011–12 school year, we served 338 youth in King County using this model, targeting the districts in King County with the lowest high school graduation rates. Over the summer, we took our original model and identified ways to further target our interventions and supports, and how to integrate the educational advocacy strategy that so many of our youth need. This year, we are expanding to serve every eighth grader in foster care in King County— going from a presence in 26 schools to 60 schools. Although this increases the number of school districts we serve, we are negotiating data-sharing agreements to make this expansion practicable.

Our plan to bring our model to full scale means that we will also expand our services to every school district in King County between now and 2015, serving all 675 foster kids we expect to engage in the services for which they are eligible. Post-2015 growth represents additional youth entering foster care as we retain the youth we already serve. Our annual service milestones for the next five years are as follows:

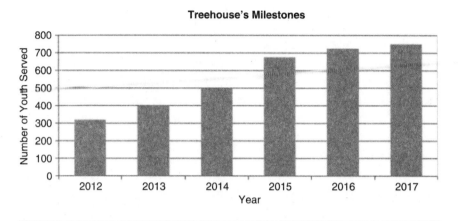

Plan Practice 3.10: Identify Key Performance Indicators

A *metric* is a measurement that follows a set of rules and definitions within a system that ensures its analytical rigor. High-performing organizations understand the old saying "You can't manage what you don't measure" and further understand that too much data is just as bad as no data at all. While it takes discipline and hard work, high-impact organizations define a small handful of so-called *key performance indicators* (KPIs) to give leaders at-a-glance information on organizational performance. KPIs are powerful tools for driving change in an organization but only if developed and applied well.

Clear quantitative or qualitative metrics that rigorously assess the impact of programs and services are essential. As noted earlier, too many nonprofits complain that "it's too hard to measure social impact," relying instead on anecdotes or even hope and faith. These organizations have more work to do on their strategy: clarity and specificity make clear measurement possible. While robust outcome measurement can still be challenging, after hundreds of nonprofit program evaluations, we have yet to find a nonprofit mission that isn't perfectly compatible with clear, concise, robust quantitative and qualitative outcome measurement.

The other barrier to good outcome measurement is the cost of data analysis. Returning to the Treehouse example, the organization followed the advice of academic experts and ended up collecting over 20 pages of data on every youth it served. There was a valid theoretical reason for every piece of data, but nobody thought about the practical challenges of processing all that information to yield evidence about what actions to take as a result. Each piece of data demands time, resources, and attention. The more data collected, the greater the expense.

The business plan should present only a handful of KPIs for financial, stakeholder, organizational, and program interventions. See Chapter 2 for an introduction to KPIs and Chapter 6 for a planning template that will guide their definition, collection, and analysis into an executive dashboard, which is a monitoring tool for business plan execution.

Case Study: Treehouse's KPIs

Our plan relies on monitoring fidelity to our program model and whether students receiving tiered, targeted services demonstrate short-term gains reflective of the change anticipated by the research behind our model. We divide these changes into short-term, mid-term, and long-term impact on the students we serve.

Short-term measure: Each year, we need to understand whether every student demonstrating a need for support in attendance, behavior, or course performance is receiving a targeted intervention. We also need to understand whether the targeted intervention results in improvement in the specific area.

- Target: 100% of students flagging a risk indicator receive tiered, targeted supports.
- Target: 75% of students receiving tiered, targeted supports demonstrate improvement.

Mid-term measure: As a result of our efforts, students who are in our program for two or more years should demonstrate increased on-track-to-graduate rates, defined as having adequate credits for their grade level and no core course failures.

- Target: Increase the number of on-track students by 20% each year.

Long-term measure: The youth we serve will graduate from high school with a plan for their future. As we reach saturation in King County, we will be able to use this measure to make assertions about our overall impact on high school graduation rates for foster youth.

- Target: In 2017, 80% of students will graduate from high school.

Plan Practice 3.11: Offer a Concise Marketing Plan

Marketing is a very broad term. As it's currently practiced in the social sector, marketing means posting on social media; running small-scale events; churning out newsletters and emails; and worst of all, sending lots of junk mail. This activity is largely wasted in an era when everyone is an information overload victim. Instead, follow the template below, writing down, in as few words as possible, short answers to these questions. The result will be a simple marketing and communication plan, which can then be summarized in 100 words or so for the business plan.

1. Why does the organization need to engage with external audiences? Why is it critical for impact and growth?
2. Who needs to be reached? Where are they, and how many of them are there? Why should they care?
3. What are the one or two short messages each audience type needs to hear and remember?
4. What does the schedule of delivery look like? Who gets what message, and when?

5. How will messages be delivered in an engaging, hard-to-ignore manner that is creative and unique?

6. What actions should each audience take, and how do they take them?

7. What does success look like? How will success be measured?

8. What will this cost be, and who is responsible for execution?

While the concepts are simple, this is yet another "easy to say, hard to do" activity. It will take time and testing to figure out how to deliver hard-to-ignore messages to the right people without spending huge sums of money. Quality beats quantity every day of the week. Be focused and creative. Don't do what too many other organizations do: "spray and pray."

As an example of a focused, creative marketing activity, see the case study below, one drawn from my very first job as a nonprofit fundraiser.

Case Study: Commitment Sunday

As the development director for an independent Catholic high school, my core market for fundraising was parents of current students. In the marketing section of the business plan we developed, we described launching "Commitment Sunday." We articulated a communication campaign to ask every parent to make a gift to the annual campaign of money, time, and/or prayer. There could be no objection to participating: Who in a Catholic school community could say no to praying for the school's success? We asked for a written commitment by a specific date we called Commitment Sunday, and we added that anyone not responding to our appeal would get a knock on their front door by a parent volunteer who would ask for the appeal in person.

This marketing campaign—an *in-your-face* activity that was also a creative and muscular way to reinforce the school's mission—was hard to avoid. We achieved 98% engagement among our target audience (name a marketing campaign with results like that!) and, even better, sent the message the school was serious about parent engagement. It was one element of the business plan that, when executed, drove the school to raise millions more dollars than it had ever raised before.

While this particular form of nonprofit marketing is not appropriate or possible for every organization, its core characteristics—focused, creative, hard to avoid—certainly are.

Plan Practice 3.12: Define Contributed, Earned, and Invested Income

Social impact enterprise income comes in three flavors: contributed, earned, and invested. *Contributed income* is philanthropic money offered in the form of gifts or grants. *Earned income* is generated from the sale of goods or services, often defined via contracts with other organizations or government agencies. *Invested income* is money generated from the organization's investments in the form of interest, dividends, and capital gains. These three types of income are generated from five different audiences: individuals, foundations, corporations, government agencies, and impact investors.

It's a complicated array of funding types and sources. Contributed, earned, and invested dollars can be generated from almost all of these funding audiences. To make it easier to think about and manage, we can consolidate all of the opportunities into six distinct buckets, summarized below along with a summary of the various subspecies of funding that comes from each domain. Later in Chapter 5: "Fund" we will discuss what strategies are effective—and what strategies are not effective—for each, with a highly detailed analysis of one particular type to illustrate how effective revenue strategies are executed. Effective nonprofit leaders must learn how to navigate the many opportunities in this complex revenue landscape and select the right ones for their organization and stage of growth:

Individuals	Tens of millions of Americans donate over $400 billion in the United States every year, ranging from millions of small dollar donations to hundreds of multimillion-dollar mega-gifts.

(continued)

Foundations	There are over 100,000 private foundations in the United States ranging from small, informal family foundations to large enterprises such as the Ford or Gates Foundation. There is about $80 billion in this space annually.
Corporations	Businesses direct over $20 billion to nonprofits each year in the form of gifts, grants, and sponsorships.
Government agencies	Federal and local governments grant over $400 billion to US nonprofits each year in the form of grants and contracts.
Earned income	Many will be surprised to learn that nonprofits earn over $750 billion annually. Yes, most of the money nonprofits make, they earn.
Impact investors	This relatively new type of funding is a type of debt: loans, bonds, or other instruments. Nonprofits borrow money and need to pay it back, but the interest rate and the risk tolerance are friendlier than in the commercial market. Where the going rate on a commercial business loan may be, say, 7%, and the borrower would need to have collateral and strong evidence of being able to repay the loan, a so-called impact capital loan might demand a lower interest rate, tolerate higher risk, or both. In other words, impact investors sacrifice interest and/or take on higher risk in return for the promise of social impact.

The business plan summarizes which of these domains to be approached for funding, along with a brief description of strategy. Before choosing which ones fit a particular mission, read Chapter 5: "Fund" carefully, consult with board members that have applicable experience, look to other organizations for examples, and consult successful social entrepreneurs. Take care to learn from successful nonprofit fundraisers as well, but only those who have raised many millions of dollars. Otherwise, you are getting narrow advice that will likely cost dearly in terms of lost opportunity. Unless consultants have raised at least, say, $50 million in funding in a particular domain for at least three different organizations, they are not experts. Most fundraisers are good at one or two of these domains. With the rare altruistic exception, the most effective consultants sell their expertise to the organizations that can pay the most for it: hospitals and universities. Credible fundraising consultants cost $25,000 a month. In sum, it is difficult to get robust, full-spectrum fundraising advice, as only the wealthy organizations can afford it.

Plan Practice 3.13: Identify Risk and Describe Mitigation

Scaling social impact is hard and risky. The following categories offer flavors of what can and does go wrong:

- **Financial risk:** Losing funding from changes in donor preference, laws or regulations that impact funding, economic downturns;
- **Reputational risk:** Negative publicity or controversy from the media, social media, or from stakeholders (this type of risk varies widely by program type; some organizations, such as activists, deliberately court reputational risk to gain attention);
- **Legal risk:** Lawsuits from employees, partners, or third parties; regulatory investigations and/or fines;[7]
- **Governance risk:** Inadequate governance policies and training in areas such as conflict of risk, financial controls, and management oversight; and
- **Operational risk:** Failed program initiatives, natural disasters, data breaches, employee turnover, among others.

Identifying and managing organizational risk is one of the chief duties of leadership and specifically the board of directors. It's the board's job to identify risk and the CEO's job to articulate how the risk will be managed, in close consultation and teamwork with the board.

---

[7]Melanie Lockwood Herman, "The Top 10 Legal Risks Facing Nonprofit Boards," Venable LLP **https://www.venable.com/insights/publications/2011/02/the-top-10-legal-risks-facing-nonprofit-boards**.

Like setting BHAGs, a fear of looking bad drives organizational leaders to hide their risks from external audiences. This is a giant mistake. All organizations are filled with risk. Failing to identify risk is foolish, and failing to talk about how it is managed is naive. The best organizations foresee risk, articulate the risk scenarios, and describe how they will be managed if they occur. Like every other planning practice in this chapter, foreseeing and managing risk communicates that the organization is led by experienced, prudent leaders. Far from discouraging supporters, it establishes and builds credibility with prospective staff, partners, funders, and volunteers.

Carefully consider what risks the organization confronts, list them as bullet points, and then detail how these risks are being monitored. Strong board policies, clear oversight, and transparent management practices are required for each of these categories. Few boards are aware of these risks, and even if they are, they are often not taken seriously enough until something bad happens.

Plan Practice 3.14: Create an Organization Chart Projection

Like most businesses, staff at social impact enterprises typically account for about three-quarters of the expense budget. However, few organizations maintain an adequate organization chart, and it is rare indeed to have a chart that projects future hires. With organizational growth milestones or phases defined, the next task is to project the number of people needed to execute by each growth phase. Here as elsewhere, experience is helpful to target the right number of positions, compensation, benefits, and support resources. That expertise must be captured and summarized in an organization chart[8] (see Figure 3.2) keyed to crawl, walk, run milestones.

---

[8]A web search for "create an organization chart" will deliver any number of good options for creating these. MS Word has a hierarchy function under its "smart art" option. Canva (**https://www.canva.com/**) is a popular solution as well.

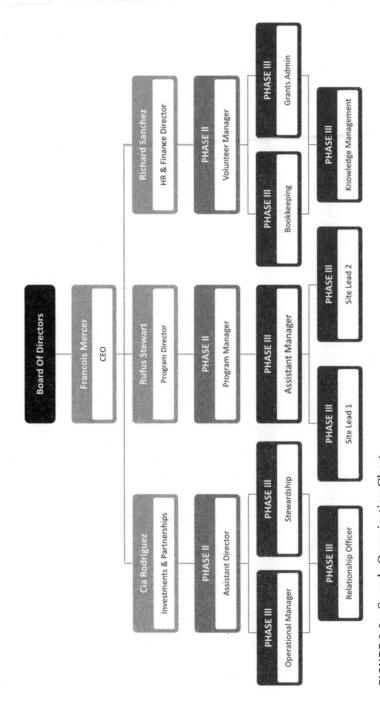

FIGURE 3.2 Sample Organization Chart.

Plan Practice 3.15: Build a Detailed Financial Projection

CEOs and executives who made it through graduate school without a class in managerial accounting or financial management can learn the necessary financial basics via any number of free online resources.[9] Basic competency includes the ability to read financial statements, create and maintain a budget projection, and understand the balance sheet and cash flow to manage money responsibly. Financing is clear and easy to understand if there are capable accountants at work and there is adequate expertise on the board. At least one CPA should be on every nonprofit board, and larger ones must have them as members of the leadership team.

To continue with the business plan development, start with the simplest possible budget that explains where the money comes from and where it goes. Figure 3.3 illustrates a typical summary-level financial projection, where only the overall categories are shown, leaving the components hidden for ease of reading.

	2023	2024	2025	2026	2027
Revenue					
Contributed Income subtotal	-	-	-	-	-
Earned Income subtotal	-	-	-	-	-
In-kind subtotal	-	-	-	-	-
Restricted subtotal	-	-	-	-	-
Total Revenue	-	-	-	-	-
Expense					
Salaries and Benefits subtotal	-	-	-	-	-
Professional Services subtotal	-	-	-	-	-
Operations subtotal	-	-	-	-	-
Total Expense	-	-	-	-	-
Contribution to Reserve	-	-	-	-	-
NET	-	-	-	-	-
# months reserve					

FIGURE 3.3 Sample High-Level Financial Projection.

[9]For example: **https://online.hbs.edu/blog/post/how-to-read-financial-statements**.

Note the line along the bottom, "# months reserve." This means the number of months the organization can continue to pay its operating expenses without any income. It is a simple calculation: add up all the annual expenses, divide them by 12 to determine the average monthly spend, and then compare this amount to cash reserves to determine the number of months of cash the organization has on hand.

Nonprofits should aim to have at least six months of cash in the bank in reserve. It depends on the type of organizational mission whether or not it is appropriate to have more than a year, however. Is there a reason for a big reserve fund or large endowment? For a university that wants to ensure its mission in perpetuity, yes, there are practical reasons. For an environmental SIE fighting an urgent mission, hanging on to huge amounts of cash may present the appearance that the organization cares more about financial stability than the urgency of its mission.

Figure 3.4 presents the next level of detail, typically the level that belongs in a business plan. This is a "goldilocks" level of detail: just enough to provide the reader with a general sense of where the money is coming from and what the proposed allocations are.

Some readers will want a lot of detail, while others will not. So the answer is to use what is known as a "grouping" function in spreadsheets, which allows the user to expand and then collapse groups of rows in a spreadsheet with a single click. All financial projections should include the smallest level of detail—projecting every income and expense category out at least three years—and this grouping function is used to present easier-to-read summaries that still allow the detail to be shown as needed.

Remember, as with every other aspect of this methodology, if it isn't easy to read, it is wrong. If an accountant insists on complicated, hard-to-read spreadsheets, find a better one. Good ones aren't easy to find, but it's critical to get the right people on the bus.

This financial projection does not go into the most granular level of detail. For example, there may be many smaller items under expense categories such as "Insurance" or "Events." Every detail should be tracked under its appropriate category, but not every detail needs to be shown. Show too little detail, and there is no transparency. Show too much, and the reader is overwhelmed with minutiae. Again, the

	2023	2024	2025	2026	2027
Revenue					
Contributed Income					
Individuals	-	-	-		-
Foundations	-	-	-	-	-
Corporations	-	-	-	-	-
Gov't Agencies	-	-	-	-	-
Contributed Income subtotal	-	-	-	-	-
Earned Income					
Product Revenue	-	-	-	-	-
Service Revenue	-	-	-	-	-
Licensing Revenue	-	-	-	-	-
Earned Income subtotal	-	-	-	-	-
In-kind					
Office Space	-	-	-	-	-
Other	-	-	-	-	-
In-kind subtotal	-	-	-	-	-
Restricted					
Other restricted income	-	-	-	-	-
Restricted subtotal	-	-	-	-	-
Total Revenue	-	-	-	-	-
Expense					
Salaries					
Executive Director	-	-	-	-	-
Fundraising Director	-	-	-	-	-
Program Director	-	-	-	-	-
Marketing Director	-	-	-	-	-
Office Manager	-	-	-	-	-
Partnership Manager	-	-	-	-	-
Taxes & Benefits	-	-	-	-	-
Salaries and Benefits subtotal	-	-	-	-	-
Professional Services					
Management consulting	-	-	-	-	-
Accounting/Bookkeeping	-	-	-	-	-
Marketing	-	-	-	-	-
Human Resources	-	-	-	-	-
Professional Services subtotal	-	-	-	-	-
Operations	-	-	-	-	-
Rent/Uilities	-	-	-	-	-
Curriculum Support	-	-	-	-	-
Communication	-	-	-	-	-
Website	-	-	-	-	-
Supplies/equipment/furnish	-	-	-	-	-
Insurance	-	-	-	-	-
Travel and Parking	-	-	-	-	-
Events	-	-	-	-	-
Misc.	-	-	-	-	-
Media & Print Campaigns	-	-	-	-	-
Operations subtotal	-	-	-	-	-
Total Expense	-	-	-	-	-
Contribution to Reserve	-	-	-	-	-
NET	-	-	-	-	-
# months reserve					

FIGURE 3.4 Sample "Goldilocks" Financial Projection.

grouping function in a spreadsheet can make navigating between summary and details easy. Offering both a summary level and full detail to every prospective partner and financial supporter is a powerful way to express organizational transparency and accountability.

Finally, remember that a financial projection isn't a contract or even a promise. It's an educated guess that reflects current understanding of the future. As each year passes, or each quarter or even month if it is early in the process, leaders continue to revise projections along with the rest of the plan. If the organization doesn't hit the revenue goals, that's okay, it will happen more often than not. Leadership can simply push the growth out into the future and go to work on improving growth strategy and execution.

Follow plan practice 3.1: "Follow Good Process," and soon enough, organizational statements corresponding to the other 14 practices will emerge. Figure 3.5 provides a template for summarizing all essential business plan elements.

PROBLEM	Define the problem being solved with concise descriptive statistics.
SOLUTION	Identify what success looks like.
VALUE PROP	Spell out why this is the best solution to the problem. Give a brief explanation of programs, and provide evidence that they work.
TEAM	Summarize executive team qualifications and provide links to career profiles.
GOAL	Articulate your vision and BHAG.
MARKET	Define how many people or parts of the planet are encountering the problem you are solving. Explain the other actors in this space and how this effort compares.
STRATEGY	Summarize impact and growth strategy: How does the organization deliver social impact? How will it execute its growth?
MILESTONES	Illustrate the phases of organizational growth toward the BHAG.

FIGURE 3.5   Business Plan Template.

METRICS	Define a small set of key performance indicators.
MARCOM	Summarize the marketing plan: Who needs to be reached? What key messages need to be delivered? What actions will be taken?
REVENUE	Explain how revenue is generated and sustained now, and how it will grow to meet the organization's resource needs.
RISK	Identify foreseeable risks and describe how they are managed.
FINANCIALS	Present a summary of three- to five-year financial projections (and keep a detailed version to share on request).
ORG CHART	Provide an organizational chart that projects the planned growth with easy-to-read color codes that align with each growth phase.

FIGURE 3.5   *(continued).*

Additional Resources

See **www.altruistaccelerator.org** for tools and examples.

Tools
- Business Plan Template
- Marcom Planning Template
- Organization Chart Projection Template
- Financial Projection Template

Examples
- Sample Business Plans
- Sample Financial Projections

CHAPTER 4

Test

The only true voyage [is] to see the universe through the eyes of another.

—Marcel Proust

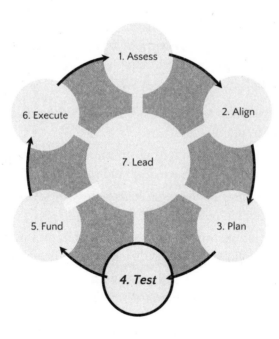

LEARNING OBJECTIVES

By the end of this chapter, you will be able to:

- Test and improve the business plan with external audiences;
- Map your most important stakeholders to identify who should provide input on your business plan;
- Identify the most effective ways to ask for advice and receive high-quality feedback; and
- Create a pitch deck from your business plan.

Business plan development begins with the CEO and board working through the align practices from Chapter 2 to articulate organizational direction in a one-page framework. Then, working with staff and others, the CEO expands the framework's content into a 10- to 15-page business plan, continuously consulting with staff and board members individually or in small groups. With these steps complete, the draft document is ready to share with select external reviewers for their feedback. This process enables you to do the following:

- Capture feedback to make the document shorter, more specific, and easier to understand;
- Validate strategy by soliciting opinions of successful entrepreneurs and people who have built and run companies before;
- Build confidence in the proposed trajectory, or, if feedback dictates, improve the plan before launching;
- Deepen relationships with the most important funders and partners by soliciting their feedback in early, pre-public plans; and
- Establish relationships and trust with prospective partners and supporters by asking them for their opinion on an internal, confidential plan.

We again return to the Treehouse case study as an example of the benefits of the test process.

Case Study: Treehouse

The initial draft of the Treehouse business plan outlined an aggressive growth trajectory detailed in a financial projection that showed the organization growing from $6 million to $12 million in a period of three years. "Wow," said Janis. "That's aggressive growth. I worry that it is not realistic. It's taken us 25 years to get to $6 million. Now we double our budget in three?"

"It isn't easy, but it is entirely possible, and isn't this what the world needs?" I responded. "You've got the courage to set the goal. Now we need to keep our courage and describe what it means to fund this effort. We must let our plans determine our budget, not let our expectations on how much money we can comfortably project determine how fast we can grow."

"I hear you, but I'm still not comfortable with such an aggressive trajectory. Can you please make it more realistic?"

"I completely understand, Janis. It's easy for me to set an ambitious trajectory, but you are the one who has to own it and answer to the board if you aren't successful. I will back it off to, say, $9 million, but do me one favor: don't get married to any rate of growth until we take this plan out and test it with our partners, funders, and other stakeholders. Let's see what our community of supporters say. They are the ones that will determine our growth rate."

The executive team defined a list of 30 people who would see a confidential draft of the plan, and the testing process launched.

A month later, as the testing process followed its course, Janis and I met to review the feedback we collected. Janis looked at me and smiled. "I am just shocked. I expected our supporters to tell us we needed to embark on such a bold vision cautiously. In practically every meeting I had, especially with the business executives, I was told our projected growth was not ambitious enough. Looks like we need to go big or go home."

Before beginning any testing phase, put a "CONFIDENTIAL" label on your business plan. It really is an early plan, not ready for public consumption. Particularly for organizations in sensitive operational spaces, it is prudent to be discreet. Reviewers will also take note of the implicit trust in being asked to review a confidential document. It's also exciting to read a confidential document.

While it is important to make a positive impression with a well-written, concise document, don't make it look too pretty. It really is a draft and can look like one. Documents that are too polished discourage reviewers from fully engaging.

Test Practice 4.1: Map Key Constituents

With these fundamentals in mind, the CEO starts the test practices by first mapping out the organization's stakeholders in a simple series of concentric circles (see Figure 4.1).

Each circle represents a stakeholder group ordered by the proximity of its relationship to the core executive team. Internally there are staff and board members. Beyond the board, key constituents might

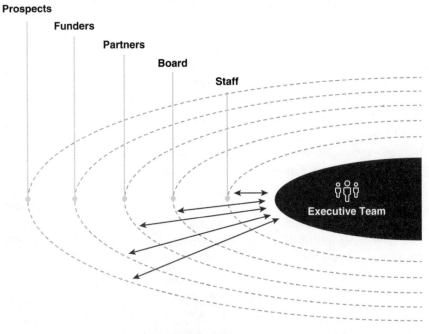

FIGURE 4.1 Constituent Mapping Model.

include corporate, government, and nonprofit partners and supporters. In all cases, both prospective funders and potential partners should be included. Balance the desire for a detailed stakeholder map with the practical demand to keep things simple and move swiftly. Note that Figure 4.1 is a model, not a prescription: the CEO can change and add to the circles, choosing additional internal and external circles as judgment dictates, such as advisory board members or former staff.

With each stakeholder group, the CEO then creates a list of the three to five most important individuals in each segment, following the judgment of the board and leadership team. The one exception is staff: all staff should be consulted, even administrative, part-time, or volunteer staff. Inclusiveness is an excellent principle. Everyone appreciates things being done *with* them, not *to* them. Furthermore, valuable insights come from surprising places, and the intimate knowledge front-line staff possess is often extremely valuable.

Apart from all staff and board members, there should now be a list of approximately 20–30 stakeholders across the various stakeholder groups. More is acceptable if time and resources allow, but going well beyond 30 makes for a heavy feedback management burden. The goal is a diverse audience of individuals representing a cross-section of stakeholder types.

Test Practice 4.2: Ask for Advice

Offer the draft business plan to all stakeholder groups as follows:

The Executive Team

- They react to the first draft and meet with the CEO to discuss their comments and incorporate changes. There are typically substantive revisions in this stage. Keep the plan among this circle until 80% satisfaction is achieved.

- Unless the executive team is larger than a half-dozen people, or there are strong differences of opinion that must be reconciled, the executive team and CEO should have a plan ready to share with staff in a couple of weeks.

All Staff

- Follow a strict need-to-know basis for sharing the business plan with staff: everyone needs to know everything, with the exception of detailed salary projections, which can be reserved for the executive team.

- Sharing the plan doesn't necessarily mean everyone gets an equal say as to what goes in the document. That is the CEO's decision.

Board Chair

- The relationship between the board chair and the CEO needs to be one of the tightest, most trusting in the organization. This does not mean long meetings or daily exchanges. It does mean 100% trust, transparency, and candor. Therefore, after aligning with staff, the CEO must ensure the board chair is in full support of the business plan details. This need for close alignment must be balanced with the realization that 80% agreement is the threshold, with action and experiment answering the debatable questions.

- This conversation, along with those with the rest of the board, should go relatively smoothly if the align practices were conducted with care.

- In some instances, particularly when the organization is facing a restructuring or other sensitive change in direction, the board and CEO may draft the plan first, with the order of operations positioning the rest of the board before the staff or the executive team. It is ultimately up to the chair and the CEO to agree on the order of review and revision.

The Executive Committee and Rest of the Board

- Start with the executive committee, and then move on to each other board member, sending the plan to each person and allocating at least 30 minutes for one-on-one conversations to review their feedback.

- Always solicit written feedback. Board members are fiduciaries and risk managers. If they don't have time to give the business plan a thoughtful edit, the board chair should be questioning their commitment to the board.

- Critique is easy and cheap. Suggested improvements are far more valuable. Ask for the latter.

Partner Organization CEOs

- Effective organizations leverage their influence and reach through partners, be they government agencies, corporations, or other nonprofits—often all three. At this stage, there is now a full business plan vetted and improved by all staff and board—but, critically, still at the 80% level. Now is a critical time to get the feedback from partners—they will often see things that staff and volunteers have missed.

- In addition to feedback, this is the time to share the plan with prospective partners. If the organization proposes a new strategy that demands significantly more corporate engagement, for example, testing to ensure the plan is attractive to prospects is best done as early as practical.

Major Financial Supporters

- There are few better ways to show appreciation for supporters—and build trust toward their future investment—than asking them for feedback on the organization's confidential future initiatives. Emphasize the goal of the meeting is advice, not money.

- These stakeholders come later in the process not because of the distance of their relationship but because they should see a plan that's validated by key partners and leaders first. In other words, they are revising a direction that has been through a reasonable degree of validation.

- This guidance is tentative. CEOs and board members may have deep relationships with major funders with subject matter expertise as well as capital that warrant their engagement at the earliest stages of the planning process—even with the business plan framework, a document that demands far less time and energy to absorb. As always, the judgment and experience of the CEO, chair, and leadership are important ingredients to this process.

- If you try to sell funders a finished product, you will be sending them the wrong message: that they are just cash machines. Remember the adage: "Ask for money; get advice. Ask for advice; get money—eventually."

Very few people are ever asked to provide honest feedback on a confidential, early-stage document. Usually, they are asked to fund an idea that is already baked, receiving little recognition for their expertise. By asking for feedback, listening with an open heart and mind, and incorporating what is learned, leaders will build new and extraordinary levels of trust and alignment with staff, board, and external stakeholders—if the conversations are conducted with integrity, humility, honesty, and courage.

Ask people for advice and feedback, and they'll become invested in the vision. People support initiatives they have a hand in creating and shaping. *Make insiders out of outsiders.*

Test Practice 4.3: Capture High-Quality Feedback

The business plan is always in draft mode as it evolves with feedback and interaction. Put "CONFIDENTIAL DRAFT" on the document (note: in the header or footer, *not* as a watermark, which is distracting), and keep it there. Remember, this is the document representing the ambitious trajectory of a social impact enterprise, not the brochure of a needy charity begging for donations.

Whenever possible, default to high-bandwidth conversations. Face-to-face meetings are best, followed by video calls, phone calls, email, and lastly text. If selected stakeholder representatives don't respond after the second prompt, delete them from the test list and find someone else. Never chase.

Always be direct and 100% transparent: "I'm leading a strong organization trying to solve this important problem with major implications for our community. Here's our plan. I respect your opinion and am consulting with selected centers of influence like you in this confidential, early stage so we can capture the best advice before we launch. I ask for 30 minutes of your time to read and critique this plan. Be as detailed as you wish, but even a few bullet points would help." No schmoozing, no begging for help. If your mission is important, your vision bold, and your strategy potentially effective, there will be many who will be interested and provide feedback.

One point about this feedback, however. As mentioned earlier, critique is easy. Ask for suggestions to make it more valuable. Ideally, get any critiques in writing.

Consider the following two approaches to feedback and consider which is more effective. Notice how testing will not just capture valuable advice and feedback but will cultivate the attention and boost the engagement of current and potential partners and funders.

Charity Approach

"Susan, I see that you are a wealthy person [or a program officer at a big foundation or a major corporate executive or the head of a government agency]. I would like to educate you about this need that we are working on. Here are evocative stories and pictures of vulnerable people to make you feel privileged and guilty. Aren't these moving? Now, please make a big gift to help us with this need. I will follow up with you repeatedly until you say yes or ignore me altogether."

Social Impact Enterprise Approach

"Susan, you are an influential member of our community. My organization has this BHAG that will deliver these benefits to our community. Does this immediately interest you? If not, no worries, thank you for helping solve other problems. If it does, we've just finished an early, confidential plan to achieve this BHAG. We are doing good work now, but we are aiming to do more, and we need advice. If this problem is a priority for you, may I ask for your wisdom and feedback on our approach? Here is our short, focused plan. With your help, we can make it better. If you like the way this evolves, and if we do a good job building trust with you, perhaps, sometime in the future, you will join us as a partner, an investor, or both."

The test practices develop the habit of thinking and acting like enterprise leaders. High-performing social impact enterprises are collective vehicles for gathering the best thinking out there, digesting it, and then acting on it. Don't sit in a room, think up a solution, and then ask people to fund it. Instead, go ahead and sit in a room, think up the best solution, and then shape it further with the best minds in the community.

No matter how important the BHAG, most people are information overload victims. Few people have the capacity to sit, read, think, and respond in thoughtful, measured ways. The most successful, caring individuals still do have that capacity, however, so the test practices are also a diagnostic for leaders to determine if they have the right stakeholders. Certainly, the initial stakeholder list can and should evolve if participants on the initial list fall low on the feedback hierarchy.

Always respect stakeholder time and move with intention and urgency. The initial testing phase shouldn't take more than six to eight weeks. If it takes longer, malfunctions ranging from the pursuit of perfection to underinvestment of time and attention should be diagnosed and remediated. Endure the cognitive dissonance of simultaneously leading a clear and sequential process and also accommodating for the inherent messiness and unpredictability of visioning and planning.

Finally, do not seek to finalize the plan. The plan is never done. It will be clear that the plan is ready to move to the next stage when external feedback is positive and iterations become increasingly marginal. Ultimately, when to move on is the judgment call of the CEO.

Test Practice 4.4: Pitch Deck

A strong business plan is a concise, 10- to 15-page organizational road map. While that length is important for internal audiences, it is still far too long for the average information overload victim. Therefore, once the business plan leaves a state of continuous iteration and settles into a state of relative stability—stakeholders have provided their feedback and signal their enthusiasm, additional edits are marginal, KPIs haven't moved lately, the financial projection has not changed radically—now is the time to boil the business plan down to a *pitch deck*, a series of 15 or so slides, each summarizing a section of the business plan. While standard practice in the business and entrepreneurial worlds, pitch decks are rarely used in the social space, and if they are done well, they will help to differentiate the organization as unusually focused and disciplined. Along with a world-class business plan, a concise pitch deck is immediate evidence that the organization is led and staffed by people not just with big hearts but with big brains as well, people who are ready to deploy powerful strategy and disciplined organizational practices in the pursuit of social good.

Create the first draft of the deck by copying headings from the business plan and boiling down the content into a couple of bullet points under each. Keeping it short and simple will always be better than generating slides crammed with information and pictures. It may take dozens of revisions to chisel the business plan down to a concise yet comprehensive deck. This focusing process often yields insights on how to improve the business plan itself. As the famous French polymath Blaise Pascal apologized to his friend, "I am sorry I wrote you such a long letter. I did not take the time to make it short."

In the world of venture capital (VC), the success of start-up entrepreneurs directly hinges on the quality of their pitch decks. Venture capital firms and investors want great pitch decks—they want to work as little as possible to find where the big investment returns are. Therefore, they offer great advice on how to create a strong pitch deck. That advice is incredibly useful for social impact enterprise leaders, even if they will never get in front of a VC.[1]

---

[1]See **https://resolute.vc/blog/2012/05/the-perfect-vc-pitch/** and **https://guykawasaki.com/the-only-10-slides-you-need-in-your-pitch**.

Additional Resources

See **www.altruistaccelerator.org** for tools and examples.

Tools
- Business Plan Testing Process
- Pitch Deck Template

Examples
- Sample Pitch Decks

CHAPTER 5

Fund

Growth and comfort do not coexist.

—Ginni Rometty

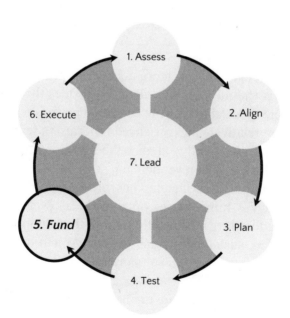

LEARNING OBJECTIVES

By the end of this chapter, you will be able to:

- Create a detailed operational system for raising money with specific, step-by-step prescriptions for planning and execution;
- Break down revenue strategy into a sequence of steps called *tactics*;
- Develop a one-page fundraising plan that summarizes how you propose to raise money, how you will develop relationships, who will do the work, and what the budget should be;
- Improve the effectiveness of your fundraising teams by giving them clear connections to both strategy formulation and execution;
- Differentiate between good fundraising strategies and poor ones; and
- Execute your fundraising activity with discipline by reviewing an activity scorecard every two weeks.

This chapter is longer and far more detailed than the previous ones. No matter what the mission, this chapter provides the design for an efficient, effective, scalable revenue engine to power increasing levels of impact. Even relatively inexperienced fundraising teams can apply the practices here and greatly enhance the likelihood they will generate substantial increases in revenue.

Every element in this chapter has proven itself over repeated deployments across hundreds of organizations. Every organization we have worked with that diligently follows this blueprint has experienced a median, sustained annual revenue growth of 25%, a figure that stands in stark contrast to so many organizations that run on a shoestring.

Before we begin, let's explore the benefits of using this system by looking at how it helped Bellevue LifeSpring, a century-old charity located a short drive from Microsoft's global headquarters.

Case Study: Bellevue LifeSpring

Bellevue LifeSpring, a nonprofit delivering food, clothing, and other financial and material assistance to Bellevue, Washington's low-income families and children, had been operating for over 100 years. In 2019, Jennifer Fischer, the organization's new executive director, realized that the $2 million organization needed to raise much more money if it was going to meet the growing need. Bellevue was next door to Redmond, the home of Microsoft, and like so many other high-tech regions around the country, sustained cost of living increases that compounded the severity of food insecurity, eviction, and difficulty providing children the activities and support necessary to foster optimal learning and development. In the city so many leading corporations called home, where no house in many neighborhoods sold for under a million dollars, over 4,000 children were living below the federal poverty line.

A performance benchmarking exercise revealed untapped opportunities for growth and impact. The consulting team worked closely with the board, executive director, and staff to sharpen the organization's program strategy, identify key performance indicators, and improve its fundraising strategy and execution. The executive director and board of directors led the process, and the resulting business plan targeted a deeper relationship with Bellevue's school district and an ambitious budget increase from $2.6 to $4.2 million.

To fuel the plan, the organization needed to transition away from its fundraising strategy that was centered on writing grants to private foundations and soliciting gifts at numerous events. After it completed a business plan, it hired a new director of investment and partnership to convert the organization's many small donors to much larger investors, launch a planned giving and endowment campaign, and rapidly expand the number of new financial supporters. Because of the organization's compelling business plan and the trust it was able to establish because of its transparent, accountable performance dashboard, the organization realized rapid increases in generated revenue: in the first year of deployment, gift and grant revenue grew 300% while the cost per dollar raised decreased by 30%—all during the first year of the global pandemic. In addition to the revenue growth, the board, executive director, and staff reported an enhanced, more focused, and supportive culture; a new focus on key metrics to drive organizational performance; and an optimism in the face of profound societal challenges.

You will recall the planning methodology laid out in Chapter 3: "Plan," providing a general framework for formulating an *impact strategy*, which may be impossible to predict given the variety of programs in the social sector. When it comes to a *growth strategy*, however, it is possible to get much more specific and even prescriptive, especially around execution. A widely applicable system for growth strategy that works is laid out in this chapter and includes KPIs, performance analysis tools, job descriptions, and compensation models, among other practical tools and solutions.

Fund Practice 5.1: Integrate Revenue Tools and Staff

If written well, a business plan and deck immediately establish credibility with sophisticated prospects. Because the business plan is an internal as well as an external document, it creates transparency and offers robust organizational accountability. It is a simple, effective way to "make insiders out of outsiders."

Now it is time to put the plan and deck to work, led by what we suggest you call your *investment and partnership (I&P) team*. We choose these words because they establish an effective framework for fundraising. *Investment* communicates that the organization promises to deliver social progress as a return on investment. *Partnership* communicates that the relationship to funders is one of equals, not one of subservience or unctuousness too often associated with gift-seekers.

Now that you have a strong label for your fundraisers—*investment and partnership officers (IPOs)*—you can add substance to that label by giving them visibility and a role in organizational planning as well as execution. For example, the *chief investment and partnership officer (CIPO)* is a core part of the leadership team, often next in line in the succession plan. The CIPO typically plays an important role in board management and development, strategy formulation and refinement, and execution. Direct work with fundraising prospects is always the majority of I&P, but additional responsibility around core planning and execution gives fundraising executives critical knowledge they need to communicate organizational value and results.

The CIPO helps lead goal setting and business plan development and often takes full ownership over the refinement of the pitch deck. In the test phase, all IPOs gather market feedback and help revise the plan. In the fund phase, as all good relationships start with asking for advice, IPOs continue as eyes and ears, collecting feedback to share with leadership and the board to fuel eventual revisions. Finally, IPOs are accountable for execution: outcomes are measured in the business plan even if they don't match aspirations, which is typical in the first business cycle or two. When the strategy isn't working, or too many investors find the metrics confusing, the IPOs communicate this and bring investors into conversation with the executive team in a collective problem-solving effort. Whether partners and investors have good advice or not, conferring with them as partners is the best way to manage inevitable execution sticking points.

Because IPOs are corporate officers with responsibility for all phases of organizational development, not salespeople given a brochure and sent out to procure auction items, their role is inherently more satisfying and durable than the traditional fundraising role. The strategic and team-oriented nature of this new model makes it much easier to attract and retain talented professionals. In dozens of deployments, job satisfaction, cost per dollar raised, and average tenure far surpass industry norms. The current average tenure of a nonprofit fundraising officer in the United States is 16 months, an enormously expensive revolving door[1] and one of the many reasons nonprofits aren't delivering needed levels of service and impact.

Fund Practice 5.2: Develop Effective, Scalable Revenue Strategy

Fundraising strategies used by most small to mid-sized nonprofits (under, say, $25 million in annual revenue) are pathways to survival, not scale. It's important to note that so many nonprofits will have a

---

[1] See Nicole Rizkallah, "Shutting the Revolving Door of Development Turnover," Philanthropy Daily, **https://philanthropydaily.com/shutting-door-development-turnover/**.

very difficult time breaking free of their subsistence-style fundraising strategies. Raffles, golf tournaments, auctions, thrift stores, and so many other grassroots, low-return fundraising strategies offer immediate gratification. The leaders who operate them are not hired to take risks or grow the organization; whether the board makes it explicit or not, they are hired to keep the operation running at its current scale, which is going to be very small due to the poor revenue strategy. While the board and staff may pay lip service to solving more of the problem they are addressing because that is what donors want, the comfort of the familiar and fear of the unknown often outweigh whatever courage brought these leaders to the organization. I have worn out my fingertips pointing to mountains of data and case study after case study showing the pronounced revenue gains, reduced staff burnout, increased stakeholder happiness, and of course profound gains in social impact that all result from better revenue strategy, but instead of being curious and intrigued, the most common reaction is reluctance or fear of change. We've spoken to many boards who, for example, respond with objections like this: "But auctions are fun!" They aren't willing to consider the huge opportunity cost of auctions. None are so deaf as the ones who do not want to hear.

What follows is a summary of the various sources of revenue available to nonprofits, with the strategies of effective social impact enterprises (SIEs) compared to those of traditional charities. After this strategy overview, we discuss how to create a specific fundraising plan, how to execute that plan, and how to measure the right performance data and use it to continuously improve fundraising performance.

Remember that social impact enterprises able to follow this rigorous, disciplined approach achieve sustained median annual revenue growth of 25%. The hard work pays off big, and there is finally adequate fuel for the social change we all want and need.

Revenue from Private Individuals

US private citizens donate over $400 billion annually to nonprofits each year (and they purchase many billions more in goods and services).

Many organizations that survive on grants or government funding overlook the importance of this major revenue stream or attempt to generate individual support with very ineffective methods. Organizations experienced with raising money from individuals are focused on conducting high numbers of high-quality, one-on-one, face-to-face meetings with current and prospective supporters. In addition, they work to ensure each relationship is authentic and of high quality, aiming for nothing less than lifelong support. While there are many strategies to reach and engage people, in this age of digital overload and low attention spans, we have found the most successful organizations focus on building strong individual relationships with the right people, not making fundraising pitches to crowds and churning out other kinds of mass appeals.

SIE Strategies

- Propose charitable investments via one-on-one, face-to-face meetings;
- Use events to educate and thank charitable investors and to identify new potential major prospects; do *not* use events as primary revenue-generating vehicles;
- Equip fundraising staff and volunteers with business plans that clearly explain how money will produce social impact, using terms and principles familiar to a business audience;
- Invest heavily in thanking supporters and demonstrating social return on investment via dashboards and concise reports;
- Monitor the right leading metrics that drive continuous improvement; and
- Use wealth screening tools to find the largest prospective investors.

Charity Strategies

- Rely on high-cost, low-return, one-time transactional events such as auctions, galas, raffles, bake sales, and car washes;
- Prioritize social media appeals, "big gift" campaigns, fundraising letters, brochures, newsletters, digital communication, and other mass marketing efforts that offer low conversion rates and contribute to message fatigue and information overload;

- Use language similar to other nonprofits: "donate," "help us," "need," "gift," etc.;
- Email multiple, repeated solicitations across the donor database; and
- Run expensive, onerous, one-time "capital campaigns" that use glossy sales brochures that frame prospects like sales targets.

Revenue from Corporations

At about $20 billion annually, corporate funding is the smallest source of revenue for nonprofits, but companies are made up of people, so winning a corporate partnership is also a gateway to the much larger pool of individual funding. However, compared to individual donations, winning and sustaining productive corporate partnerships demands a very different set of approaches. An SIE must be able to do at least one of three things for corporate funding prospects: (1) provide a significant boost to their marketing or brand, (2) offer specific ways to make their employees measurably happier, or (3) offer a promising solution for a real business problem the company is having.

SIE Strategies
- Deliver evidence that the partnership can solve their business problems, add marketing and brand value, or create a broad platform for meaningful employee engagement;
- Recognize corporate supporters frequently and publicly;
- Develop personal relationships with decision makers;
- Appeal to the marketing department or corporate social responsibility leader, not the foundation office; and
- Show how their business competitors are benefiting from partnership (use with caution).

Charity Strategies
- Approach corporate foundations with a "need";
- Solicit one-time sponsorships or small grants; and
- Limit interaction to mid-level managers and not core decision makers.

Revenue from Foundations

While there is about $80 billion in the private foundation world, this money is the most expensive to attract and the hardest to sustain. Always consider grant funding a one-time event—grants support new ideas or data-driven initiatives, not core programs. When the possibility exists to meet with a foundation decision maker, take it, and then pursue a careful strategy of fostering a strong individual relationship. Otherwise, outsource grant research and writing to proven professionals.

SIE Strategies
- Rely on experienced, proven grant writers to research and write grants (expect to pay > $125/hour) (in-house grant writers make sense only when they are each bringing in $500,000 to $1 million in annual revenue); and
- Ensure *all* grant proposals fund projects already in the organization's business plan.

Charity Strategies
- Start a new program or project because there is grant money to support it (chasing grant dollars destroys one of the most important prerequisites for success: focus);
- Modify or fudge current program description or program outcomes to fit the grant requirements; and
- Manage the time-consuming grants process in-house, leaving no time left for higher-return fundraising domains and strategies.

Revenue from Public Agencies

Local, state, and federal agencies provide hundreds of billions in grants to nonprofits every year, and the nature of the funding opportunity varies greatly by organizational size, type, and location. Over the past decades, governments are increasingly outsourcing their work to nonprofits, especially in the health and human services fields. At the same time, budget pressures have led to cutbacks for fields such as arts and education. Despite the considerable variance and complexity in the public funding landscape, public agencies generally advertise where and when they are willing to grant funding. So just like private foundations, it's critical to get the advice of seasoned grant professionals. Note that, just like the foundation space, you should be looking for any and all possibilities to establish and build personal relationships with decision makers.

SIE Strategies

- Use experts to review the federal grant register and target new grant opportunities (while the largest nonprofits have dedicated teams in Washington, DC, smaller groups can discover large pools of funding with the right help);
- Research state agency funding prospects and engage decision makers with personal attention and careful relationship management;
- Hire government relations experts with established relationships to key decision makers;
- Go beyond reporting requirements and engage agency leaders with concise reports and evidence demonstrating the impact of agency funding; and
- As public grants rarely pay for the full cost of delivering services, build adequate operating margins into program models or ensure the availability of cross-subsidization from other funding domains, such as individuals.

Charity Strategies

- Executive staff work on grant proposals and/or reporting;
- Pursue public agency grants without adequate funding margins or the means to supplement the funding with other revenue;
- "Trim programs to fit"—that is, customize program outcomes based on what grants are looking to fund; and
- Opportunistically pursue multiple disconnected grant-funded initiatives without an integrated strategy.

Earned Revenue

Many are surprised to learn that approximately half of the nonprofit sector's annual ~$2 trillion revenue comes from fee-for-service activity, just like any other type of business. The opportunities are, of course, highly dependent on organizational type. Health care and human services organizations rely on Medicaid funding, for example. There are many other flavors of earned income, limited only by the board's and executive team's entrepreneurial imagination and skill.

SIE Strategies

- Launch and scale a for-profit subsidiary (for example, environmental groups can build certification models and deliver the certification process via a for-profit subsidiary);
- If there is valuable intellectual property, secure it with a patent, copyright, certification program, or other method and generate revenue through a licensing campaign; and
- Purchase real estate and sublease to for-profit tenants.

Charity Strategies

- Manage low-margin subsidiary businesses (restaurants, thrift shops, etc.); and
- Fail to charge people who can afford to pay because "we are a nonprofit."

Revenue from Impact Capital

Hundreds of billions of dollars are flowing into the "impact" space.[2] Some estimates even put that number into the trillions of dollars. Broadly defined, impact capital can be any asset class—from debt to private equity to fixed income vehicles—that's looking for a measurable social return in addition to a financial one. While few nonprofits can provide truly commercial rates of return to compete for all these dollars, there may be philanthropically minded investors—individuals or foundations—willing to accommodate sub-market rates of return or take on higher levels of risk in exchange for social impact. SIEs can potentially access these investors if they have an earned income stream. Note that this is an emerging and highly specialized space, and

---

[2]See The Global Impact Investing Network website (**theginn.org**) for an excellent overview.

while there is significant capital here, few nonprofit organizations are equipped with the specialized expertise needed to access it, and there is a very small number of expert consultants with a significant track record.

SIE Strategies

- Use organizations such as Semble (**semble.com**), a community-sourced impact-focused loan program;
- Solicit *program-related investments* (PRIs)—loans that are often convertible to grants—from private foundations;
- Secure risk- and/or rate-tolerant loans from individuals, family offices, or institutional investors; and
- Secure social impact bonds or other pay-for-success initiatives.

Charity Strategies

- None (access to the debt markets typically requires the tools to pass investor due diligence, such as business plans, detailed financials, and evidence the organization can repay the debt, typically via an earned income strategy).

To conclude this overview of strategy, complete fund exercise 5.a at the next board meeting.

Fund Exercise 5.a: Are We on Track for Growth?

Discuss the following questions and write down the best answers for each. Task the CEO with developing a plan to implement conclusions. (The next section provides a templated process for implementation.)

- Which of these domains are appropriate for our mission?
- Do we possess the in-house strategic insight, staff expertise, and operational acumen to execute on the success strategies?
- Can we access proven third-party experts to help us develop and execute our revenue strategy?
- How will we monitor our execution to ensure it is on track? Do we know the leading indicators for each of our strategies? Do we have the capability to track and report them accurately?

Fund Practice 5.3: Develop an Investment and Partnership Plan

An *investment and partnership plan*, or *I&P plan*, is a one-page spreadsheet that details each execution step of each strategy for every segment in every domain. The revenue domains are listed in the rows, and the sequence of steps to access them are listed in the columns. Each of the components to this document are explained below. An excerpt from a sample I&P plan is shown in Figure 5.1, one that focuses on one segment of the "individual" revenue domain, showing it in full detail.

There are other segments in the individual domain as well as different domains entirely: corporations, foundations, government agencies, and earned income. Each of these other domains may contain multiple segments as well. This chapter aims to give practitioners a detailed look at *just one* of the segments from start to finish: major investments from individuals. The full template, which includes detailed examples of all the other revenue domains, is available at **altruistaccelerator.org**.

While this chapter explores the Individual domain, other revenue domains require different strategies and skills. Some lean heavily on marketing and communication; others require deep relationship-building expertise; still others may be outsourced. Typically, there is more growth to be had by improving performance in one domain versus beginning efforts in a new one. Most small to mid-sized nonprofits access two or three of these funding domains, with only the largest hospitals and universities possessing the fully staffed fundraising teams able to access more or even all of them. And some organizations, particularly those that rely on government funding, can become quite large in only one of these funding areas. It is quite case-specific whether or not an organization can fund its BHAG via one domain or multiple domains.

Furthermore, an organization's ability to access the various types of revenue can change dramatically over time. For example, Treehouse launched its growth strategy with 90% emphasis on individuals, as the data indicated that's where the opportunity was. As evidence of their impact became stronger, the organization was then able to enter

Domain	Segment	Goal	Average Investment	Prospects	1. Acquire	2. Build Trust	3. Propose	4. Accept	5. Deny	6. Report	Volunteers	Staff	Staff Budget	Ops Budget
Individuals		$2,285,000												
		$500,000												
	Major Investors	$400,000	$10,000	120	1. Current investors	1. Advice on business plan	1. Offer to provide a draft proposal	1. Define closing steps	1. Remove	1. Gift receipt, personal thanks from CEO	1. Board of directors	1. CEO (.2)	30,000	
					2. Wealth scan	2. Face-to-face meetings	2. Include plan for tracking results	2. CEO thank you	2. Return to stage 2, build trust	2. Customized reporting	2. Advisory board	2. Dir, I&P (.2)	20,000	10,000
					3. Referrals from board members	3. Site visits	3. Get to the No	3. Board Chair thank you	3. Move to monthly supporter segment	3. Recognition at events, annual report, newsletter		4. Event staff (.25)	15,000	10,000
					4. Advisory board members	4. Events				4. Quarterly dashboard updates				
					5. Events	5. 1-1s with board, CEO				5. Personal updates from CEO/Chair		6. Admin (.25)	10,000	5,000
					6. Annual Investors	6. Dashboard				6. Prepare for another proposal when ready				
						7. Stories of inspiration / impact								

FIGURE 5.1 The Individual Domain from the Investment and Partnership (I&P) Plan.

and win in the corporate domain, and after that, the government one. Continuous testing of the business plan with representatives of the various domains provides the best indication of potential funding in a given domain.

"Marry the goal; date the strategy" is a truth that applies to both unit-level as well as organization-wide execution.

With initial revenue domains selected, the next task is to break down a strategy into specific steps so it can be executed with clarity, consistency, and effectiveness. Consider a good fundraising strategy for individuals: *deliver proposals via one-on-one, face-to-face meetings.* While this gives a general idea of what to do, it leaves important details unanswered, such as (1) how to find individual investment prospects, (2) how to engage them and what to say, (3) when and how to deliver proposals, (4) what happens if they say no, (5) what to do when they say yes, (6) how much time and money are required, and (7) who is on the team.

We address these details by completing each box in the I&P plan for every domain. When complete, it will serve as a start-to-finish guide, including each step in the fundraising process, who is involved, and what it will all cost.

Remember, a strategy is just an abstract concept until the entire fundraising team—the executive team, board members, and staff—work together to create, document, and follow a specific, step-by-step process of applying the strategy in a series of steps (which we will call *tactics*), all organized from beginning to end. The result is a breadcrumb trail for each member of the team to follow. This does not mean creating a rigid, militaristic operation: on the contrary, when everyone knows what to do, fundraising becomes a joyful, uplifting, and even fun and creative undertaking.

Let's start by explaining each of the column headings in the I&P plan below.

Segment

In each major revenue domain, there are various sub-domains, which we call *segments*, each for a different type of audience that is best approached with unique tactics. For example, in the individual domain, there are typically three distinct segments: *major investors* (a smaller number of wealthy prospects with investment capacity above, say, $10,000 annually), *monthly supporters* (a much larger number of smaller prospects), and *planned gifts*[3] (typically larger sums of money; the average planned gift is $75,000, given through wills, trusts, and a variety of other financial and estate planning vehicles).

- Assign a revenue goal for each segment based on historical performance plus 25%—a healthy stretch goal. If the organization has never done anything but event-based fundraising, enter modest figures for major investment and monthly supporter categories.
- For mature fundraising operations aimed at individuals, 95% or more of the revenue will come from a small fraction of individuals—5% or less. If there is no history of major investor work, it can take a year or two to get started, but the investment in the effort will be well worth it.
- Don't overthink the goals or get stuck on the details. Be biased toward action and experiment, not reflection and analysis. After 6 to 12 months, you will have built solid trend data, enough to start setting more accurate goals and, eventually, even make predictions on how much can be raised.

Goal

Identify the fundraising dollar goal for each domain. You should already have a number for this in the financial projection in the business plan. This is an interconnected system: the business plan defines the revenue goals. Now the task is to link each of the revenue targets in the business plan with the specific steps and resources needed to generate the funding.

---

[3]The typically problematic term *gift* works well for this particular revenue segment. These truly are gifts as they are made when people pass away: they won't be around to see the results. Furthermore, the term *planning giving* is far less tainted than so much other social sector terminology, primarily because it is a difficult and complex revenue space to enter and is thus dominated by the most capable and sophisticated nonprofits.

Average Investment

Make a forecast of the average investment amount for each domain. Base it on historical data or make another guess. A reasonable guess is $10,000 for an average major investment, $100 for monthly supporters, and $75,000 for planned giving. Again, don't overthink it. After a year of execution, real data will make next year easier.

Prospects

No matter the revenue domain, there is an individual out there somewhere who must be approached. Divide the fundraising goal by average investment, and the total number of people who need to say yes to proposals emerges. However, not everyone will say yes, so account for a *conversion rate*, the percentage of people likely to say yes versus no. Historical data yields this rate, but as few organizations know about conversation rates or collect or monitor them, start with a conversion rate of 30%, a reasonable baseline. If everything is recorded properly, 6 to 12 months will yield a conversion rate and enable more precise predictions.

For example: If the goal is to raise $500,000 from individuals, assign $400,000 to the major investor segment (the remaining $100,000 will be obtained through other sources). If the average major investment is, say, $10,000, you will need 40 successful proposals to reach your funding goal. Not every effort will be successful, however. Assume a conversion rate of 25%—which means one out of every four proposal requests will result in a yes. Do the math with this conversion rate to find the number of people you will need to approach to get 40 people who will say yes ($0.25x = 40$, so $x = 160$), and you will find that you need 160 investment prospects to get to our 40 successful ones.

Now we have a very specific task: find 160 prospects and figure out how to get at least 40 of them to say yes to a major proposal. That is still not easy, but the task is clear and measurable.

Partnership Stages

Now that we have targets for revenue, prospect population, and average investment size, we can go into detail about how to find the right prospects, how to engage with them, and how to turn prospects into supporters.

Raising money means talking to dozens, hundreds, and even thousands of people and keeping track of many individual, simultaneous, complex conversations. Organizations that do it well can build close, trusting relationships with large numbers of people who, as a direct result of these relationships, make big investments of time, treasure, and talent to support the mission. With deep relationships come deep commitments.

Note that the types of relationships are dependent on what type of people we are talking about. While we will go into great depth in this chapter about relationships with private individuals—for many nonprofits, this is the greatest source of revenue growth—strong relationships can be built with other types of funders: foundations, corporations, public agencies, and impact investors. The strategies and tactics for all those other types of relationships are different, but the overall mechanism for establishing and building them is the same.

The first step in creating a good relationship management system is defining each of six categories that represent the most important stages of the relationship-building process from start to finish: (1) acquire, (2) build trust, (3) propose, (4) accept, (5) deny, and (6) report. Each is explained below. It is critical that everyone in the organization develop a shared understanding of each of these stages.

Partnership Stage 1: Acquire

Now that we have estimated how many prospects we need, we need to find them. In this domain, we need to find major individual investment prospects with money to invest and who also care about what the organization does. In other words, we must find prospects with *capacity*, meaning they own enough wealth to make a charitable investment appropriate for this segment's average investment size; and (2) *affinity*, which is some evidence that they care about the mission. The organization must also be able to get in touch with the prospect, so at least an email address is required, but mobile numbers and physical addresses are ideal.

Prospects for whom there is contact information and reasonable evidence of capacity and affinity, and for whom some contact information is known, are said to be *qualified*. These are the people who belong in this relationship stage—the organization hasn't attempted to get in touch with them yet, but together they make up people who are the most likely to make a major investment.

The concept of "prospect qualification" is critical. Don't fill the prospect domain with people you can't get in touch with. Don't write down the names of wealthy people with no evidence they care about your mission. Gaming the process and fudging the numbers must never happen. Doing so cheats the organization out of the essential performance data it needs to help other people.

Time is precious. Qualify your prospects carefully. An international malaria treatment organization is correct in presuming Bill Gates has both capacity and affinity, but if their only contact information for him is **info@gatesfoundation.org**, he doesn't qualify. In addition, don't confuse your own desire that a prospect possesses capacity or affinity with reality. Be conservative with qualification, or you will waste time and energy talking to the wrong people.

Once a prospect is qualified, they are recorded in the database as belonging to the "1. Acquire" stage. Now that we've covered who belongs in this relationship stage, we will explore the particular tactics on where to find them.

Acquire Tactic #1: Current Investors

The first place nonprofits should look for major investors is the people currently supporting them. In the drive to raise money, in the urgency to find new donors, it is all too easy to overlook the individuals who already support the organization. Nonprofits must recognize that individuals who have already made a donation are likely to do so again—if they are shown the impact of their support and how even more of their support can do even more good. Any organization that receives $500 or $1,000 gifts from individuals as a result of events or other mass appeals can typically generate $5,000 or $10,000 from these same individuals if they take the time to build a trusting relationship. "But I don't have time to spend on all of these relationships!" is the standard objection we hear from executives. However, this objection springs from ignorance of how to set up an efficient, effective relationship management system. Properly designed, staffed, and operated, relationship-based fundraising is proven to be the most efficient and effective way to raise money, which is why it is a fundamental fundraising strategy for successful organizations.

Acquire Tactic #2: Wealth Screens

Once the fundraising strategy is focused on building long-term partnerships, then the organization must make wise decisions on where to invest its time and energy. Of course, there is no time to build deep, lasting relationships with everyone. Leaders must be selective with whom they seek as long-term partners. Therefore, spend time where it is likely to be most productive: with people who are most likely to have wealth they can contribute and who demonstrate a pattern of doing so.

The easiest and fastest way to do this is with a *wealth screening service*. The one we like is iWave (**iwave.com**), which uses sophisticated analysis of dozens of publicly available data sets to rate individuals in any nonprofit database on their capability and willingness to support fundraising efforts. They can identify small donors with much larger potential and even help identify new prospects. Importantly, this isn't spying or doing anything remotely unethical, as all the information used is public; it is just efficient research. These services typically return many multiples of the dollars they cost within the first fiscal year.

Acquire Tactic #3: Referrals from Board Members

Among the many desirable attributes of a good board member is access to capital. In the private sector, people with significant investment capacity are known as *accredited investors*,[4] qualifying as such if they own at least $1 million in liquid assets besides their house or they

---

[4]US Securities and Exchange Commission, "Accredited Investor," **https://www.sec .gov/education/capitalraising/building-blocks/accredited-investor**.

earn more than $200,000 annually ($300,000 as a couple under present rules). Accredited investors are strong board assets because they can make a major investment themselves and know others who can. "Felicia, you've been such a strong supporter. Who else might you know who cares about what we do and could support us like you do? We will treat them with the same consideration and respect we treat you."

If the accredited investors on a board aren't willing to make an investment or make referrals, either they don't trust staff or they are on the board for appearances only. CEOs must attract and retain board members who consider the organization one of their top two charitable priorities. Once the evidence of strong social return on investment is produced, the onus is on the CEO to ensure the organization has a strong plan and evidence that funding will be used well to bring onto the board members who make deep commitments of their time, talent, and treasure. For board members who continue to defer or deflect, graciously suggest they join an advisory committee or the emeritus board.

Acquire Tactic #4: Referrals from Advisory Board Members

Unlike boards of directors, advisory boards have no legal status or formal duties. They are simply a group of influential and wise supporters that CEOs rely on for occasional help and advice. Properly designed, built, and maintained, they can be a rich source of guidance, financial support, and referrals to investment prospects. There is an entire class of powerful, wealthy, and influential people who might care about social impact and would be willing to help but who are also uninterested in the heavy lifting of being a director and fiduciary. "Javier, you are an influential leader who cares about our work. I'd like to publicly recognize your care and concern by nominating you to our advisory board. All you need to do is return my phone calls—I won't ask you for help often, but when I do, please carve out a little of your expensive bandwidth for me and our mission." Build the relationship, and soon Javier could be making investments and referrals too. Furthermore, advisory boards are excellent vehicles for identifying and cultivating future directors.

Acquire Tactic #5: Events

Fundraising events can be an effective means of finding new major investment prospects—if they are designed properly. But in the urgency to raise money *now*, nonprofits often design them poorly. They overlook the opportunity to identify and inform major potential investors. They pack everyone in a room, ask them for money, and send them thank-you letters, repeating the process at the next event. These kinds of ineffective fundraising events treat attendees like cash machines.

Investment prospects who can make six-, seven-, and eight-figure contributions don't do so because they are asked at an event. They need to trust the organization, and that level of trust must happen carefully, over time.

So what can you do? You can design events to attract and educate prospects as part of an empathetic and genuine relationship-building process. If the events are unique and interesting, they can be a fabulous part of the acquire, build trust, and report stages. Effective leaders focus on nurturing deep, honest, trusting relationships, with the event as a starting point for new investors and a means to recognize and thank the current investors. Ineffective leaders treat the events as the finish line, blurting appeals over loudspeakers, realizing a fraction of what each person could contribute if they were treated as individuals. The economics of typical event-based fundraising make this clear: events might raise two dollars for every dollar it costs to produce them. The type of ongoing relationship-based systems described here typically returns ten dollars for every dollar invested.

Bottom line: Don't treat events as a small-time cash grab. Pursue order-of-magnitude larger investments 6, 9, or 12 months from now, with people whom you introduced to your mission at a fun, educational, and creative event.

What does this look like? Consider this example: "Good evening. We aren't here to do another awful rubber chicken dinner and shout guilt-inducing *asks* at you over loudspeakers. Our time tonight will be a creative journey to bring our mission to life and demonstrate our strategy to solve this whole problem. We aren't dreamers or wishful thinkers whose main strategies are hope and passion. We aren't patting ourselves on the back for serving marginally more people each year. We are going big. We've got a robust business plan that details the work. And we have a team in place that is ready to execute and deliver evidence our proposed interventions are both efficient and effective. But before we launch, we'd like to follow up with you in the weeks and months that follow tonight to meet with you in person and get your advice on our strategy. This room is filled with leaders who have done difficult things, and you know how hard it is to scale up an organization. We want to build trust with you that, if you care about this social challenge, over time, you will come to trust us as the leading solution provider for this challenge—just check out our powerful value proposition or our plans to produce evidence our programs are the best out there. We seek to enroll you as our partners and investors and work with you to create more social impact in this space than has ever been attempted before."

Acquire Tactic #6: Monthly Supporters

As these tactics make clear, the "major investor" segment focuses on establishing and nurturing trusting, personal, one-on-one relationships with high-capacity prospects. A source of major investor prospects comes from another investor segment entirely, which we call *monthly supporters*—all those people who don't necessarily pop up on wealth screens or the referral lists from accredited investors. Monthly supporters are defined as anyone and everyone who might potentially care about the mission and support it with small to medium ($1 to $100) monthly donations. (These dollars add up fast, and like all the other revenue domains and segments, this one demands unique tactics, staffing, and budgeting.)

Monthly supporters often create new major investment prospects by word-of-mouth. They tell their wealthy Aunt Mae about the work and, if prompted by the organization, might even encourage her to get involved. The more monthly supporters, the more reassured major investors are that the organization enjoys a broad base of support. Furthermore, for purposes of our acquisition tactics here, they can become major investors themselves for many reasons: they may have a hidden source of wealth, they may inherit money, or they may provide small dollars forever until they name the organization in their will. Continue to run all supporters through wealth scans to ensure no major prospect is missed. In these ways and others, the monthly supporter population is the foundation for the major investor segment.

Other Acquire Tactics

British news publication *The Economist* is well known for the quality of its writing. It publishes its own style guide, well worth reading, which contains one memorable principle: never use a phrase that's been used somewhere else. In other words, be unique and creative. It takes more skill and energy, but the rewards are worth the investment. Do *not* do what all the other nonprofits do. Instead, focus on being unique and creative, and do not try to do too many things. A team with too many tactics executes none well.

Partnership Stage 2: Build Trust

Once major investment prospects have been fully qualified, the next stage in the relationship is a longer process of earning and deepening their trust that the organization presents a solution worthy of their investment. Individuals with larger charitable investment capacity—people who can write five-, six-, and seven-figure checks to the charity of their choice—don't make these decisions on a whim.

The time required to make a decision is typically proportionate to its size or importance. Go to a supermarket and consider how long it takes to choose between one type of peanut butter and another. Then consider how long it would take to decide whom to marry or what house to buy. High-capacity investors don't think more than a few seconds about writing a check for $1,000 at an auction. These checks are expressions of *affinity*. They simultaneously demonstrate *capacity*, but that capacity will be tapped only if the social impact enterprise does the work to build the trust that the money will be used effectively. Concerns that won't stop a high-capacity prospect from writing that

$1,000 check are far more likely to surface when the investment in question is $100,000 or $1,000,000—concerns such as the following:

- Is this charity capable of using such a large sum of my money effectively? Don't charities waste a lot of the money they are given?
- Do I trust the CEO? Is the staff competent? How do they attract quality staff with such low pay and long hours?
- Who else is writing big checks? Has anyone whose judgment I respect made a big investment in this organization?
- How do I know they won't come to depend on my money?
- How do I know the numbers and figures they are showing me are real and not made up?
- Who is on this board, making sure no one is stealing or goofing off?

These are the same types of questions any private sector investor considers before making a financial investment in a company. The process is called *due diligence*. For major investment prospects, it may take anywhere from 1 or 2 trust-building conversations to 30 or more—it is an unpredictable and dynamic process, like any human relationship. The job of everyone on the I&P team is to act explicitly, intentionally, and transparently to build this trust. Start by following another old and very helpful adage: it's not fundraising; it's "friend-raising."

Begin building trust by listening and learning. Prospects will explain how to earn their trust if asked nicely. Sample questions are as follows:

- Why is the mission important to them? What's their backstory? People love talking about themselves and what they believe in.
- What is their vision of personal success? Are they inspired by religious faith? Wesleyan utilitarianism?[5] Or do they want to bask in the public recognition and flaunt their wealth?

---

[5]The Effective Altruism movement has been around since at least the sixteenth century. Consider John Wesley's guidance: "Do all the good you can / By all the means you can / In all the ways you can / In all the places you can / At all the times you can / To all the people you can / As long as ever you can."

- How do they come to trust other people? By conversation and personal dialogue? Or by investigating data and facts? Or both? Or something else?

An important foundation for fundraising professionals is grounding the work in a deep sense of humanity and empathy. While the term *consultative sales* accurately describes the mechanics of the process, it also carries psycholinguistic baggage: the insincerity, manipulation, and deception associated with too many bad businesses. For many in the social sector, the term *sales* is quickly associated with used cars. Below are a set of principles that, if taught, absorbed, practiced, and reinforced by organizational leaders and staff, not only will ensure the fundraising effort is humane, moral, and empathetic but will also lead to significantly better results.

One of the most gratifying aspects of fundraising is that pushy salespeople perform badly. The most effective fundraisers are leaders of the highest integrity, people who are highly empathetic listeners and passionate about the mission. Building genuine trust with prospects cannot be faked. Each of the principles below applies with every interaction fundraisers will ever have with prospective partners and supporters.

- **Be yourself.** Be genuine, authentic, and transparent when talking with potential investors. If interactions feel contrived or manipulative, stop. Take a break and focus on the mission. Insincerity is hard to hide, and the struggle leads to burnout.

- **Treat everyone as a potential major investor.** Don't judge by appearance. Qualify with care and intention. Don't give up too soon. At the same time, don't chase after people unwilling or unable to grant trust.

- **Develop the relationship first.** Investment proposals come later. Major investments happen because the organization has spent time building trust with the investor. Prospects have been asked for their input on the business plan and are updated on progress and setbacks. Only after a relationship based on trust, integrity, and transparency has been established should a proposal be made.

- **Be interested in your investor prospects.** Relationships are authentic and two-way. Never use a script. Discover their interests, family, and so on. Ask about preferences for frequency and mode of communication (email, phone, etc.) and honor those. Do more listening than talking. Be the person they want to have another meeting with because the conversation is fun and stimulating.

- **Always leave a meeting with the next one scheduled.** The goal is to keep the dialogue moving forward toward an eventual proposal. Maintain momentum and engagement by having the next step mutually defined. Always ask for the names of others the investor prospect knows—always be networking.

- **Follow the platinum rule.** It can't be overemphasized: Never treat people like targets or cash machines. Don't tolerate even informal dialogue that dehumanizes prospects ("Hey, that guy is a really big fish...").

- **Remember your proof points.** There is no substitute for clear, concrete, and compelling measures of social impact. No matter how good the fundraising strategy or execution, every fundraiser's most important tool is clear, compelling evidence of strong social return on investment.

One last piece of hard-earned wisdom before reviewing the "build trust" tactics in more detail: One of the biggest reasons small nonprofits fail to raise significant capital is because their boards and executive teams think those $1,000 checks really are a lot of money. Unless one comes from a wealthy background or has spent a significant amount of time around the wealthy, it's easy to be intimidated. It can also be hard to imagine anyone ever voluntarily giving away the equivalent of a large suitcase filled with $100 bills. This fear and uncertainty will go away with time and practice, and it goes away faster with successful proposals. Until then, take a deep breath and seek the guidance of the team and colleagues who have done it before.

Build Trust Tactic #1: Ask for Advice on the Business Plan

Business plans are powerful tools for "making insiders out of outsiders." With it, leaders can begin by demonstrating rigor, transparency, and humility.

"Jordan, I'm the investment & partnership officer at this special social impact enterprise, and we have just drafted a plan with some exciting potential to solve this problem. I would like you to review this plan and give us your honest feedback. I will not ask you for money. We're still in a draft stage with this and we are looking for the input of leaders to give us their suggestions and critique."

Ask for money, get advice. Ask for advice, get money, eventually, if trust and respect are earned.

Build Trust Tactic #2: Aim for Face-to-Face Meetings

Always default to the highest-bandwidth, most personal interaction possible. Always aim to speak to people in person. Unless you can tell the prospect enjoys email—some do—use it as little as possible, keeping everything short and leaving detail to conversation. A Zoom meeting or a phone call is fine for follow-up meetings, but don't rely on them. Influential people are busy, so act considerately.

While fundraising uses the exact same mechanics of a typical sales operation (beware people who tell you differently, and many will), remember that this isn't an ordinary transaction. The build trust process involves creating awareness that it is possible to solve a major problem in the community, and that higher purpose must always be kept top of mind for every fundraising professional. Focus on the problem being solved, the urgency of the challenge, and the benefits to the community—the profoundly important social return on investment—if the BHAG is achieved. This focus will lead to face-to-face meetings.

If there is no prior relationship with the prospect, seek an introduction to them via a friend or work colleague. Fundraisers are passionate users of LinkedIn. A reputation as an ethical person who is trying to make the world a better place makes it easier for board members and current investors to introduce their friends.

Finally, remember that in any meeting, the prospect should be talking at least 50% of the time. The goal is to listen and learn. Here are a list of good questions to ask during these intimate conversations:

- What are your most important causes?
- What's the biggest philanthropic gift you've ever made, and what motivated you to make the investment?

- What did that nonprofit do to earn your trust?
- Has a nonprofit ever broken trust with you? What happened?
- You've read our plan, you've visited our site, and you've met our board chair and CEO. Is there anything else we can do to earn your trust? We'd like to have a series of very careful discussions with you, all at your own pace, to explore how we could enroll you as one of our major supporters.

Build Trust Tactic #3: Arrange Site Visits

Showing is more powerful than telling. Demonstrate the value proposition as it is happening. Having a great business plan is a distinct advantage, but almost every major investment prospect will be curious to see things in action. Furthermore, a substantial number of major prospects may need more than plans and cash flow projections to build trust.

"Guillermo, thank you for your great advice on the business plan. Next week, we've got a number of the community's leading lights coming to our office to hear directly from the children we have helped. We expect the mayor will be there. Care to join us and see our work for yourself?"

Build Trust Tactic #4: Host Events

The most effective events are the ones that are designed to be the start of the fundraising conversation, not a one-time ask. Remember, change the script from "I want everyone in this room to dig deep and make a stretch gift!" to "We welcome your support, and if you have been moved this evening, of course we welcome you to make an investment. But importantly, we will follow up with each of you after this event: we need to get your feedback on our goals and strategies. This is a hard problem to solve, but with your advice and participation, we can get it done. We are all in this together. For many of you just getting to know us tonight, we look forward to building a relationship with you."

Build Trust Tactic #5: Arrange One-on-One Meetings with the Board Chair and CEO

Keeping it personal is the strongest way to build a relationship. "Amanda, thanks for coming to our event. And thank you for the terrific feedback on the business plan. I'd like to get you together with our CEO so he can hear your feedback in person. Our chair is also having a small dinner at her house. Would you like to see if you can attend?" These conversations may be almost entirely about personal matters at first—often the most sophisticated prospects want to know the character of the leaders first. Savvy judges of performance often focus on *who* before *what*. If a prospect probes for character and background, that's a good sign. Follow the energy and use good judgment.

Build Trust Tactic #6: Ask for Feedback on the Dashboard

As Chapter 6: "Execute" will demonstrate, an executive dashboard is a one-page snapshot of the organization's performance, a visualization of goals and KPIs measuring the organization's impact and growth. Measures may include trends around program reach, program quality, financial health, and revenue generation measures.

When it is ready, not only will the dashboard help staff and board continuously improve, but it will offer tremendous power as a fundraising tool. So many nonprofits struggle to show their impact, often leaning on long, confusing documents, videos, and so forth. Like a business plan, a dashboard is a clear, comprehensive, concise tool to convey managerial competence and acumen. Dashboards are compelling visualizations of how resources are deployed to generate impact. Because they use evidence-based numbers, they are credible.

"Shawna, have you ever supported a charity and then had no idea what they did with your funding? You get a lot of uplifting stories, but then they come back not long after, asking for more money. With us, it's very different. We treat donors as investors, and we have a comprehensive, concise dashboard that shows you how well we are doing and what specific results we are producing with your funding. What do you think of this approach?"

Build Trust Tactic #7: Talk about Anecdotal Wins

Stories that illustrate impact are still important. Business plans and dashboards are critical tools that are very compelling for the most sophisticated audiences. But everyone likes a good story to put all the data into human context. Just as this book uses the case study of Treehouse to illustrate abstract concepts, you can do the same with your programs. Most charities need little help with this tactic as they are already heavily socialized to tell stories.

Partnership Stage 3: Propose

When someone says, "I don't like asking people for money," it's probably because the phrase *asking people for money* puts things in a very negative frame, one that evokes stereotypes of panhandling or pushy salespeople applying pressure and manipulation. Reframe the question as follows: "Do you like leading people to investing in partnerships that result in profound social progress?" Or "Can you build trust with influential leaders and show them how to help others?" Fundraising is a sophisticated, high-minded profession. Like anything, it is easily debased by cynics. Stay in a positive frame of mind with positive language.

With the prevalence of negative terms such as *the ask* or *solicitation*, it's not surprising that many nonprofit executives are fearful of raising money. Five minutes viewing the psychopathic salesmen in the brilliant 1992 film *Glengarry Glen Ross* is enough to permanently damage anyone's affinity for sales. Therefore, executives and staff who approach fundraising with fear and suspicion should recognize that establishing, maintaining, and reinforcing a culture of humanity and empathy are the keys to success. Only the small percentage of humanity afflicted by psychopathic impulses can practice guilt and manipulation over the long term with no loss of energy or enthusiasm.

Hence the word *proposal*: we aren't twisting someone's arm; we aren't making a *gotcha* ask. We are learning that person's goals and determining if our organization is the right one to enable them to express their desire to make the world a better place. It is a peer relationship and a noble pursuit, perhaps among the most noble of all. Consult with prospects. Learn their needs. Share evidence of impact. Determine if there is a fit. Walk away if there is not.

There must *never* be coercion. Apart from being morally repugnant, it is a poor tactic. What makes the fundraising profession so enjoyable is this: the right thing to do is also the smart thing to do. There is never any compromise between being effective and being a good person. This is a truth that is applicable to most other fields as well.

Remember an important positioning element: the fundraiser is not a supplicant. Fundraisers are sophisticated professionals, social entrepreneurs, people working hard to make the world a better place. That work demands resources. People with affinity and capacity are ready and willing to give those resources to fulfill their own need for significance and life meaning. When it comes to major investments, the good fundraiser approaches major prospects as a peer who can help a colleague make a decision that makes the world a better place. "Anna, you are a successful person. What do you do for significance? What are your goals for making the world a better place? Here is how we work with successful people like you to help them capture significance. I love this work. It's evangelizing for a good cause. Are we a fit for you? If not, I won't chase you—we aren't pushy salespeople."

Always treat everyone as a unique individual. Someone with deep trust may need only a few steps before being ready for a major proposal. Others may need months or longer. While never forgetting that there is a high degree of variance in the number of trust-building conversations necessary before moving the conversation toward proposal, we can say with a reasonable degree of confidence that most prospects will need between 10 and 15 interactions with staff, volunteers, board members, and events, typically over the course of about six to nine months, before trust is built. How long does it take, and how many interactions are required, before anyone feels they know someone else? The answer is: it depends. Treat everyone as an individual.

Propose Tactic #1: Offer a Draft Proposal

Even for someone with high capacity and affinity for the organization, it's a big decision to make a major investment. So break down the process into smaller pieces, reducing a big decision into smaller, easier ones. The approach with tremendous utility is the *draft proposal*. Ask your potential investor, "We've had terrific conversions, and it seems clear that our mission aligns well with your passion. May we send you a draft proposal—something cast in Jello, not concrete? We're going big here and aiming for major investments. We can structure this in a number of ways, and we will do our best to find something that works for you. If not, no worries. What we don't want to do is waste time— our mission is urgent."

Assess the prospect's giving potential with data if possible, bearing in mind their history of support. Also, no one is ever insulted by being asked a number above their capacity. Finally, get to a specific number— and then stop talking. It is easy to spot an inexperienced fundraiser because they are nervous and fill silence with chatter. For example:

- "Carly, would you consider a $250,000 charitable investment in the initiative we've been discussing? Bear in mind we could do this in installments—start with, say, $50,000, and it's on us to demonstrate the impact you are looking for. If that pilot works, we can explore doubling it—or adding a zero. We never want to go beyond your trust and passion." (Followed by silence and patient waiting for a response.)

- "Carly, I'd like to send you a draft proposal for a substantial investment—mid–figures. Please consider the substance of the proposal before reacting to the number, if you would be willing to do so." (Again, followed by silence and patient waiting for a response.)

Follow up with the potential investor in a timely manner, politely asking them when they will make their decision and if there are any concerns or doubts they may have. If they don't respond, never over-prompt. Have the CEO, board chair, or volunteer follow up. Investment and partnership are a team activity.

Propose Tactic #2: Include Options for Tracking Results

One of the biggest concerns prospects will have before making their first large investment in a nonprofit is this: "How will I know you will use the money well?" First, the business plan should already contain clear performance measures, so be sure to include all the key performance indicators that the prospect cares about in your major investment proposal.

How do you know which ones to include? Ask, "What measures would give you confidence that we are performing to your expectations?" Also, ask how you should deliver this information: "We will certainly send you our standard impact reports. What other information would you like to see?"

The next chapter will provide a robust process for measuring and reporting organizational performance and especially social impact using an executive dashboard. A dashboard will do a great deal to secure prospect confidence that the organization will be transparent and accountable to results. There are other reporting options as well, and each of them are explained below. Each provides a different format with unique appeal, so learn each of them carefully, explore the differences around each with your prospect, and include the right ones in the draft proposal.

Propose Tactic #3: Get to the No

Successful fundraising means not spending too much time chasing reluctant prospects. A common mistake made by inexperienced fundraisers is "chasing the money" or otherwise trying to convince reluctant or disinterested parties to provide support. Remember, fundraising is about building partnerships; it is a relationship among equals. Focus time only where there is genuine interest and engagement. "Your time is very valuable, and we don't want to waste it exploring an opportunity you are not truly passionate about. Don't hesitate to let me know if this is not the right time for you." A fundraiser's expressed willingness to accept *no* for an answer is a powerful signal of integrity and, counterintuitively, often helps get to *yes*.

Partnership Stage 4: Accept

Prospects say, "Yes, I will make a major investment" in many ways. The transition from proposal to acceptance may be nuanced, but as long as each conversation ends with a specific next step, things will go well: "Susan, I'll send you that draft proposal, but first may we schedule time to discuss? This is an important process, and we shouldn't leave it open-ended. We are very deliberate in these conversations."

There is a lot of advice out there about using various psychological tricks to induce prospects to say yes. But nothing is more effective than being simple, direct, and straightforward. "Susan, is this proposal to your liking? If not, we will revise it until it is. Let us know what we need to do to get to yes. Having you as an investor and partner will mean we can do substantially more good."

The pathway to yes will be unique to each individual. As elsewhere, be empathetic, transparent, and concise. Whatever the pathway, if the prospect accepts the proposal, remember another useful piece of wisdom: when getting to the end zone, behave as if it is familiar territory. "Thank you, Susan, that's very gracious—we are delighted." Then follow the accept tactics below.

Accept Tactic #1: CEO Thank You

Once the closing steps of the investment are confirmed, the CEO should call or write with short, genuine expressions of gratitude. Don't go into details. The formal acknowledgment document and receipt come later, once the investment has been completely transferred. Until then, ensure this happens no later than the next business day. A swift, immediate acknowledgment of the commitment is not only polite and proper, but it also helps ensure the commitment actually is fulfilled.

Accept Tactic #2: Board Chair Thank You

Another expression of gratitude should come from the most senior leader in the organization: the board chair. There should be good communication between the I&P team and the chair around when to acknowledge new, major investments. The board chair should respond with another personal call or email. It doesn't need to be as fast as the CEO's: within a week is fine. However, the longer it takes, the less gratitude it communicates. A timely, short personal call or email is better than a late, long letter. When an investment prospect in the accept stage receives additional, separate thanks from the CEO and board chair, their pathway from prospect to established investor is made easier and more certain.

Partnership Stage 5: Deny

Another valuable piece of wisdom to remember when soliciting major charitable investments: About two to three times as many people say no as say yes. Even the most carefully qualified and trustworthy group of prospects may yield conversion rates around 30%.

Embrace the hard truth that, as a fundraiser, you will hear *no* many more times than you will hear *yes*, and don't be ashamed or awkward when it happens. Novice fundraisers fear getting turned down—or they may even feel resentful, as they worked hard and deserved a yes. "How could anyone turn down an opportunity to invest in us, especially after all these building trust meetings where we were getting encouraging signals!"

Here is the response to these concerns and others: be grateful for the no, as you can now spend your time on a prospect that might say yes. So when no is the answer, show gratitude for the opportunity to explore the partnership. The faster you proceed to the next promising prospect, the more funding will be generated for the mission.

Deny Tactic #1: Remove

When a prospect turns down a proposal, offer to remove them from the list of prospective organizational partners. "We understand this isn't the right time for you. If you wish, we will take you off our list of potential major supporters and not bother you again with these in-depth conversations with our executives and board members." This shows respect for the prospect's time. What's more, it provides an opening to turn their "no" into a "not yet." Many prospects may just need more time, and the finality of an offer of "we won't bother you anymore" is likely to prompt them to think twice. Remember, there is no bad outcome to this process. You either save valuable time to spend with a more promising prospect or you deepen the partnership.

Deny Tactic #2: Move to Build Trust Stage

If the prospect does not want to be removed from consideration completely, then their refusal opens up the opportunity to discover why they said no. It is the fundraiser's job to understand that "no" often means "not yet." The task is now to identify where there is a lack of understanding or a breakdown in communication around the proposed investment's social return or the strategy. Perhaps there are deeper, hidden issues such as a lack of trust in one of the team members or even a clash of personalities. "Tamara, does your no mean, no, not ever, or are there some basic objections or concerns that we haven't addressed? In other words, can you share more?" In this case, there is more work to be done to build trust with the prospect, so slow the process down, return the prospect to the building trust stage, address the objections, and try again. Never argue! It's wisest to come back another day and see if there is another opportunity to address objections. Look at every "no" first as an opportunity for the I&P team to interrogate and improve their own building trust process.

Deny Tactic #3: Move to Monthly Supporter Segment

Perhaps the prospect has too many other philanthropic obligations. Perhaps, despite all indications of significant charitable investment capacity, there are unknown financial constraints—an investment just went bad, there's a looming divorce on the horizon, and so on. Perhaps the qualification process broke down somewhere. Or the prospect just stopped responding to calls and emails. Many things can and will go wrong. Just stay away from dehumanizing metaphors ("We couldn't hook that one"). Continue to build trust and propose a smaller, recurring monthly donation. Celebrate any commitment of support, large or small.

Partnership Stage 6: Report

It would seem obvious that building and maintaining a predictable, steady stream of financial support is extremely important for any social impact enterprise. No money, no mission. A chief measure of the predictability and sustainability of financial support is *donor loyalty*, the percentage of financial supporters who support a nonprofit year after year. But here is a sobering statistic: fewer than 45% of donors who give to a charity renew their support the following year.[6] There is tremendous individual generosity every year—individuals give away nearly half a trillion dollars annually—but as this statistic makes plain, it is not too much of an exaggeration to characterize the nonprofit fundraising strategy as *churn and burn*: treating financial supporters like cash machines, subjecting them to a relentless drumbeat of messages entreating them to "renew your support!" before any effort has been made to convey gratitude or report the social return on investment.

No matter how small the donation, the smart social impact enterprise makes a significant investment in *reporting*: the simple act of showing the social return on investment. In traditional fundraising terms, the phrase is *donor stewardship*, the sustained expression of gratitude, care, and consideration for people who provide their time, talent, and treasure to the organization. The best way to ensure an individual fails to "renew their gift" is to spam them with "renew now!" emails. Instead, demonstrate the positive results of their support. Tactics for doing so are outlined below.

Report Tactic #1: Acknowledge Gift with a Receipt

Respond within 24 hours to every donation, large or small, with a letter, electronic or otherwise, continuing the standard gift receipt language and expressing gratitude for the support. Keep it short and to the point. A common practice, and a hackneyed one at that, is

---

[6]"Fundraising Effectiveness Survey," Fundraising Effectiveness Project, **https://afpglobal.org/fepreports**.

for the executive director to jot a little personal note at the end of a form letter expressing a second thank-you, a sort of "you get special attention" signal. There are many ways to do this better, however. Pick up the phone. Write a separate email. But get the donation receipt out fast.

Report Tactic #2: Customize Investor Reporting

Now that the prospect is a charitable investor, the very next thing to ask, after expeditiously getting out a gift receipt, is this: "What is your preferred way to learn the impact of your support? We offer very clear, concise reporting once a quarter, including a dashboard with our KPIs. Others prefer examples of the lives we've changed. Or one-on-one personal updates from our board chair or our CEO. What works for you? It's essential that we demonstrate the social impact you make possible—if we are successful, you will keep supporting us, and we will grow our impact and ultimately solve this difficult problem."

Report Tactic #3: Publicly Recognize Investors

Public recognition of financial support is important as it communicates that the organization's mission is made possible through generosity. Recognize your supporters following a low-dose, high-frequency pattern—mentioning names at events, listing new supporters in your newsletter, or interviewing supporters and featuring their stories and reasons for their investment. Many vehicles are at your disposal. Investor preferences on public acknowledgment range from requesting strict anonymity to naming buildings or entire organizational units, as is common with hospitals and universities.

As elsewhere, avoid trite, hackneyed tactics: "You, too, can be a member of our Platinum Club!" There's an entire industry of so-called donor premiums, which are gifts, tchotchkes, plaques, certificates, and any number of other gimmicks that nonprofits can use to recognize and reward donors. If you've seen it before, avoid it. As elsewhere, creativity and personalization are important, but nothing is as important as following the wishes of the supporters.

Report Tactic #4: Produce Dashboard/ Quarterly Reports

Given the pervasive lack of trust in nonprofit effectiveness and the saturation of emotional appeals across the social sector, it makes sense to secure the loyalty of financial supporters through clear, concise expressions of concrete evidence that their dollars are being put to the best use possible. Treat major financial supporters like investors and provide them with quarterly reports and dashboards (see Chapter 6: "Execute") that visualize KPIs and demonstrate progress toward milestones in the business plan. The same reports that go to staff and the board can be sent to supporters. Make insiders out of outsiders.

Report Tactic #5: Provide Updates from the CEO/Chair

Supporters who deliver major chunks of an organization's budget deserve periodic updates from senior leadership. These are all at the discretion of the investor, but a simple email from the board chair goes a long way. "Jiang, we had a great quarter and are building momentum with some positive developments. I'd be happy to review these with you if and when you are interested. Next week? In any event, your support remains critical. Thank you."

Report Tactic #6: Move Back to Partnership Stage 2: Build Trust

While the term *investment and partnership pipeline* is used here to describe the process from acquisition through building trust to proposal and reporting, in truth, it is perhaps better described as a circle, not a line. This is because one investment, if properly acknowledged and carefully stewarded, will lead to another one, and another after that, each often larger than the previous one, with donations growing over time as trust and relationships deepen. A prospect acquired at an event or via a referral or other tactic makes an investment after an appropriate, personalized series of trust-building interactions. Then with proper reporting, they make another, even larger investment, repeating the pattern over a lifetime of loyalty that ends with the investor leaving assets to the social impact enterprise via estate planning.

When are supporters ready to consider making another investment? Ask. If there are strong, trusting relationships, supporters often make longer-term pledges—over, say, three to five years. It's all very individualized and case-specific. We recommend no fewer than three "reporting" conversations before moving back to building trust to ensure there is no "gimme gimme" dynamic.

See Figure 5.2 for a sample investment cycle.

With all the stages of the prospect relationship defined and tactics explored in each stage, we can now discuss the final elements of the I&P plan: volunteers, staff, and budgets.

Volunteers

Volunteers are a terrific resource when it comes to raising money, but only if they are provided with a well-structured role with adequate staff support. Traditionally, the volunteers who have a direct role in identifying, cultivating, soliciting, and reporting on investments are those who sit on the board of directors and the advisory board, if there is one. To be successful, provide them with simple tasks and crystal clear expectations. For example, board members can be asked to share the business plan with one new prospect every month, simply to ask for feedback. Or they can reach out to current partners to ask if the organization is performing to expectations. Set an easy, memorable goal: have one personal, face-to-face conversation per month with a current or prospective investor. That's not a lot of work, and it's easy to remember.

Even with such a light lift, volunteers are often leery of "asking people for money," associating the work with all sorts of negative tactics. No amount of exhortation and encouragement will get them over this hesitation. Instead, ask them where they feel most comfortable. Even the most cautious board member should feel no hesitation to contact current investors and make sure they feel the donation is being used well. These conversations fall directly within their legal status as fiduciaries and, as they are distinct from the proposal process, offer less

(start here ⬇)

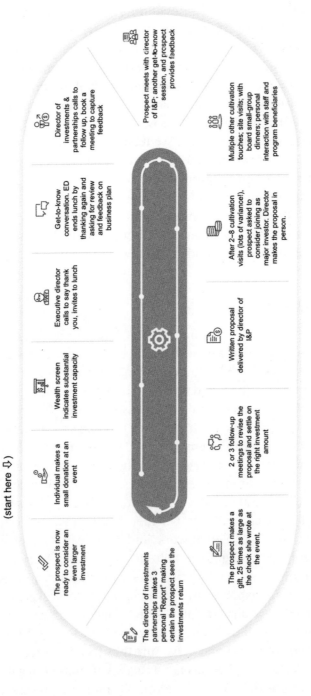

FIGURE 5.2 The Cycle of Social Investment.

opportunity for anxiety to blossom. In short, the volunteer is gathering feedback on the potential or actual use of the investment, detailing whom they spoke with and what was said. If they feel awkward about doing it themselves, they may join the executive director or fundraising staff. That said, if too much handholding is required, it is a sign that the individual may lack the confidence, stature, and/or commitment that board leadership demands.

Nonprofit staff often waste tremendous amounts of time and energy hectoring their boards around time-consuming responsibilities such as filling tables at the auction. The most effective boards are staffed by very busy people who want to help, and often their highest and best use is to introduce executive staff to their friends and colleagues, signaling their support via their board membership alone. Effective boards spend the bulk of their energies providing organizational insight, oversight, and foresight, making contributions during the acquire stage (see acquire tactic #3), not scrounging the community for auction donations.

In our work with boards, we do not hesitate to pivot away from the old "give/get" requirement. While a requirement that board members make major philanthropic contributions is a good idea on large arts or foundation boards, we have found success splitting off fundraising duties to an advisory or ambassador board, where it becomes the only focus. This has produced good results and eliminates the hectoring involved with getting reluctant board members to participate in investment and partnership activity.

As leaders develop their I&P plan, they must be specific about volunteer expectations and include volunteers only after they are aligned on process and agree to participate. As this is a significant contribution of their time and talent, don't forget to thank and recognize them.

Staff

Fear or ignorance on how to hire, train, manage, and support top fundraising teams is a primary reason why boards and executive directors never break free of their financial constraints. As soon as fundraisers become successful—that is, as soon as they win their first few six-figure investments—their market value skyrockets. Unless their compensation packages reflect this, they will very likely follow the richer pay and benefit packages offered by larger organizations.

Because successful fundraising teams build and maintain deep, long-term relationships with their prospects, a critical feature of the I&P plan is competitive compensation for fundraising teams. Boards and executive leaders can simply look to the hospitals and universities in their region for compensation benchmarks. Hesitate to pay top fundraising staff that extra $25,000 or so, and the penalty will likely be many multiples of that in lost revenue. The overhead myth and the myth of uniqueness are such effective wrecking balls for nonprofit growth and impact because the first things they target are competitive salaries for fundraisers. While the nonprofit fundraising profession's rules of ethics[7] rightly prohibit pay based on a percentage of dollars raised, it is not hard to devise incentives and reward packages with a holistic view of staff performance.

It may take anywhere from 12 to 24 months to establish a mature I&P pipeline. Once it is up and running, however, each fundraising officer is typically able to manage a portfolio of 150 prospects and up to $1 million or more in projected charitable investments running at peak efficiency.

Determine the approximate proportion of staff time devoted to each of the revenue domains. Start with the best guess and refine from there. Note that it is a team, with the CEO, fundraisers, and event and administrative staff working together. Be sure to allocate significant time on individual investments. This is where the funding typically is, but this is only a generalization. Revenue strategy may be wholly dependent on earned or agency income, for example. Whatever the staffing allocation, the point is to measure action and be intentional about staff time. Start with a best guess, measure, and improve the accuracy of allocations. This is important preventative medicine for burnout.

---

[7]"Code of Ethical Standards," Association of Fundraising Professionals, **https://afpglobal.org/ethicsmain/code-ethical-standards**.

Staff Budget

Typically, about three-quarters of revenue generation expenses are salaries and benefits for staff. Be thoughtful and deliberate about where fundraising staff should spend their time and allocate a portion of their salary as budget in the appropriate categories.

Note: The number one barrier to fundraising performance is poor compensation and a lack of incentives for fundraising staff. In the private sector, salespeople are among the most well compensated professionals in any company. The same applies to the social sector. High-performing organizations must invest heavily to create teams of dedicated professionals.

Operations Budget

Revenue generation expenses are typically events, websites, and the CRM (customer relationship management software—the fundraising database). Don't bother printing fancy brochures. Attention spans are limited, and it is a waste of paper in the digital age. Spend money on bringing people together in the community to explore and celebrate the work.

Almost every nonprofit has a CRM, but only a tiny fraction use it effectively, because it is hard to do, particularly with frequent staff turnover. Even though there are only a few fields that must be tracked for each constituent record, CRMs come loaded with a confusing array of features. The pre-formatted ones are not much better. Among all the packages out there, the Nonprofit pack that comes with Salesforce is likely the best option for most small to mid-sized nonprofits, but it requires an investment in training that few organizations make. The market is filled with CRMs that purport to already be set up for nonprofit fundraising teams, but these are often simplistic and limiting. The ideal pathway, but one that demands some significant budget allocation, is to bring in a CRM expert to incorporate the measures provided here and give administrative staff the guidance around care and maintenance training necessary to keep the CRM from becoming a digital dumpster.

Total Budget

It's important to track the time spent on raising money to determine an important figure: cost per dollar (CPD). Add up all revenue and divide it by all expenses. Smaller and newer I&P teams will have CPDs about $0.50—meaning that every dollar spent raises two. However, if the execution goes well, major investments will start to flow, typically between 12 to 24 months at the longest, and as revenue goes up, so does efficiency, with CPD over time reaching an optimal level of $0.15 to $0.20. CPD is a powerful KPI—but beware; it is a lagging indicator. Substantial investment in staff pay and operations is often required first before this number comes down.

Other Revenue Domains and Segments

The goals, prospect numbers, average investment amount, tactics, and staffing for each revenue domain and segment will all vary according to strategy. The above examples illustrate a beginning-to-end planning sequence only for one segment, major investors, of just one revenue domain, individuals. This chapter focused on this segment as it is typically where there is the most amount of accessible funding for most mission types.

The challenge for boards and executive teams is to understand what other segments they also need to access or how to allocate scarce resources to the most productive ones. Many nonprofits have access to sophisticated revenue streams around earned income: they could leverage their tax-exempt status to build up real estate assets, they could license their intellectual property, or they could create for-profit subsidiaries. No one has perfect visibility into all the right ways a nonprofit could and should be funding its programs, so as soon as executives have a reasonably complete draft of their I&P plan, they should consult with proven experts in each domain.

Bias conversations to the most experienced fundraisers who raised at least $50 million for least three distinct organizations. It takes many years to develop true expertise in the field, so ask people with gray hair and a long, successful track record for advice. Nonprofit revenue professionals are typically generous altruists eager to share best practices and help their peers.

Another good way to develop and improve domain specific strategies and tactics is to consult with aspirational peers. For example, a community food bank that is just starting up can easily find much larger, well-established organizations with leadership happy to share best practices. Universities and hospitals are filled with altruists who are willing to share insights into their strategies.

Fund Practice 5.4: Drive Performance Improvement with an Investment and Partnership Scorecard

Just like a business plan, even the best I&P plan is a pile of dots on a screen until people use it to take action. And put any plan into action, and things are guaranteed to go wrong, per legendary boxer Mike Tyson's famous quip: "Everyone has a plan until they get punched in the mouth." Therefore, execution needs to be carefully measured and continuously monitored, all in a lean, efficient manner that takes minimal time away from conversations with prospects and investors.

Therefore, all plans must have scorecards. This is a fundamental truth of effective management. *Scorecards* are exactly what they sound like: they are ways to keep score and to track team performance. Without them, there is little other than intuition or anecdote to guide performance.

This all-important mutual dependency between a plan and a scorecard is universal. This section will describe how to create a scorecard for just the I&P plan. However, that same connection between a plan and a scorecard applies to the broader organizational business plan, which is measured by an *executive dashboard*, a process that will be covered in Chapter 6: "Execute."

The sections below go into what are likely excruciating levels of detail for identifying everything that needs to be measured and how to measure it. If the organization wants to become a truly high performer, that same care must be applied to everything else the organization pursues. It takes months of hard work and continuous improvement to transform an organization from a team of loosely connected people pursuing their own hazy understanding of an ambiguous goal into a disciplined team collecting and following an agreed-upon set of KPIs. The reward is worth the effort: dramatically improved social impact delivered by happy, well-compensated people who are living their best lives and making the world a better place.

Early in my consulting career I had a good appreciation for planning and strategy but limited experience getting teams to execute. We created strong plans that everyone liked, but the plans sat on the shelf. Frustrated with the challenge of executing plans, I patched together an execution guide, a primitive scorecard outlining checkpoints and milestones that indicated progress. It was slow, frustrating work, well outside my natural capabilities. Years of effort resulted in a patchwork system that, while better than nothing, was still obviously inadequate.

And then something wonderful happened, a moment of discovery that remains among the most powerful of my career. I discovered the book *4 Disciplines of Execution*,[8] a clear, concise, turnkey process for executing strategy. The book fixed the biggest hole in my consulting practice and helped propel the development and impact of the many nonprofits I touched in the following years.

The four principles of *4DX*, as it is known, are simple and easy to memorize:

1. Set a clear, quantitative goal (the book calls them *WIGs*, for wildly important goals).
2. Act on the lead measures (things you do today that will produce the outcomes you want tomorrow).
3. Keep a compelling scorecard.
4. Follow a cadence of accountability (consistently analyzing the scorecard to improve execution).

The I&P plan will include a specific dollar goal and all the associated actions to get to that goal. The task now is to translate those proposed actions into a simple, easy-to-understand scorecard, what we call the

---

[8]Chris McChesney, Jim Huling, and Sean Covey, *4 Disciplines of Execution* (New York: Simon & Schuster, 2015), **https://www.franklincovey.com/the-4-disciplines/**.

I&P pipeline. Every two weeks, everyone associated with investments and partnerships (the CEO along with all marketing, administrative, and fundraising staff) come together and use this scorecard as their performance measurement and guide for continuous improvement.

The sections below provide specific, step-by-step instructions on what to measure, how to produce the scorecard, how to read it, and how to capture trend data that shows which fundraising tactics are working and which ones need improvement. By preserving the summary data from each scorecard, teams can build trendlines that can then be used to improve strategy and forecast revenue.

Scorecard Step 1: Set Up the Database

This scorecard methodology requires no advanced information management skills. It does require a commitment to carefully track and record a modest number of elements for each prospect. Also, the recording and reporting of this information may require some manual labor at first. When the recording and reporting processes are fully understood, organizations with access to adequate technology and information management resources can then automate them.

Start by configuring the database to record each of the fields below in each prospect record. Whatever software package is used, adapt or configure it as needed, a task that is not as onerous as it sounds as there are not that many pieces of information to record and track. If there is no database, a simple spreadsheet will work until the organization is ready to invest in a CRM. I've raised many millions of dollars with simple spreadsheets, no CRM required.

Scorecard Step 2: Record the Right Data

A database is like a collection of index cards, with each card being a record and all the information in each record called *fields*. Track the following fields for each record:

- **Prospect:** Name, address, email, and related personal information.
- **Segment:** Put a simple one-letter code in every prospect's record that describes if they are a private individual; part of a corporation,

foundation, or agency; or a purchaser of the organization's goods or services. (These codes depend on what segments are tracked. There may be others: for example, if the organization relies on churches to get the message out, and recruit and retain more of them is a goal, set up a pipeline for them and use "C" to represent "Church Partners.") Below are examples of typical segment codes:

F:	Foundation
C:	Corporation
I:	Individual
A:	Agency
E:	Earned income
P:	Program partner

- **Stage:** Every I&P prospect is assigned a 1–6 numeric code that describes their current relationship status. Use numbers to represent the stages in the database for a useful shorthand to describe where investors are in the pipeline.

Code	Stage	Definition
1	Acquire	Prospects who are (1) qualified (for affinity and capacity) and (2) for whom there is contact information.
2	Build trust	The prospect has personally responded to an acquisition tactic. Do not move into this stage without this indication or expression of interest.
3	Propose	A stage of negotiation or consideration of a draft investment proposal.
4	Accept	A verbal or written yes but not yet transferred funding.
5	Decline	Declined the proposal.
6	Report	Transferred funds. The prospect is now an investor. Record how the investor wants to receive reporting on their charitable dollars.

- **Proposed Investment:** Even if there is little knowledge, make a guess on how much that prospect will invest if all goes well. Don't fail to take a guess. Starting with a wild guess is better than zero, and this will motivate those who don't like ambiguity to learn more about the prospect and get to a more accurate number. For prospects that have never been engaged one-on-one, base the goal on (1) a wealth screen, (2) the current understanding of their affinity for the organization, and (3) 5 to 10 times any previous charitable donations. Don't get stuck in analysis paralysis. Conversations with the prospect will give insight on affinity, and investment goals can be modified as the relationship deepens. For example, if the prospect reveals she just sold her company to Apple and loves the mission, it would be safe to increase the proposal amount accordingly.

- **Probability:** This is a simple percentage that describes the overall likelihood of the prospect accepting the proposal by writing a check. Assigning probability enables the ability to make cash flow projections, which will be illustrated in the scorecard section below. While it is possible to assign specific probability ratings to every prospect, doing so would require many subjective judgments. Over the course of an entire team, things would get messy very quickly. Therefore, it's easier and more robust to simply assign one probability rating for each stage of the relationship building process, as follows:

  o Assign a 5% probability for prospects in the acquire stage. While there must be some indication of prospect affinity and capacity to even be included in this prospect list, there has been no communication yet, and thus there is no certainty the prospect will even respond to build trust tactics. Account for that with a steep discount of 95%.

  o Assign 25% probability for prospects in the build trust stage. As all prospects in this category are engaging someone in the organization around one or more of the build trust tactics, there is moderately more confidence a proposal may be successful, so we apply a 75% discount to the proposal value.

  o Assign a 50% probability if the prospect agrees to review a draft proposal in the propose stage.

- Seventy-five percent is assigned as a probability when the prospect says, "Yes! I love the proposal. I'll be overjoyed to make a $10,000 investment in this terrific organization!" There is still a 25% discount applied to everyone in the accept stage: not everyone follows through on a verbal or even written commitment, so a conservative estimate here is prudent and reminds everyone that the investment is made until the funding is received.

- The only instance where there is 100% certainty of money being received is when it actually lands in the bank. Therefore, only record investments in the report stage when they are deposited.

Scorecard Step 3: Assign a Relationship Manager

Every I&P prospect should be assigned a *relationship manager* (RM), who is a member of the I&P team responsible for monitoring the relationship and ensuring it is developing in a positive direction. RMs make sure the prospect is actively engaged in the work of the organization, that communication and exchange happen at minimum once every quarter, and that every conversation leads to a next step that strengthens the relationship. Relationship managers are accountable for the progress of the prospects under their watch. They do everything in their power to ensure prospects have a good experience and touch many different parts of the organization to learn more about the good things their investment could do. They are never the only person to speak to a prospect: good relationship building involves many touch points.

No one person should have more than 150 to 200 prospects for whom they are the relationship manager. This means you need to be selective about who goes into the I&P pipeline. Being selective about adding prospects with the highest capacity and affinity is the whole point of the major investor segment. There may only be a vague idea of who should belong at first. It may take months of removing prospects who don't respond and finding new ones before the pipeline begins to take shape. Even after then it will be continuously dynamic as people move on and new people join. This is normal. Always remember: continuous improvement.

Scorecard Step 4: Assign a Close Date

Another guess is required: how long it will take to win the investment, typically somewhere between 3 and 12 months depending on estimates of affinity and capacity. If uncertain, write down six months and change it as indications of the strength of the relationship are revealed. Just like many other data points, update the information as more is learned. The best way to learn is by asking the prospect: "Karan, what's the largest charitable gift you've ever made? Is our program a priority for you? How long would you need to get to know us before you feel you would have confidence to make an investment in our work?" Obviously don't fire all these questions off at once. Empathize and use good judgment. But also don't be shy. Only through experience will that balance point be discovered. And that balance point will be different for every person. This is why being a good observer and listener are important fundraising skills.

Scorecard Step 5: Define and Count Relationship-Building Contacts

A *relationship-building contact*, or *contact* for short, is just what it sounds like: a personal interaction (preferably in person, but phone calls and substantive emails qualify as well) between the organization's staff or volunteers and a current or prospective investor that substantially deepens that investor's understanding of how the organization is solving important problems and how their solutions align with the partner's or investor's own goals.

Record all contacts accurately and consistently. The number of contacts the organization records is the most important fundraising KPI. Getting it wrong or gaming the definition will ruin the analysis. The entire I&P team must understand and deploy a consistent understanding of what contacts are and how they are entered, not just for the major investor segment but for all revenue segments—individuals, corporations, foundations, agencies, earned revenue, and any others appropriate for any particular I&P plan.

Follow these rules:

- Record every contact within 24 hours of occurrence.
- Do not enter contact reports for interactions that are not substantive or do not show a deepening of the relationship. Saying "hello" to a prospect at an event or exchanging a casual email does not merit a contact report.
- Always aim for the highest-touch, most personal interaction possible. In-person meetings are best; video calls are the next best thing; phone calls are better than emails or texts, which are better than nothing.
- Describe each contact succinctly: what was discussed, why it is significant to the relationship, how it affects the proposal under consideration, the next step and date, and any change in the investor status.
- Contacts are counted organization-wide every two weeks and reported as a KPI in the I&P scorecard.
- Don't forget about activity for investors in the report stage. Every investor who has made a contribution should receive at least three separate report contacts before any consideration of a new proposal is discussed. Do not treat your donors like cash machines.
- Example contact report:

"I met with Hiroshi today to discuss her feedback on the business plan. She is positive overall but remains concerned about our program overlap with partners. I invited her to meet with our school team and see the work in action. Next step: propose a site visit in the next 3 weeks. Stephan to call 10/5 to invite; Alice to follow up."

Scorecard Step 6: Define the Next Step

Don't leave a meeting without being absolutely clear on what happens next and when it will happen. Every contact is a link in a chain that builds trust and a mutual understanding of how the mission and work align with the prospect's own desire to make the world a better place.

Here are two examples:

- "Dmitry, thanks for meeting with me today. I'd like to learn more about why you supported us at our recent event. I'd also like to ask for your advice on our organization's future plans. What's your availability look like in the next couple of weeks?" (Next step: Dmitry will review the business plan and you will meet in two weeks to review his feedback.)
- "Dmitry, thank you for that terrific feedback on the business plan. When we revise it next, I'll give you an updated copy. Please come see our work in action—this firsthand experience will be exciting. The mayor is going to be there, and I'd love to introduce you. Does March 18 work for you? If not, we've got other great opportunities to see our work up close." (Next step: In six weeks, Dmitry will join a select group of community leaders to see the program in action.)

Scorecard Step 7: Produce the Prospect List

Take the time to properly configure the database records with all the fields above. The next step is to produce a list of all current I&P prospects (see Figure 5.3).

An organization with a mature I&P pipeline may have many hundreds of people currently under relationship management. Whatever the total number of prospects under management, the next challenge is to ensure a dedicated staff person has the capability to produce this

prospect	segment	stage	goal	probability	RM	contact date	next step
Dan Smith	I	1	$50,000	5%	Jeff	10/15	event 6/2
Juan Tun	C	2	$75,000	25%	Farhad	12/1	meeting 6/7
Mei Lee	C	2	$25,000	50%	Farhad	9/1	proposal 6/9
Jo Vasque	A	3	$100,000	75%	Lin	10/1	call 6/25

FIGURE 5.3   Sample Prospect Output from Database.

list every two weeks. Be disciplined. For example, designate 9 a.m. on the first and third Monday of every month to produce this list.

Scorecard Step 8: Produce the Investment and Partnership Scorecard

The *I&P scorecard* is a single table that boils down all your fundraising prospect information in a concise and measurable way so readers of the scorecard can quickly understand if the organization is making adequate fundraising progress and there are enough prospects in the pipeline to meet goals.

The correct way to create and use scorecards is to use the *4 Disciplines* discussed earlier. These disciplines translate directly to the I&P process:

1. The wildly important goal is the annual fundraising goal.
2. The lead metric is the number of high-quality contacts with prospects.
3. A compelling scorecard will look something like that shown in Figure 5.4.
4. Every two weeks, the I&P team gathers to review the scorecard.

stage:	1 - acquire	2- build trust	3- propose	4- accept	5- decline	6 - report	Totals:
Individuals	5	15	10	7	3	4	44
Foundations	2	3	1	0	4	2	12
Corporations	1	4	0	2	1	3	11
Agencies	0	0	0	0	0	0	0
Earned Income	0	0	0	0	0	0	0
June 15 TOTAL	8	22	11	9	8	9	67
(30-May)	4	20	9	8	7	7	55
(15-May)	3	15	6	2	6	4	36
(1-May)	1	11	2	1	2	3	20
Dollars by stage:	$95,000	$375,000	$430,000	$175,500	$0	$950,750	

Revenue vs. goal: 50%   Fiscal year elapsed: 30%   # contacts this period: 47   # potential contacts: 90

FIGURE 5.4 Sample Investment and Partnership Scorecard.

Producing a scorecard from a long list of prospect records demands expertise with a spreadsheet function known as a *pivot table*. There are many guides on the Internet on how to use a pivot table, so we will not reproduce them here. They are a little tricky at first, but once learned, they are simple and powerful. In Figure 5.4, the rows represent partnership stages, the columns are investor types, and the figures themselves are the number of prospects in each cell.

Read the Investment and Partnership Scorecard

With the scorecard produced, the executive team and board can quickly grasp a clear, comprehensive picture of fundraising progress and get answers to the following questions:

- Are we on track to meet our fundraising goal?
- How many prospective investors are we talking to in each segment? What stage are they in? Have we engaged enough to reach our revenue goals?
- How well are people responding to our efforts to build trust and solicit their support? Are prospects progressing well from stage to stage, or is everyone just sitting there, not responding?
- Are we fulfilling our goals for the numbers of conversations we need to be having? Is everyone on the team engaging in the necessary number of relationship-building contacts?

What follows is an outline of the important data the scorecard provides and the performance conclusions that can be drawn from this example.

Trend Data

Produce this scorecard every two weeks, which is the correct cadence of accountability. Every time this report is run, copy the total number of prospects by stage and paste into a separate table with each date. Over time, this simple trend data will show the overall movement of the prospect population through the relationship stages and highlight successes to be expanded and sticking points to be resolved.

As shown in Figure 5.4, the organization is doing an excellent job acquiring potential major individual investors. Notice the numbers going up every two weeks. Alternatively, if that number were flat, the team would have reason to question the acquisition tactics and begin to make adjustments.

There is much more that can be said about analyzing trend data. This is only the most simple, high-level analysis. If the organization has the time and capability to go deeper, track the prospect numbers for each revenue domain, track the dollar totals, or track the contact activity. Each separate trendline can yield fruitful insights if the data is recorded and produced with fidelity to this process.

Prospect Diversity

Notice the organization isn't doing much when it comes to identifying foundations, corporations, agencies, or earned income prospects. Is this good or bad? It depends. If the organization is intentionally pursuing just individuals, great. If there's a big earned income initiative featured in the business plan, then the team knows it needs to put more effort into those tactics or change them if they aren't producing results.

Income Projections

It will take a little more manual labor manipulating data, but it's not too hard to add up the proposal goals by stage, apply the associated discount rate, and designate the total discounted dollars by stage at the end of the scorecard. This gives another at-a-glance look at where the current opportunities are and whether the organization is on track to meet the revenue goal.

Proposal Activity

Examine how the numbers of people in stage 3: "Propose," continue to rise. This team is doing a good job at proposing investments. There should be movement over time across all stages in the pipeline. Don't read too much into the numbers until there is at least six months of trend data. And be aware that it is better to move prospects at their pace, not yours. While there is tremendous variability around how long it may take individuals to progress from stage 1 to stage 6, in general, a period of six to nine months is a typical investment cycle.

Conversion Rates

Compare the number of prospects who have made an investment (in stage 6: "Report") versus the people who have declined (in stage 5: "Decline"). Note that there are nine prospects in the report stage, while eight are in the decline stage. This is a conversion rate of over 50%, which is very good. Aim for conversion rates between 25% and 50%. If conversion rates fall below 25%, that's an indicator the team should start to consider the following:

- Are we properly qualifying prospects, or are we including prospects in the pipeline with inadequate capacity, affinity, or both?
- Are any of our building trust or proposal tactics not working?
- If it's not a qualification or tactical issue, perhaps the performance issue is in the quality of our delivery. Are we failing to build relationships with timeliness, professionalism, and empathy? Do one or more of us need more training and support?
- Enough interviews with prospects in stage 5 will yield insights into the above.
- If conversion rates fall below 25%, don't despair. Whatever happens, don't beat people up with the data. Use the data to direct curiosity around where the team can improve. Ask people who say no to be brutally honest about why they aren't saying yes.

Key Performance Indicators

Note the information displayed at the bottom of the scorecard. Examine each of these numbers carefully:

Revenue vs. goal:	25%
Fiscal year elapsed:	30%
# contacts this period:	47
# potential contacts:	90

The "revenue vs. goal" is quite simple: how much money have we raised? This organization has raised $950,750 so far—the amount of money in stage 6. It is 50% of the revenue the organization is aiming for, or $1,901,500. And good news, it's only 30% of the way through the fiscal year, so this organization is in good shape. Sync the I&P scorecard with the beginning of the fiscal year, carrying over all the prospects in stages 1–3 and resetting stages 4–6 to 0.

Consider the final two KPIs: the number of contacts this reporting period and the number of potential contacts. This information is so critically important it deserves a detailed explanation below. In sum, understanding an organization's potential capacity for contacts and measuring how many it actually records in a given period is one of the most important pieces of revenue performance data there is. Every two weeks, the I&P team should consider not just their conversion rates but the level of activity they are able to accomplish. The CEO should keep a careful eye on activity levels and continuously cheerlead the team to reach full potential.

Warning: do not use numbers to create a sweatshop. Using metrics to drive team performance always comes with the danger that managers and leaders will take a shortcut and start demanding that teams "hit their numbers." Pressure tactics lead to burnout and failure. Metrics are great, but when discussing how to drive improvements, encouragement, training, and incentives are always better than scolding and threats.

Contact Numbers

While we have already mentioned that recording and monitoring the number of contacts is critical to creating and maintaining high-performing teams, we will revisit this topic again for a simple reason: every two weeks is an opportunity to see if the team can generate more positive contacts. Along with conversion rates, contact activity is the most powerful fundraising KPI.

Because measuring contact activity is simple and powerful, there is also strong staff temptation to manipulate the contact reports to show high levels of activity. Creating and maintaining the discipline that results in clear and accurate contact report entry is difficult and demands continuous positive reinforcement. Every prospect should have a relationship manager assigned, and every relationship manager is the directly responsible person for ensuring a positive relationship is being built and that all contacts are documented and of appropriate quality. Wave hello to a prospect at a party? That's not a contact. Meet with a contact and get valuable feedback on that prospect's likelihood to make a major investment? That better get recorded right away and not two weeks later, when essential details may be forgotten.

Therefore, every two weeks, run a report (or use whatever process that is simple and that works) to count the precise number of contacts that have occurred over the last two-week period. Well-communicated guidelines such as "All contacts must be in by the first and third Monday of every month by 9 a.m. or they will not be counted in the next report" have to be understood and embraced by the team. If not, an old expression applies: garbage in, garbage out.

Not all of this will go smoothly at first. I&P leaders will need to continuously and positively reinforce team discipline until the behaviors become habit. But then a wonderful thing happens: teams can accurately measure how many contact reports have been filed every two weeks. This is a major milestone. All that is left is to compare the number of actual contacts with the number of potential contacts the organization should be recording if everyone is working to their full potential and not distracted by other tasks and burdens. The I&P team is on its way to becoming the revenue engine for a world-improving social solution.

Position		Biweekly Total	Annual Total
Board Member goal: 1 per month	⊖	.5 each	12
Advisory Board goal: 1 per month	⊖	.5 each	12
CEO goal: 5 per week	⊖	10	250
I&P Director goal: 5 per week	⊖	10	250
I&P Officer goal: 15 per week	⊖	30	750

FIGURE 5.5   Sample Organizational Contact Potential.

Examine Figure 5.5. It depicts the staffing at a small social impact enterprise that has made a basic investment in its I&P team: in addition to the CEO, there is a director and two officers. It provides levels for optimal contact activity that are derived from years of testing, ones that are deliberately stretch goals (which our highest-performing clients regularly exceed, so we know these are not unrealistic). That said, consider these as starting points only—teams should set their own performance goals.

Notice that, while these levels ask that the paid staff work hard, it's an easy lift for the board members. They are volunteers and their best value to the organization is strategic engagement and the other duties listed in Chapter 7: "Lead." Far too many nonprofits burden their boards with onerous fundraising expectations. It is much more efficient and effective to pay staff. Directors are of course free to volunteer more activity—this is a floor, not a ceiling.

With this nominal contact potential for each I&P team member in mind, the next step is to determine the average number of contacts to close an investment. While there is great variance, Figure 5.6 shows a reasonably conservative estimate.

Now, count up the total number of potential annual contacts by the entire team: eight board members and eight advisory board members

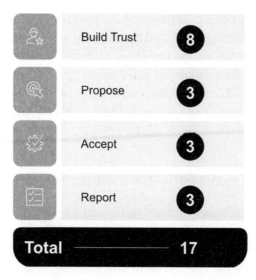

FIGURE 5.6   Typical Number of Contacts to Close an Investment.

equals about 190 annual contacts, the CEO can do about 250 annually, and each I&P officer can do 750. This means an organization-wide annual contact total of 1940.

Keep doing the arithmetic: at 17 contacts per major investment, this means the organization conceivably has the capacity to propose about 115 major investments every year. If 40% convert with an average investment size of $75,000, that's well over $3 million in annual revenue. What may seem like a heavy investment in the I&P team now makes sense: look at the annual revenue they produce. Compare this to similarly sized organizations that run transactional fundraising events and pursue gifts and grants: they will rarely raise more than $1 million annually, and they will do so at a *much* higher cost. *This* is why small nonprofits stay small: (1) ineffective strategy, (2) inadequate investment in their fundraising team, and (3) failure to measure leading and lagging indicators along with the other elements of 4DX.

This hypothetical example highlights the importance of measuring contact numbers, conversion rates, and average investment size. Every organization must first establish a baseline by implementing this system with fidelity for at least six months before the beginning of valid trend data appears, and a full fiscal year before solid benchmarks emerge. The scorecard gives immediate, near-term insights into how to improve, however, particularly if the team has the discipline to carefully document contacts and measure team activity. The next section outlines the agenda for using this data in the I&P pipeline meeting.

Running the Biweekly I&P Pipeline Meeting

All of the above is empty theory until teams apply the system: collect the data, record it in the database, produce the scorecard, and meet as a team every two weeks, like clockwork, to review performance. A sample agenda for the I&P pipeline meeting is shown below. This one works very well, but as elsewhere, adapt it as needed.

Sample I&P Pipeline Meeting Agenda

Goals	1. Review face-to-face contacts and progress toward moving investment prospects through the relationship stages.
	2. Use data to analyze and improve the effectiveness of the tactics for each segment.
	3. Share the feedback we are hearing from prospects: What do they like? What isn't working?
	4. Set individual and group goals for the next 2 weeks on contact activity and next steps with the 3 most important prospects.
Frequency	Every other week. Choose a specific day and time (first and third Monday at 9 a.m.); set the calendar for the year. Stick to the meeting schedule.
Duration	One hour at first; 30 minutes when everyone is up to speed.
Attendees	CEO, IPOs, database coordinator, marketing staff, others involved in I&P work. Rotate in all other organizational staff as observers to socialize the group's work with the rest of the organization's staff: *they will be running their own scorecard meetings soon.*
Materials	Organization-wide pipeline report; individual pipelines for every IPO.

Agenda	Go around the room—5 minutes for each attendee.
	1. Look backward: How did I do the last 2 weeks on the quantity and quality of my contacts?
	2. Look forward: What are my priorities, both in terms of quality and quantity of contacts, for the next 2 weeks?
	3. Who are my most important 3 prospects right now who are closest to a proposal?
	4. Here's what I have done to deliver a high-quality report to a current investor—the report stage activity is important to us, and we make sure to cover it.
Culture	Keep it professional, supportive, and inspiring.
	1. Keep it disciplined and focused: talk in headlines only.
	2. Don't beat people up with the data. If the team only did half of expected contacts in the last two weeks, how can the team do better in the next 2?
	3. Is the mission world-changing? Bring the fire. If this meeting is boring, leadership needs to start cheerleading and focusing on the problem the organization is solving.

Advanced Analytics

The measures described above will produce a powerful I&P scorecard. Tracking these basic KPIs and trends is a proven way to capture actionable and highly valuable performance insights. Teams that use these practices effectively will raise increasingly more money year after year. It is the same basic methodology behind all sophisticated fundraising operations.

As teams get comfortable with this compelling scorecard and the cadence of accountability and use it to drive continuous performance improvement and revenue growth, they may choose to explore adding additional measures to capture finer-grained insights. For example, the chief I&P officer may ask the team, "Okay, after a lot of hard work, the scorecard is solid. In the spirit of kaizen, let's experiment. What do you think about coding our acquisition tactics and then recording in each prospect record which one led us to each prospective major investor? We can then run a baseline report to establish the percentages of prospects we are acquiring from particular acquisition tactics. It will take us at least six months to build useful data as we've all seen, but then this additional date might yield new insight into which tactics are the best. We can then put more resources into those to see if that drives up our acquisition rates. We will take this slowly, making sure that, if we measure something, we fully commit and do it well. But if this works, it will improve our entire strategy, and we can explore expanding it to our other pipeline tactics."

Wise leaders know that every measure comes with the cost to collect it and the even more expensive cognitive bandwidth to analyze the measure and do something about it. Therefore, high-performing teams err on the side of *parsimony*, pursuing deeper analytics only when and where there are the resources to service their costs. If valuable performance insights may be captured, the cost of the additional KPI may yield multiples of new revenue down the road. If that happens, the organization can invest further.

Additional Resources

See **www.altruistaccelerator.org** for tools and examples.

Tools
- Revenue Strategy Template
- Revenue Scorecard Template
- Investment and Partnership Protocols
- Pipeline Meeting Agenda
- Prospect Brief Template
- Investment and Partnership Staffing and Budgeting
- IPO Hiring and Orientation
- Questions by Stage
- IPO Compensation Framework
- Sample Major Investment Proposal

Examples
- Sample Completed Investment and Partnership Plans
- Sample Revenue Scorecards
- Sample Job Descriptions

CHAPTER 6

Execute

Good business planning is nine parts execution for every one part strategy.

—Tim Berry

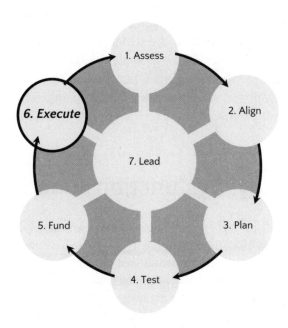

LEARNING OBJECTIVES

By the end of this chapter, you will be able to:

- Build awareness and consensus among staff to encourage adoption of effective execution practices;
- Design, build, and improve dashboards to monitor and improve growth and enhance strategy along with the other targeted areas of organizational performance; and
- Understand how to nurture a culture of performance, trust, and effective teamwork.

While many nonprofits can describe their program or services, most struggle with delivering them as promised to funders, partners, and supporters. Many for-profit organizations struggle with execution as well: it is obviously easier to promise something than to deliver on that promise. As elsewhere, there are very effective practices and tools used by high-performing for-profit organizations that, with some adaptation, are directly applicable to the social sector, and this chapter will describe what they are and how to apply them. First, it may be useful context to explore what happens when these execution practices go unused, as they do today by even very large and apparently successful, well-funded nonprofits.

Case Study: Dysfunction Junction

Save the Animals (STA) is a multibillion-dollar environmental conservation NGO launched in 1973 by the famous English conservationist Sir Winston Trufflewhite, who late in his life abandoned his career as an industrialist and big game hunter to dedicate his enormous personal fortune to the cause of wildlife conservation. "As I rested my boot on the dying carcass of the rhino I had just shot, I had an epiphany," he wrote in his autobiography, *I'm for the Animals: Are You?* "I would dedicate my life and my riches not to slaughtering, but to preserving these and all other magnificent creatures." He founded STA with a $100 million gift, dedicating it to the organization's mission to "study, preserve, and protect the glorious abundance of wildlife in our planet's oceans, forests, and skies."

The organization grew dramatically in the 1980s as a result of a large contract with the United Nations, and it grew even further in the 1990s and 2000s with billions more from government agencies such as USAID, the German development agency GIZ, large private foundations, and most recently, a $250 million grant from a technology entrepreneur. Today, the organization runs a sophisticated multinational fundraising enterprise that raises over $7 billion annually, a sum that funds the work of over 100 distinct conservation programs.

"We generate cutting-edge science and policy papers that model the forefront of global conservation," observes STA's CEO, Davis Carter. "Our ideas hold out the most hope that we can enjoy the variety of Earth's species for decades to come."

By the early 2000s, long standing partners and funders began asking STA for its goals and plans around implementing the policies and science it generated. Disturbing reports in scientific journals began making their way into the general media. According to a recent report in the *Economist*, since 1970, nearly three-quarters of the world's animals have died as a direct result of industrialization.

In response to increasing pressures to focus the organization on concrete indicators of progress, Carter, a zoologist by training, created a series of donor-funded internal programs that he said would "create and enhance STA's ability to directly implement our cutting-edge science to battle extinction on the front lines, wherever it occurs in the world. This will give us the capability to apply the solutions we create."

In a few years, the organization had launched multiple internal-facing service units focused on program execution. First was the Theory of Change Lab, chartered to produce detailed graphical documents that explained how the science at each program unit would be implemented. Another was the Impact Center, an initiative to collect, analyze, and report program outcomes. A third was the Center for Great Teams, founded to focus on providing professional training and development. A fourth was the Improvement Group: staffed by former teachers, it would convene the various groups to provide training and capture helpful findings that could be disseminated to other groups.

"What we've done is create a huge goddamn mess," observes Patricia Gonzalez, one of the organization's most successful fundraisers. "Every member of our C-suite is a brilliant scientist, but not one of them has substantial experience in organizational execution. They confuse confidence in their opinion with actual knowledge of how to apply our science. Now we have these absurdly designed, overlapping initiatives, none of which conform to organizational best practices. Until we get someone in leadership who has real-world execution experience, we are going to struggle. Our board members are full of famous people who have no clue what their C-suite is doing. But since our leaders all blame business for creating the mess we are in, it's unlikely to happen. I'm looking for another job. I just can't waste any more donor money in good conscience on goals we have no chance of meeting. It's sad, though. This organization is our biggest effort to save all our animals."

As any capable CEO will agree, plans and ideas are easy and cheap. Execution is hard and expensive. Ideas on paper are worthless until put into practice by teams of people who demonstrably deliver clear, measurable, evidence-based, independently verifiable results, ones that are significant against the size of the challenge. Getting a group of people to work together effectively on big challenges with consistent focus and energy over long periods of time is extraordinarily difficult, and even the most successful organizations find maintaining success long term extraordinarily challenging.

This chapter provides practices for small nonprofits to help them tackle the execution challenge. Recall how the fund practices laid out a clear, step-by-step execution pathway for raising money by setting a goal, carefully planning out how to get to the goal, and then measuring the execution with a scorecard that provides the platform for continuous improvement. In the same way, the execute practices offered here show how to embed these same principles of clear goal setting, disciplined planning, and continuous analysis and improvement across the rest of the organization: with front-line staff, with unit-level managers, and with executive leadership.

Beware the risk that, after all the effort required to work your way through the assessment, alignment, planning, and fundraising steps in earlier chapters, nothing actually changes. Plans get put on shelves. Even if more money starts coming in the door relatively quickly, as it often does in the fund phase, it is easy to seduce yourself with the illusion that the organizational transformation is complete. "We've got a plan. The money is coming in. Phew, past the hard part! I'm tired. We are good."

As we have seen many times, organizations that complete the growth and impact methodology through the fund phase may indeed enjoy a short-term bump in revenue. However, if an execution management system has not been established for programs and other key parts of the organization, there is a great risk that the organization will not hit the goals of its business plan. Without a clear means of ensuring that the business plan actually gets implemented, the organization likely will not be able to follow through on promises of impact made to investors and partners. When that happens, investors and partners withdraw and fundraising suffers.

The best way to ensure that plans are actually executed is with what we will call an *executive dashboard*, which is another type of scorecard. To be clear on the terms, we define a *scorecard* as any continuously updated measurement document that is used to monitor and improve organizational performance. The *investment and partnership pipeline* is an example of a scorecard, one covered in great detail in Chapter 5. In this chapter, we explain how to build an *executive dashboard*, which is an organization-wide scorecard that allows executives and boards to track KPIs in the business plan.

The first step to creating executive dashboards is to make sure that everyone in the organization knows what they are, why they are important, and how they will be used to support people, build teamwork, and create a more trusting, supportive environment. This careful process of building buy-in is critical. If they are designed and used properly, executive dashboards will help make everyone's job more effective and meaningful. The idea of performance management can be scary at first, so this orientation is important to reduce fear and pave the way for adoption and use.

Execute Practice 6.1: Inform Strategy with an Executive Dashboard

Dashboard sounds like a fancy business term, but the concept is simple. Everyone with a driver's license already knows what a dashboard is. Drivers need quick, at-a-glance information on speed, miles traveled, engine or battery status, and so on. Measurements like these are KPIs for a car, and they are laid out to be read quickly. Driving is dangerous, so long reports won't work—there need to be warning lights before the brakes fail or the engine blows up.

Executive dashboards are just like automobile dashboards. Instead of speed and mileage, executive dashboards track the KPIs from the business plan and perhaps a handful of other measures that boards and executives want to track. They are short, simple, and designed to be updated at least every quarter, with monthly updates being typical.

Executive dashboards are shared with everyone in the organization. They are used by the board, management, and staff to monitor progress and make decisions. They are shared with partners and investors to report on organizational progress and to make adjustments and improvements. In addition, they have a powerful fundraising function. Share them with prospects as a powerful trust-building tactic, and share them with investors to report on performance and demonstrate the social return on investment.

An important resource that will help organizations explore what an executive dashboard is and what benefits it can deliver is the seminal article by Robert S. Kaplan and David P. Norton: "The Balanced Scorecard—Measures That Drive Performance."[1] This article is a summary of Norton's 1992 book of the same title, an oldie-but-goodie of business literature. Sharing it with boards and staff will help orient them to key concepts.[2]

While Kaplan and Norton's article is a great introduction to what scorecards can do, there is another resource already mentioned in Chapter 5, one critical to understanding how to build and create dashboards: *The 4 Disciplines of Execution*. The I&P pipeline is one example of a scorecard; now we are expanding that measurement process here to encompass the rest of the organization. It's work, but here is why executive dashboards are mission-critical investments:

1. Access immediate, direct, and continuously updated monitoring and evaluation of growth and impact strategy;

---

[1] Robert S. Kaplan and David P. Norton, "The Balanced Scorecard—Measures That Drive Performance," *Harvard Business Review*, January–February 1992.
[2] Remember, the terms *scorecard* and *dashboard* can be used interchangeably.

2. Enable teams to take control of their own performance improvement: evaluation is owned and driven by staff and built into
operations, minimizing the need for slow and expensive external
evaluations;

3. Foster a culture of *kaizen* (continuous improvement), supporting
the foundation high growth and impact;

4. Support clarity of role and purpose for everyone in the organization, from board members to front-line staff (dashboards illustrate
the importance of everyone's work);

5. Provide comprehensive, concise, compelling insights for stakeholders, partners, and funders.

Like every other part of this methodology, a robust executive
dashboard demands a considerable up-front investment in time and
resources. Like the big payoff offered by 4DX, the rest of these practices
offer major returns in accelerated growth and impact.

Execute Practice 6.2: Nurture a Culture of Performance and Trust

Launching a dashboard with teams that have never been part of a
culture of performance measurement and improvement is risky.
Peter Drucker, the influential management theorist, wrote, "Work
implies . . . accountability, a deadline and, finally, the measurement
of results—that is, feedback from results on the work and on the planning process itself."[3] This sounds fine as theory, but bring up the words
accountability and *deadline* in a nonprofit staff meeting, and it is very
likely that the response will be fear and distrust. Therefore, the number one rule of using scorecards to improve performance is this: *don't
beat people up with the data.* So many companies use scorecards as
tools of fear and oppression: *hit your numbers or you are fired!* People

---

[3]Paul Zak, "Measurement Myopia," Drucker Institute, July 4, 2013, **https://www
.drucker.institute/thedx/measurement-myopia/**.

perform well when they have positive, supportive feedback on their performance. Fear and negative consequences only result in a loss of morale and employee engagement.[4]

Start by addressing potential fears around performance monitoring. Drucker recognized this and quickly followed up his comments about deadlines and accountability with this guidance for CEOs:

> *Your first role . . . is the personal one. . . . It is the relationship with people, the development of mutual confidence . . . the creation of a community. This is something only you [the CEO] can do. . . . It cannot be measured or easily defined. But it is not only a key function. It is one only you can perform.*[5]

High performance is rooted in trust. Courageous change makers are out to solve problems no one has solved before. Trusting, tight-knit teams are a critical success factor. Some leaders try to build trust by describing their organizations as families. That's a poor analogy: family members don't get to choose each other. Family members must love each other no matter what. And trust isn't very common in too many families! A better analogy for the trust that needs to be created is the professional sports team. The organization invests heavily in top players who get on the field with a sophisticated game plan to score goals and win. As Google's research on building strong teams reveals, staff thrive best when they can speak up and explore and share ideas without fear of punishment or censure.[6] The CEO is responsible for establishing and maintaining that trust and safety.

With an awareness of the tools, an appreciation of their great usefulness and power, and a trust that the transparency and accountability

[4]Colin Lecher, "How Amazon Automatically Tracks and Fires Warehouse Workers for 'Productivity,'" The Verge, April 25, 2019, **https://www.theverge.com/2019/4/25/18516004/amazon-warehouse-fulfillment-centers-productivity-firing-terminations.**

[5]Paul Zak, "Measurement Myopia," Drucker Institute, July 4, 2013, **https://www.drucker.institute/thedx/measurement-myopia/.**

[6]Charles Duhigg, "What Google Learned from Its Quest to Build the Perfect Team," *The New York Times Magazine*, February 25, 2016, **https://www.nytimes.com/2016/02/28/magazine/what-google-learned-from-its-quest-to-build-the-perfect-team.html.**

they make possible won't be abused, staff can proceed into the strategic and technical aspects of building, operating, and continuously improving scorecards. When they are owned and driven by staff and tied to a strategy that works, the organization will be on its way to adding to the list of dramatic social impact success stories in the opening pages of this book. The hard work is worth the effort.

Execute Practice 6.3: Analyze Three Levels of Performance

Imagine that an explorer has discovered a new land, one hundreds of thousands of square miles in size, one that takes her hours to traverse even by jet. She will need to fly at 30,000 feet to look at the entire terrain to navigate and to watch out for mountains and storms. But that view is incomplete: it doesn't give enough detail to get an understanding of what's below. She can swoop down to 500 feet, where details on the ground are much easier to see, but then it will take much longer to see the entire landscape. At 5,000 feet there's a good balance of terrain and detail, but some risks are hard to spot and other levels of detail are still lost.

No one view is perfect. What's needed are three airplanes flying as a team, communicating to each other what they see well and relying on the others for their respective advantages. Everyone gets a complete set of information, and they can explore the landscape effectively, but only if they stay at their assigned altitude and communicate regularly.

Providing every team in an organization with clear visibility to what the other teams or people are doing is one big point of the dashboard: clear, constant communication of key performance data without the need for meetings or emails. Leaders stay at high altitude, looking ahead to chart the overall course and watch out for opportunities and risks. Department managers stay at middle altitude, monitoring the performance of their teams and ensuring unit-level goals critical to overall success are met. Finally, staff on the front lines are closest to ground-level altitude, doing the essential work to deliver on the mission and look out for execution problems and strategy and measurement improvements.

Organizations larger than a dozen staff typically need to monitor these three perspectives: the executive, program or unit, and staff level. (In smaller organizations, program and staff levels are typically the same, and in start-ups, a few people do everything.) Number these, and a clear order emerges—*three levels of analysis*:

Level 1	**Organization:** Foci such as BHAGs, goals, strategy, KPIs; headlines from the business plan; content of the pitch deck
Level 2	**Team or business units:** Programs; revenue; finance; HR; culture; professional development
Level 3	**Individuals:** Day-to-day execution at the front-line staff level across the organization

These levels are easily remembered and become useful shorthand to toggle back and forth between information altitudes, keeping everyone clear about what level of focus to maintain in meetings and day-to-day discussions. As will be discussed in more detail in the final chapter, people have natural differences in brain wiring that make them more comfortable and skilled at particular levels, and they are drawn naturally to those perspectives. Therefore, it's critical to have labels to create intentional direction on a level of analysis. It helps everyone recognize diverse skills and act more collaboratively.

Execute Practice 6.4: Identify Mission-Critical KPIs

With these three levels of information in mind, the executive dashboard presents all the level 1 information that the board and executive team pull from the business plan, along with other measures they judge necessary to gauge progress. See below for the most basic set of level 1 KPIs that belong on an executive dashboard:

1. **Quantity**
   - How much of the problem you are solving versus your goal; and
   - KPIs related to growth strategy.

2. Quality

- The differences made with each person or thing being served; and
- KPIs related to impact strategy.

3. Finance

- Budget versus actual income and expense for each month since the beginning of the fiscal year; and
- Number of operational months of cash in the bank were all income to stop (months of cash reserve).

4. Revenue

- Pipelines for each revenue domain (individuals, corporations, etc.);
- Number of face-to-face contacts you are making with current or prospective investors; and
- Percentage of the revenue goal for the year that is in the bank versus the percentage of the fiscal year that has elapsed.

If Chapters 2 and 3 were followed, there should already be an initial set of KPIs. Creating the Executive Dashboard provides another opportunity to revisit and refine them, and this is normal when building the first version of the dashboard. If they do change from the business plan, remember to go back and update the business plan with the new KPIs.

Once the organization has all of this information in hand, these measures are often presented visually. Figure 6.1 presents a general example of how this information might be presented visually. This type of quick, at-a-glance visualization of information is often more engaging than lists of numbers, and it also helps those who have a hard time reading numbers to understand what all the numbers actually mean.

Where does one find KPIs for the dashboard? From the business plan! But remember, measurement takes time and effort, so choose only the most important measures that everyone will pay attention to. Pick too many, and no one can track them all. Pick too few, and miss critical performance areas. Different people will want to track different things, so attempting to arrive at 100% consensus is usually a waste of effort.

Therefore, now is the time to reread the business plan and pull out all the growth and impact measures, along with other KPIs around organizational performance, seeking to arrive at 80% consensus among

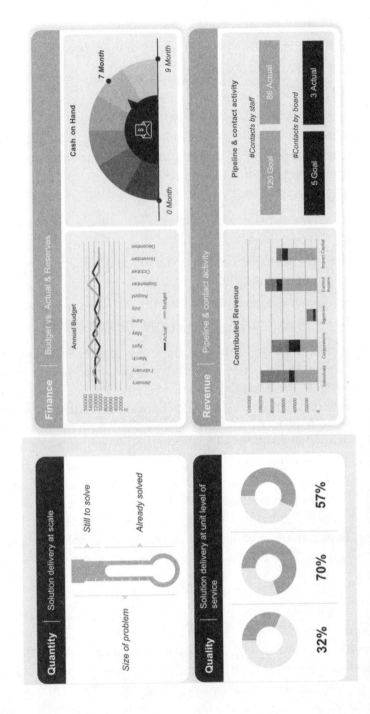

FIGURE 6.1 Sample Dashboard Visualization.

the board. The practices that follow offer a pathway for doing this. But remember: whatever is targeted are only *draft* measures. They can be changed later. Even the most expertly created business plan and dashboards will be wrong, and no one will know where they are wrong until they are used. So don't make the common mistake of spending a lot of time trying to get everything perfect. Stay biased toward action and experiment. Once the initial dashboard is put in action, board and staff will have a much better idea about how the KPIs and their representation in the dashboard can evolve. Now that everyone knows what a dashboard is and what they are for, it is time to start creating them.

Execute Practice 6.5: Create a Dashboard Plan

Just like the I&P plan divides revenue strategy into domains, segments, tactics, and the sequence of steps, a dashboard plan describes a start-to-finish series of steps to identify, collect, and report on execution performance. Like the format of the I&P plan, it is a simple table, in which rows correspond to the management domain (programs, revenue, finance, etc.) and columns correspond to each of the workflow steps. The columns are defined as follows, and an example is shown in Figure 6.2.

Column Headings and Definitions

1. **Domain:** The management category in question
2. **Level:** 1, 2, or 3
3. **KPI (lag):** The outcome measure that signifies success
4. **Lag Goal:** The desired result
5. **KPI (lead):** The activity that is performed to get to the lag—the cause of the success
6. **Lead Goal:** Quality or frequency of desired lead activity
7. **Source:** The single person who inputs that piece of data
8. **Input Freq.:** How often the source inputs the data
9. **Responsible:** The manager responsible for improvement and reporting of results

1. Domain	2. Level	3. KPI (lag)	4. Lag Goal	5. KPI (lead)	6. Lead Goal	7. Source	8. Input Freq.	9. Responsible	10. Report Freq.	NOTES
Graduation Success	1	Graduation Rates	80%	ABC+	95%	Caroline	Biweekly	Gelkha	Quarterly	
	2	Attendance	95%	Support Delivery	24 hours	Jamal	Biweekly	Devon	Monthly	
		Behavior	95%	Support Delivery	24 hours	Jorge	Biweekly	Devon	Monthly	
		Coursework	95%	Support Delivery	24 hours	Stephan	Biweekly	Devon	Monthly	
		Psychosocial Dev.	100% in place	Plan Milestones	weekly	Caroline	Biweekly	Devon	Monthly	
	3	Delivery Time	24 hours	Response Time	24 hours	Ed Coord	Daily	Ed Coord	Biweekly	
		Solution preparation	100%	Partner Engagement	100%	Ed Coord	Daily	Ed Coord	Biweekly	
		Caregiver engagement	100%	Engagement Contacts	10	Ed Coord	Daily	Ed Coord	Biweekly	

FIGURE 6.2 Treehouse Dashboard Plan.

10. **Report Freq.:** How often the relevant teams meet to discuss results and improvement

11. **Notes:** Scratch pad for next steps, sticking points to be resolved, etc.

This example presents all three levels of a dashboard plan for the Treehouse ABC+ goal to support foster youth to attain 80% high school graduation rates. The ABC+ strategy is broken down into lags and leads, and each KPI measure is carefully calibrated among the team to ensure everyone knows exactly what is being measured.

Importantly, not every domain will have three levels. Small organizations may have only one. In larger organizations, some units may only have two levels, such as finance, which is a fairly straightforward record keeping and analysis function with smaller staff and less of a need for leads and lags.

Execute Practice 6.6: Align the Board with the Dashboard

In the align phase, the board makes the high-level, long-term decisions that undergird the business plan framework. Next, in the plan phase, executive staff developed a full business plan based on the framework, revised it with the board's approval, and moved it into the test phase. A similar process happens with the dashboard. A strong start toward the necessary level 1 KPIs should already be in the business plan. Consolidate these into a scorecard and be certain to circle back to the board. "Okay," says the CEO. "We've done a lot of development work to get to this stage, so now is the time to put our plan into action. Here is your at-a-glance executive dashboard to track our progress toward our BHAG and to help diagnose the problems that will inevitably occur as we execute."

Once the dashboard plan is 80% complete, the CEO should meet in person with the chair, spread out the business plan and dashboard plan, and consider how well the dashboard plan scores progress on the business plan. This is an extremely important conversation that is worth multiple discussions until the chair and CEO are happy with the interrelationship of both documents (always keeping the 80%-is-good-enough agreement threshold in mind). The dashboard plan still needs to be reviewed by the rest of the board and staff and then be put into action for at least six months until there is hard evidence about what should be changed. The biggest risk is this process gets bogged down in argument and details, especially around various level 3 measures, so the CEO needs to remind the board to stay in its lane and focus on level 1 only. It is the CEO's job to manage the rest.

With the chair and CEO in at least 80% agreement, the CEO repeats this review process with the executive committee and then the entire board. This incremental approach is safest. Put a dashboard plan in front of an entire board all at once, and odds are excellent that the group will plummet into endless and unproductive meetings. While this process takes time, once the dashboard is ready for use, it will pay back all the invested time and effort by taking the place of endless board reports and thick meeting packets.

Now, with the entire board and CEO in at least 80% agreement on level 1 KPIs, the CEO can now take the plan to the staff team, discuss any adjustments, and secure the initial commitments from each team member who is either entering or reporting the data. While adjustments can always be made, these are serious, long-term commitments for a core part of the organization's performance accounting. The CEO must make sure staff has the time and support to stay committed to the work.

Then, once the measures are understood and the workflow to collect them is in place, it should be a relatively simple task to document activity in a database. For organizations that don't enjoy good data management practices or a culture of documentation, this will be a heavy lift. For others with these basic competencies, the primary barrier is staff time and attention. Should staff object due to a lack of time or energy, something has obviously gone wrong in execute practice 1, 2, or 3. Revisit the loss of opportunity if no such system is adopted, or challenge staff to create a better alternative. Ultimately, the organization's culture of teamwork and basic discipline must triumph.

This stage is where implementations succeed or fail, so leaders need to spend the time on change management. For some organizations, perhaps it is best to pick one business unit at a time to add to dashboarding after the I&P process is complete. Others may find a complete transition to be wise. Leadership, cheerleading, and tenacity will be required in any change management process. (See Chapter 7 for more on change management.)

Execute Practice 6.7: Build the Visualizations

Building good data visualizations takes skill, especially if the datasets have multiple points in a trendline. As always, simple is best. While there are any number of data visualization solutions out there, organizations should not go anywhere near them until they first develop a rock-solid understanding of what data they are collecting and have a good process to support it. Start with Google Sheets, which is 100% free and easy to use. It includes basic charts and graphs functions, and it's simple to build the charts in one sheet and put the data in other tabs or subsidiary sheets. A level 1 executive dashboard can include links to level 2 and even level 3 data. Teams can put together a very useful and functional dashboard with subsidiary scorecards and data entry sheets with only modest effort and expense.

The biggest challenge is to keep the executive dashboard functionally "at a glance" so viewers don't have to work hard to read it. Done well, people with very little familiarity with the organization can get a basic sense of what the organization does just by looking at the dashboard. This will take time and practice. If visualizations prove too difficult, skip them entirely and just go with numbers. Any nonprofit with a consolidated list of goals and KPIs that represents all major organizational domains is already at the very top of the social sector in terms of managerial capability, so don't worry about looking bad if there are no fancy charts and graphs.

Below are two early examples of the Treehouse visualizations. The first (Figure 6.3) was primarily used as an external report to partners and investors and was updated quarterly. It was clear and simple and presents the three ABC lead measures of graduation clearly. Take a look at the third measure: the youth on target for course performance was only 34%.

	Graduation Success Report Card
treehouse	Semester 1: September 2012-January 2013

Youth Served	2013 Goal	YTD at Semester
8th Graders (Class of 2017)	67	47
Total King County	400	318

Schools Served	2013 Goal	YTD at Semester
Number of In-School Mentors	14	14
Number of Schools	60	52
Number of Districts	11	7

ABC Plus Snapshot – End of Semester 1	
Youth on target for Attendance	64%
Youth on target for Behavior	88%
Youth on target for Course Performance	34%
Youth accessing Enrichment	93%
Youth with Student Centered Plan	Complete by Aug 2013
Self-determination, sense of belonging, & engagement	Standardized assessments beginning Aug 2013

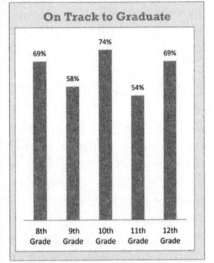

On Track to Graduate

8th Grade	9th Grade	10th Grade	11th Grade	12th Grade
69%	58%	74%	54%	69%

What We're Learning

- Students at most risk receive 1.5x – 2x the amount of service hours as their peers

- Fidelity and observation monitoring visits with Mentors and Specialists are improving service and data quality

- Our custom-designed Microsoft Dynamics client database will allow for more effective and efficient service coordination and program monitoring – implementation in August

8th Grade Cohort

- As of April 15th, the number of 8th graders served has increased to 67

- All 8th graders have a plan for the summer and their transition to High School

FIGURE 6.3   Treehouse's Early Dashboard.

Treehouse's CEO, Janis Avery, was never afraid of looking bad. It was a new effort, so unsurprisingly the numbers were low. And because she was unafraid to confront reality, her courage to show a work-in-progress effort engendered tremendous trust and buy-in among her partners and funders. The dashboard was a powerful tool to show transparency, and it created conversation points with partners, prospects, and investors about what was being done to push the numbers up.

The second dashboard, shown in Figure 6.4, reflects the organization's ambition to create a more comprehensive dashboard. While it's

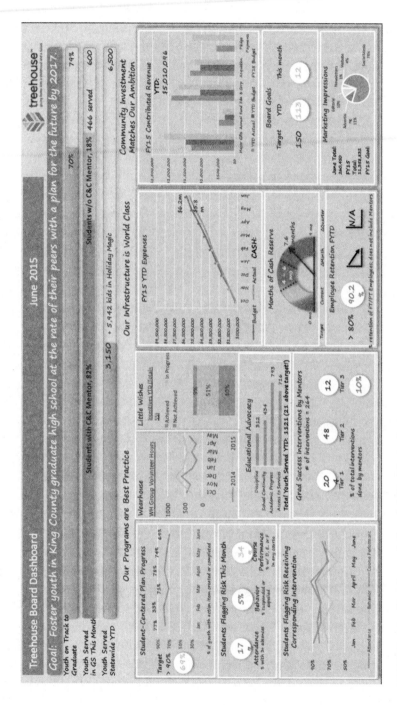

FIGURE 6.4 Treehouse's Second Dashboard.

not quite "at a glance," it reflects a drive to experiment and evolve and an understanding that it's not about the graphics; it's about creating an accurate platform for continuous discussions about how to better execute strategy.

Execute Practice 6.8: Establish a Cadence of Analysis

It's easy to spend too much time tweaking the visualizations and marginally improving the measures. Don't be caught in that trap. Get the dashboard to 80% visual accuracy certainty on the goals, leads, and lags, and then launch the cadence of accountability meetings as articulated in *4DX*.

In general, level 2 meetings, where teams get together and talk about front-line results in marketing, fundraising, programs, and other key operational areas, happen every two weeks. That is the *Goldilocks* cadence, shorter and there's not enough trend data to be meaningful, longer and there isn't enough room for analysis and adjustment. Level 2 meetings that consider higher-level organizational goals and strategies happen once a month and level 1 meetings once a quarter. As elsewhere, these are starting points. Here is what is most important:

1. Staff gain confidence in the lead and lag measures as authentic evidence of progress toward the goal.

2. Each cadence of accountability meeting uses the same type of disciplined agenda as shown in fund practice 5.4: "Drive Performance Improvement with an Investment and Partnership Scorecard." Whether the meeting is on a biweekly, monthly, or quarterly cadence, all relevant members of the team need to have clear, crisp, evidence-based conversations from both a numerical and qualitative perspective:

   a. Look back at the last period and determine what went well, what didn't, and what the implications are, if any, around adjusting the strategy or the execution.

    b. Look forward to the next period of execution to discuss how to implement any needed strategy improvements.

    c. Set specific goals for the entire team on the leading activity.

3. Teams support each individual positively to help them hit their goals, and if one or more individuals really show great progress, the team can study it and see if there are any innovations that can help the rest. Anyone that struggles gets positive support. Anyone that succeeds raises the bar.

The entire point of the dashboard and all its measures is to clearly and regularly analyze what is working and what isn't and set clear improvement goals for the next period of analysis. This is the secret sauce, the magic behind the curtain of all high-performing organizations: focus and discipline.

Execute Practice 6.9: Improve the Data Collection Process and Infrastructure

It often requires significant staff time to collect, report, organize, and visualize information. Tremendous cost and efficiency savings are possible if the organization sets up consistent patterns for collecting and reporting the information. Once these patterns are put in place, there are likely any number of technology solutions that can make the work more efficient and effective.

But don't start investing in a new database or a major technology upgrade until there is a very clear reason about what needs to happen and why. We have seen so many organizations pursue new software applications and fancy technology before they know what they want to accomplish. Powerful tools create powerful messes.

Small organizations can use Google Sheets to give all staff secure data-entry portals, which can then feed into scorecards and then into simple executive dashboards. Larger organizations can explore the utility of business intelligence tools such as Tableau, Smartsheet, and PowerBI. The real genius behind any dashboard is in its selectivity and simplicity, not in fancy graphics. That said, business people with advanced workflow, logistics, supply chain, and analytics expertise can be very helpful in optimizing data collection and reporting, but only if the targets are clear and the data collection and analysis process is reasonably well established.

Execute Practice 6.10: Evolve and Improve

The first version of the dashboard will likely be only partially functional. Some KPIs will have easily accessible data—others will need to be built from scratch. The leadership team should set specific goals for building the dashboard each month to make it more and more comprehensive with respect to what the organization wants to measure and how it is measuring it.

Once the dashboard is moderately functional—say, half of the KPIs have data and trends are starting to emerge—then it can be shared at every board meeting for continuous feedback for improving its content and structure. Each meeting should result in specific improvements until the dashboard's data is fully populated and representative of what's in the business plan.

After all this work, the organization is now ready to start using the dashboard to do what it is intended to do: present trend data and give direct insight on what is working and what is not.

In addition to continuous improvement from staff and board members, another audience can provide a terrific source of advice on how to improve the dashboard: investors and partners. First, sharing a draft dashboard even in relatively early stages of development with the organization's biggest financial supporters to get their feedback is a very smart way to make sure this tool is developing in a way that can demonstrate transparency and accountability. Further down the road, when the dashboard is fully functional, it becomes a powerful trust-building and reporting tool for the entire I&P team. Most nonprofits cannot concisely present evidence of impact. Annual reports are too long, too vague, and quickly out of date, and long documents rarely get read.

Furthermore, I&P officers are an organization's most active external eyes and ears, and they are the best source of stakeholder feedback. They can also bring along program officers or other executives to confer with the largest prospects, partners, and investors, with the dashboard being the primary focus point of conversations. All these meetings will be potential sources of improvements to the dashboard, so incorporate feedback and continue to align stakeholders around the goal and vision.

This is an incredibly powerful process that is light-years ahead of organizations yet to break free of the bake sale and auction mentality. Share the model with those organizations as well! This is not a zero-sum game. We are all in this together. The more nonprofits that use these disciplined, powerful tools for transparency and accountability, the better off we will all be.

Additional Resources

See **www.altruistaccelerator.org** for tools and examples.

Tools
- Dashboard Development Worksheet

Examples
- High Quality KPIs
- Sample Dashboards

CHAPTER 7

Lead

You manage things; you lead people.

—Rear Admiral Grace Murray Hopper

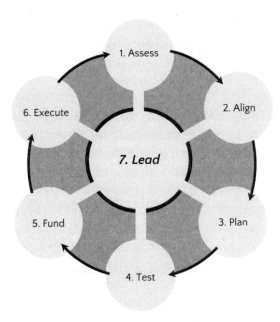

LEARNING OBJECTIVES

By the end of this chapter, you will be able to:

- Understand the fundamental cultural underpinning for any organization that seeks to improve its performance and accelerate growth: psychological safety;
- Apply the principles of good change management to your organization;
- Identify and manage disruptive people;
- Create a clear, actionable, and comprehensive job description for board members;
- Balance capabilities on the leadership team by recognizing the four different work styles and how to integrate them to improve team performance and minimize conflict;
- Understand the criticality of adequate staff pay to organizational performance; and
- Review good practices around robust succession planning.

While it's easy to spot bad leaders if you work for them, defining what makes a good one—and providing specific direction for leaders who sincerely want to improve—is hard. There is an enormous literature on leadership and governance best practices, but no one busy running teams has time to absorb even a fraction of it.

So, while the lead practices presented in this chapter are not comprehensive, they are concise, easy to remember, and actionable. We will start with a dysfunctional case study to highlight the criticality of good leadership. A small set of lead practices follow, along with some implementation tools and resources. We've found each of these practices essential for supporting the practices in the other phases.

Case Study: Dysfunction Junction

Pro Mentors is a 501(c)3 social services agency founded in 2010 that today has an annual budget of $2.2 million and the mission to recruit and train retiring corporate executives to serve as mentors for low-income youth in New York City. At the urging of the board, the CEO commissioned an organizational performance evaluation to ascertain why the organization has been unable to reach its recruitment goals.

The backstory: Two years ago, the organization's largest individual donor, also a member of its board of directors, made a $1 million philanthropic gift and presented the organization's CEO and staff with the following challenge: "We have been trying hard, but fact is, we have never been able to recruit more than 200 mentors in any given year, despite being at it for over a decade. We are spending more than $10,000 on each recruit. If we are going to help these kids, we need to scale up our operations, and that means being more efficient and effective. So I am making a $1 million donation now to provide you with the additional resources to improve our performance. Use the money however you want—with the one restriction that you immediately hire expert consultants to help you diagnose and solve our recruiting challenges. If they and you can solve our constraints and get our recruiting levels to 400 mentors per year in the next 18 months, I will make an additional unrestricted $1 million donation."

The consulting team was swiftly hired and launched an evaluation process that included confidential one-on-one interviews with all board and team members, analyzing organizational financials and documentation and collecting answers to a brief diagnostic survey.

Susan Masterson, the lead consultant for the engagement, spoke first to the CEO, Frances Busiva, and then to the program director, Ellie Bennet, and the marketing director, Felicia Timentes.

Busiva, the CEO, presented as calm, polite, and professional. Yet during the interview, she pointed to "weak staff" and "a dysfunctional board" as the core reasons behind the organization's inability to reach its recruiting targets. "I am getting migraines. I keep asking the board for help, and all they do is tell me to figure out a better recruiting strategy. I get no help from my team, which just makes excuses."

In the interview with Timentes, Masterson got an earful: "Frances seems great when you meet her, but one-on-one she is emotionally manipulative, domineering, and borderline abusive. I've been here five years, and however much I love this mission, I can't stand it anymore. The number of times she's gaslighted us, telling us our problems are our fault! Just yesterday she called me up crying because she said I betraycd her with my last quarterly report. I can't take this anymore. I love this mission and the impact we have had, but in all honesty, I'm looking for another job."

As Masterson progressed through the interviews, she found substantial evidence to support Timentes's observations. Furthermore, during the interviews with board members, several of the directors said, "I've been saying this for years. Frances needs to go. She's not performing."

Masterson asked the board chair to call a special executive session and presented the recommendation: "It is past time to transition the CEO. The evidence we have gathered indicates that the organization will not make progress until there is a more capable leader in place, one who starts by creating an environment of teamwork, not blame."

Fast-forward six months: a new CEO was recruited, and Masterson got an email from Timentes, who had previously complained so bitterly: "Thank you!" she said. "We've still got our challenges, but our new CEO is doing things *with* us, not *to* us. We finally have an environment where we can work together as a collaborative team."

Masterson forwarded the email to her colleagues with an additional note: "It never ceases to amaze me how some of the most sophisticated directors, those with fabulous private sector experience, fail to detect a classic kiss-up, kick-down behavior, especially in the context of ongoing flat growth. It's up to the directors to support and supervise the CEO, and so often, like in this case, this duty goes unfulfilled. Impact suffers."

Lead Practice 7.1: Establish and Maintain Psychological Safety

The first characteristic of good leaders and perhaps the most critical foundation to accelerating organizational growth and impact is the imperative that all board members and everyone on the leadership team establish and maintain an environment of **psychological safety** among themselves and all the other members of the organization: staff, volunteers, and stakeholders. First articulated by Amy C. Edmondson in *The Fearless Organization*, psychological safety describes the state that exists when everyone in the organization feels it is okay to take risks, speak candidly about difficult topics, and constructively critique and challenge the status quo, all without fear of reprisal, recrimination, or shaming. Amy Gallo (previously Edmondson) summarizes how psychological safety is established: (1) making clear employee voices matter; (2) leaders admitting their own fallibility; (3) leadership actively inviting input; and (4) leadership responding to input productively.[1]

One way to immediately examine an organization's level of psychological safety is to consider what happens when front-line staff discover bad news. Imagine your nonprofit is halfway through a major one-year grant from your largest funder, and front-line program staff have discovered evidence that one of the most important programs isn't working as well as promised. What happens to this information? Do staff ignore it? Fear bringing it to the attention of management? If it is brought to management, are staff blamed or criticized? Is there apathy? Perhaps the problem is reframed by management so it appears not to be a problem at all. Or it might be solved at the specific point of occurrence only, with no further investigation or thought about it reoccurring.

Figure 7.1, created by sociologist Ron Westrum,[2] describes the range of potential reactions to bad news along a spectrum that ranges from "suppression" to "inquiry."

This framework is incomplete: a more comprehensive table would include more categories on the left end of possible negative reactions, such as *panic, anger,* and *despair*. Nitpicking aside, why do some organizations shoot or isolate the messenger, while others look for global solutions or root causes?

Like doctors and teachers, those who work in nonprofits often consider their jobs an important part of their identities. Work in a nonprofit is not just a job for pay; it is often an expression of an altruistic

[1]Amy Gallo, "What Is Psychological Safety?" *Harvard Business Review*, February 15, 2023. **https://hbr.org/2023/02/what-is-psychological-safety**.
[2]R.A. Westrum, "Typology of Organisational Cultures," *BMJ Quality & Safety* (2004), 13:ii22–ii27.

Suppression — Harming or stopping the person bringing the anomaly to light; "shooting the messenger"

Encapsulation — Isolating the messenger so that the message is not heard

Public relations — Putting the message "in context" to minimize its impact

Local fix — Responding to the presenting case, but ignoring the possibility of others elsewhere

Global fix — An attempt to respond to the problem wherever it exists. Common in aviation, when a single problem will direct attention to similar ones elsewhere

Inquiry — Attempting to get at the root causes of the problem

FIGURE 7.1   Spectrum of Reactions to Bad News.

worldview and deeply held values. Because of the altruistic nature of the work, nonprofits have significant job-recruiting advantages, and many leverage applicants' values into concessions around pay and conditions. The attraction of the work is further evidenced by the many people who work hard for nonprofits for no pay at all, such as the board members and thousands of other volunteers who make up a core part of almost every nonprofit organization.

While the centrality of passion for making the world a better place is obvious to almost everyone who works in the social sector, what is not obvious at all is how all this very same passion can quickly become a barrier to effective teamwork. When someone's identity and value system are bound up in the work they are doing, it makes it easy for constructive criticism and analysis to be misconstrued as a personal attack. What leaders may view as *generative* might be easily interpreted by staff as *pathological*. Therefore, to ensure a generative culture, discussion of organizational performance challenges can be made less risky and more productive if they are framed as *clinical*. Defined as "objective and devoid of emotion; coolly analytical,"[3] *clinical behavior* may be understood as the other side of the coin of psychological safety. Just as everyone should be made to feel invited to share their thoughts

---

[3]*The American Heritage® Dictionary of the English Language*, 5th Edition.

and speak freely and without fear of negative consequences, so should the discussion of problems and challenges occur in an atmosphere of detached professionalism and calm, impersonal analysis. This does not mean leaders should repress passion or institute a robotic environment. Save the passion for the successes. When there are problems and challenges, however, leaders must reinforce that calm, clinical analysis will help maintain everyone's psychological safety and promote diagnosis, resolution, and ultimately prevention.

There is typically one person responsible for ensuring the organization is rich with psychological safety and open, clinical inquiry: the chief executive, who, as "chief culture artist," sets the tone by demonstrating and continuously reinforcing productive behaviors: avoiding blame, celebrating people, acting with empathy, encouraging diverse viewpoints, and others.[4] Like trust, psychological safety is complex and fragile—hard to create and easy to break—and maintaining it requires continuous exertion. Unlike many for-profit enterprises that are more likely to be at risk of authoritarian, top-down cultures, the challenge among many nonprofit organizations is an overemphasis on personal comfort and a reluctance to criticize. In their desire to ensure their teams feel safe, leaders may mistakenly foster a feel-good atmosphere in which fear of giving offense constrains speech and behavior. Those who attempt to deliver constructive criticism can be isolated and silenced by oversensitivity and avoidance of conflict, malfunctions every bit as destructive to mission fulfillment as authoritarian environments. Psychological safety is about optimizing teamwork, not avoiding hard conversations.

A final word about psychological safety: it is best measured indirectly. Direct conversations about fostering and maintaining it are important to have with all team members initially, but it is best practiced not with constant direct inquiry—Are you psychologically safe today?—but as an underpinning to *all* organizational conversations and exchanges. Leaders who focus on the concept itself without consistently demonstrating it risk getting branded as hypocrites, so executives must be truly prepared to practice what they preach.

[4]Rakshitha Arni Ravishankar, "A Guide to Building Psychological Safety on Your Team," *Harvard Business Review,* December 1, 2022.

Lead Practice 7.2: Practice Intentional Change Management

As this methodology represents a radically different way of thinking and running a nonprofit like a scalable social impact enterprise, the first order of business for leadership is to ensure that strong change management practices are put in place early in the transformation journey. People are tricky. Leaders can deliver the right strategy and the right tools, but if they don't get the change management processes right, nothing will stick.

John Kotter's 1995 article "Leading Change: Why Transformation Efforts Fail"[5] presents an effective eight-step model we have used repeatedly (see Figure 7.2).

Kotter's framework meshes well with this methodology. The first three steps, "creating the climate for change," are covered by the assess and align phases. The next three, "engaging and enabling the organization," line up with the plan and test phases. And the last two, "implementing and sustaining for change," match well with fund and execute. Kotter's change management framework is one of many, with

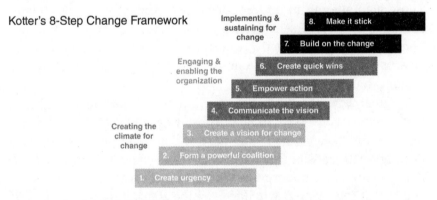

Kotter's 8-Step Change Framework

Implementing & sustaining for change

Engaging & enabling the organization

Creating the climate for change

8. Make it stick
7. Build on the change
6. Create quick wins
5. Empower action
4. Communicate the vision
3. Create a vision for change
2. Form a powerful coalition
1. Create urgency

FIGURE 7.2   Kotter's Eight-Step Change Framework.

[5]John P. Kotter, "Leading Change: Why Transformation Efforts Fail," *Harvard Business Review*, May–June 1995, **https://hbr.org/1995/05/leading-change-why-transformation-efforts-fail-2**.

Lee Bolman and Terrence Deal's "Four Frames Analysis"[6] presenting a useful alternative perspective. While Kotter's approach is arguably the most clear, simple, and easy to follow, leaders should review the literature to develop a richer understanding of organizational psychology and various change methodologies.

Lead Practice 7.3: Identify and Manage Disruptive People

The biggest barriers to creating alignment and teamwork among a board, executive, and staff team aren't strategic and technical; they are personal and emerge from the quality and character of the individuals inside the group. Risk aversion is only one of many personality factors that damages the trusting and supportive teamwork essential for this methodology to take root. In addition to all the cultural and practice barriers articulated in the introduction, board members are also often unpaid volunteers distracted by full-time jobs, the work sparks passion and emotion and may be intensely personal or even triggering, most nonprofits are already resource- and time-starved, and investments in trust and team building are hard when there are fires to put out.

This environment is vulnerable to *power players*, people who, consciously or not, spark conflict, deflect and distract from key issues, and disrupt team building and trust. Therefore, for this impact and growth methodology to take root, both the CEO and board chair must identify and either resolve or remove disruptive people.

The Dominator

Dominators are the easiest to recognize. They are the people who speak the loudest and most often. We've all met dominators. They are often quick to judge, whether it's because of actual knowledge or perhaps

---

[6]Lee G. Bolman and Terrence E. Deal, *Reframing Organizations: Artistry, Choice, and Leadership*, 5th ed. (San Francisco: Jossey-Bass, 2013).

just an abundance of confidence in their own opinions. But regardless of whether their attempts at control come from a benevolent sense of responsibility or toxic narcissism, dominators prevent a healthy flow of diverse perspectives, especially when it comes to quieter, more introverted group members.

The Interrogator

Interrogators are harder to recognize. They are the cousins of dominators, but they are sneakier about seeking power. While all organizational members need to ask questions, interrogators use questions to seek power, quizzing and probing other members or staff to disrupt or stall any initiative they don't like. One common interrogator strategy is *creative obfuscation*, where interrogators sidetrack an initiative with confusing or shifting narratives and constant requests for more detail or evidence. Those with black belts in interrogation, plentiful in political arenas, may even *frame shift*, presenting a new and startling perspective to cast doubt on the entire enterprise. With doubt sown on other perspectives, they present their path as the only one that is safe and sound.

Another tried-and-true interrogator strategy is the *orbital referral*, a tongue-in-cheek label for shifting the discussion skyward, asking big philosophical questions that can never really be answered with certainty. Interrogators deploying the orbital referral may seek to have nuanced, extensive discussions around, say, the organization's mission or values statements when that is not the purpose of the meeting. They pursue the seemingly important work of aligning the group on a grand purpose or design but do so with no practical expression or operational implementation.

The Aloof

The aloof individual is common and easy to spot. The aloof are just that: hard to engage. They miss meetings; they are unresponsive to email. They don't have strong opinions and don't put a shoulder down to help with organizational development, fundraising, and so on. They may have significant surface value by virtue of their talents, wealth, or influence, but they aren't really on the team. When executive directors or board chairs complain about "board engagement," they are likely dealing with the aloof.

The aloof often have good reasons for their behavior. They may be "crazy busy" and even express regret at their lack of participation and responsiveness. If confronted, they will often promise to do better in the future. But if their aloof behavior becomes a pattern and they don't take the initiative and volunteer their resignation, then they are sending the group a clear message of, "I want to stay on this board for the prestige or because it makes me feel good, but I am not going to do much work, and I certainly am not going to raise money, engage in the analysis of complex matters, or offer my own opinion for potential criticism."

The Victim

Victims may be the most difficult to resolve. The victim won't assume responsibility for making a decision or authentically engaging in a challenging group conversation because of, well, the "great difficulty of life." And there is always something terrible or onerous in the way, and certainly none of it is their fault.

We hasten to say that there are obviously terrible and huge numbers of genuinely traumatized people who authentically are victims. We are not including them in this classification. We refer to the board and staff members who, to varying degrees, adopt the pose or stance of a victim, presenting exaggerated or distracting matters as reasons for their failure to productively engage.

Dealing with victims is fraught with risk. Because consciously or not, the victim will take advantage of the kindness and sympathy of others.

So what should leaders do about power players? Standing up to a dominator can be scary. Interrogators just might be asking very important questions. And is it reasonable to expect everyone to answer every email and attend every meeting? Finally, the potential of being an insensitive jerk or, worse, causing genuine additional harm to someone who may already be struggling to stay afloat, makes it very difficult to steer a victim toward a more productive style of group participation.

With these caveats in mind, we return to the fundamental first step of creating high-performing organizations: get the right people on the bus. Organizational leaders are often confronted with the difficult choice of pursuing organizational excellence or tolerating disruptive board members or staff. As most nonprofit leaders are kind and empathetic, and termination is such a difficult process, leaders too often fail to make the hard choices and transition out those who can't function as part of a high-performing team.

Lead Practice 7.4: Define Good Governance

SIE performance begins and ends with the board of directors. Boards hire and fire the CEO and have a duty as fiduciaries to operate the organization in the public interest. If a nonprofit is not performing well, it is the immediate fault of the board and no one else. Therefore, boards bear great and ultimate responsibility for nonprofit impact and growth. The topic of good governance is an enormous one, and the role comes with great responsibility and little to no training, a critical gap which this methodology aims to bridge. Board members who hold their CEO accountable to implementing the practices defined in Chapters 1–6 will be doing everything necessary to promote growth and social impact. Board members should use this handbook in close, supportive partnership with the CEO.

Remember, this chapter is not a comprehensive guide to board governance. It covers what we have found are the most important leadership and governance practices to support impact and growth.

Start with Equity

Social sector organizations are typically proactive when it comes to advancing diversity, equity, and inclusion (DEI) into staffing, governance, and programs, yet there are far too many well-meaning organizations that have yet to advance beyond policy statements. In other words, equity is too often given lip service and not operationalized beyond the occasional workshop or training session. DEI is successful when it is a core component of the organizational strategy, knit into the business plan, reflected in the metrics, and allocated appropriate resources in the budget projection. A few concrete activities that go beyond the workshop level are offered here:

1. Ensure equitable and inclusive hiring and promotion processes at all levels of organizational management, from the board and executive team through front-line employees. Benchmark current diversity statistics, set goals, and ensure hiring practices are targeted to the goals. Diversify the talent pipeline through targeted recruiting and mentorship programs.

2. Implement a zero-tolerance policy for discrimination and harassment.

3. Establish metrics to track progress on DEI goals, with boards holding leadership accountable for gathering and analyzing data workplace culture, attitudes, and norms.

4. Create flexible work arrangements and parental leave policies.

5. Elevate DEI leadership into the C-suite, and ensure it is led by employees from underrepresented groups.

6. Foster a culture of belonging and inclusiveness through intentional communication.

7. Continuously evaluate and adapt DEI efforts to remain relevant and influential.

This is only the sparsest of outlines for operationalizing equity; it is up to the board and CEO to ensure recommendations like these go well beyond information sessions and talking points to become deeply embedded in both organizational culture and daily operations.

Establish Clear Roles and Responsibilities

A significant proportion of organizational dysfunction springs from ignorance of roles and responsibilities and how everyone should be working together as part of a team. Board members don't understand their role; CEOs micromanage or fail to keep the board informed; staff don't have visibility to important organizational decisions. While there are many resources on how boards can ensure proper organizational function, what's missing is a clear snapshot of optimal roles

Role	Board	CEO	Management	Staff
1. Set goals	Provide foresight	Cheerlead	Leaders	Supporter
2. Define strategy	Offer insight	Lead architect	Execute & revise	Execute & refine
3. Assess risk	Exercise oversight	Risk taker	Risk advisors	Risk monitors
4. Implement strategy	Exercise oversight	Obstacle remover	Leaders	Drivers
5. Assess results	Constructively critique	Chief quality officer	Assess results	Generate results
6. Monitor finances	Oversight, contribute leads	Chief revenue officer	Leaders	Drivers
7. Compliance	Exercise oversight	Head compliance officer	Leaders	Drivers
8. Culture	Exercise oversight	Lead culture artist	Leading culture artists	Culture artists
9. Talent	Select and supervise CEO	Select & support mgmt	Select & support staff	Support each other
10. Decisions	all As, some Bs; all 1s	all A&Bs all 1&2s	all A&Bs all 2s; some 1&3s	some Bs; all 3s

FIGURE 7.3 Organizational Roles and Responsibilities.

and responsibilities, and who should be making what kind of decision. To help cut through the information overload around governance and fill this gap, Figure 7.3 offers a one-page snapshot of 10 key organizational responsibilities, segmenting them across the CEO, manager, and front-line staff layers.

Board members can glance down their column and absorb their job descriptions in fewer than 25 words, with most of the categories being self-explanatory (except for the decisions category, which is explained below). Furthermore, they can immediately grasp the nominal relationship with the CEO and how the CEO should be orchestrating relationships with management and staff.

This chart is also useful for the rest of the team. It gives everyone clarity on how they contribute to organizational performance. Perhaps most important, staff can quickly grasp their critical importance to the organization: they are the ones who must support the goal; they are the ones who execute and refine strategy; and they must watch out for risks, produce results, and contribute to financial monitoring, culture, compliance, and mutual support. If the rest of the practices in this methodology are in place and everyone in the organization stays in these lanes, the organization will be well on its way to truly becoming organized—and effective.

In addition to these simple, clear organizational roles, a taxonomy of decision types helps clarify who needs to be involved in particular kinds of decisions, along with how much time and effort need to be expended on those decisions. Figure 7.4 illustrates the decision types listed along row 10 of Figure 7.3.

Class A decisions are rare in organizations: like a rocket launch or cutting down a tree, they are impossible to reverse. These are the decisions that should involve managers, CEOs, and board members, and they should be made after careful study and deliberation. Examples include a sale of major assets, closure of a business unit, or dissolution of the company. Class B decisions are reversible and should be made with much more speed. Using this filter,[7] the organization can avoid dreaded analysis paralysis and proceed with the speed that successful entrepreneurial efforts demand.

----

[7]Originated by Jeff Bezos in a shareholder letter (see **https://www.sec.gov/Archives/ edgar/data/1018724/000119312516530910/d168744dex991.htm**).

Type	Characteristics	Risk	Occurrence	Pace
Class A	irreversible (rocket launch)	high	rare	slow
Class B	reversible (business strategy)	moderate	annually/quarterly	moderate
Level 1	org-wide	high to moderate	annually/quarterly	moderate
Level 2	unit-level	moderate	monthly	fast
Level 3	front-line or roles-based	moderate to low	weekly/daily	fast

FIGURE 7.4 Organizational Decision Types and Speeds.

Finally, level 1–3 decisions, covered in Chapter 6: "Execute," can be assigned to their appropriate organizational lanes. Of particular importance, the board is involved with all level 1 decisions such as goals, strategy, and so on, but is *not* involved in level 2 or 3 decisions, which are left to the CEO. A CEO can point to this guide to help prevent board micromanagement, a common board malfunction. Likewise, this chart helps management keep the CEO from micromanaging.

Board Characteristics, Skills, and Behaviors

High-functioning boards exhibit ethnic and gender diversity, represent all the domains of subject matter expertise required for adequate governance, behave in a manner that projects deep commitment to the mission and respect for other directors and staff team, and make decisions based on data.

Diversity   Board gender, ethnic, and cultural diversity is critically important for organizations choosing to lead with equity. Studies produced by McKinsey[8] claim a business advantage for such diverse

---

[8]Sundiatu Dixon-Fyle, Kevin Dolan, Dame Vivian Hunt, and Sara Prince, "Diversity Wins: How Inclusion Matters," *McKinsey Featured Insights*, May 19, 2020, **https:// www.mckinsey.com/featured-insights/diversity-and-inclusion/diversity-wins-how-inclusion-matters**.

leadership, but these studies do not meet standards of proof and appear to confuse correlation with causation.[9] Nonetheless, the experiential, cognitive, and cultural variety presented by diversity is undeniably beneficial and a core driver of equity and inclusion, qualities of immense importance in a social setting.

Skill   In addition to interpersonal diversity, skill depth and distribution are also critical success factors and ones that are widely acknowledged. Many boards understand they need gifted professionals in all relevant domains—law, executive leadership, finance, accounting, HR, marketing and sales, technology, logistics and operations, and subject matter expertise relevant to the organizational mission. However, a second standard of expertise is too often overlooked: successful entrepreneurial experience. As stated earlier, only 3% of companies of any tax status ever make it past $1 million in annual revenue. Individuals who have launched and built successful companies possess courage, wisdom, and grit that even very smart, experienced managers don't. Given the lack of growth and impact in the social sector, the applicability of an entrepreneurial tool kit should be obvious, and given the difficulty of applying a growth strategy, there is no substitute for experienced entrepreneurs, who are plentiful in the private sector. There are profoundly positive differences in organizational performance and impact among the subset of organizations that enjoy experienced entrepreneurs on their board.

Commitment   Another board standard is engagement and commitment. A CEO may be a highly successful entrepreneur, but if he sits on his local board just so he can boast about it at cocktail parties, he's not the director the organization needs. All directors should conduct themselves as if the success of their organization were critical to their financial futures—as if the organization's impact equated to their retirement funding. For starters, this means showing up for meetings,

---

[9]Katherine Klein, "Does Gender Diversity on Boards Really Boost Company Performance?" *Knowledge at Wharton*, **https://knowledge.wharton.upenn.edu/article/will-gender-diversity-boards-really-boost-company-performance/**.

responding to emails in a business day or two, and working hard and demanding the best of one's self and one's colleagues. Too often, skilled board members appear to confuse board membership with social impact tourism, and focused commitment is something the CEO and especially the chair must demand and receive. The alternative must be a swift transition off the board. Otherwise, the organization will pretend, not perform.

Performance Improvement   With these foundational pieces in place, the board can focus on overseeing and supporting the CEO, who creates and maintains the executive dashboard to inform decision making and ensure continuous performance improvement. The board and CEO's significant investment in building the dashboard should help optimize board insight, oversight, and foresight and return multiples of invested hours in saved meeting time.

Administrative, Legal, and Policy Guidance

Nonprofit boards are volunteer groups, but too often they operate casually, like a book club. Providing necessary levels of financial, strategic, operational, execution, and risk oversight demands a tremendous investment in administrative, legal, and policy infrastructure: technical documents that are difficult to get right and hard to read and remember. As a result, too many boards cut and paste mission critical documents such as conflict of interest policies and never pay attention to them until bad things happen.

A trusted resource for the policy and administrative side of nonprofit boards is BoardSource (**boardsource.org**), a small nonprofit established in 1998 to strengthen social sector governance. It offers a library of diagnostics, policies, assessments, and other resources to enhance board performance.[10] Guidance on planning, strategy development, and fundraising skews toward legacy nonprofit practices, however; while adequate for maintaining stability at organizations already functioning

---

[10]Tristan Colyar, "Board Policy Checklist—Charter Boards," BoardSource, **https:// boardsource.org/resources/board-policies-checklist-charter-boards/**.

at their desired scale, BoardSource is less useful for entrepreneurial boards seeking growth and performance management tools.

The most robust guide to the legal, administrative, policy, risk management, and fiduciary responsibilities of nonprofit directors is the 2019 *Guide to Nonprofit Governance*[11] produced by Weil, Gotshal & Manges, a large and highly respected law firm. While it runs nearly 300 pages long, much of the length is due to useful policy and corporate templates and worksheets of the highest quality. It is an important resource for executive committees and CEOs.

Lead Practice 7.5: Ensure Balanced Thinking Styles

Not everyone thinks alike. Genetics and upbringing result in great variations around different ways of learning and knowing. This neurodiversity has been with us for a long time and manifests in many ways that are often subtle and easy to overlook. When it comes to the critically important organizational task of building and sustaining high-performing teams, considerations of neurodiversity are crucial. Each of the practices in this methodology are mission critical, yet perhaps none is so subtle and powerful as this one: boards and CEOs must make sure that executive teams are balanced across the four major kinds of thinking styles—what can be called *neurobalanced* teams. Furthermore, everyone in the organization needs to be aware of these thinking differences and how to work collaboratively with someone with a different style. What often seems like a character flaw or lack of professionalism or focus is really just another way of looking at things, one that has unique strengths.

Only a summary is provided here, but no board member or executive should feel prepared for management until reading and reflecting on Ichak Adizes's *How to Solve the Mismanagement Crisis*.[12] He surfaces

---

[11]"Guide to Nonprofit Governance 2019," Weil, Gotshal & Manges LLP, **https:// www.weil.com/~/media/guide-to-nonprofit-governance-2019.pdf.**
[12]Ichak Adizes, *How to Solve the Mismanagement Crisis* (Homewood, IL: Dow Jones-Irwin, 1979).

the underlying reasons that organizations are so disorganized, and he offers a clear set of solutions to create stronger executive teams and more harmonious working environments. We provide the briefest of summaries below with encouragement that leaders review the entire work.

PAEI (producer, administrator, entrepreneur, integrator) is Adizes's acronym for four different thinking styles, ones that appear in different combinations and at different strengths (see Figure 7.5). Some people are strong producers: they can get the work done, and that makes them happy. Others are most capable at being an administrator: they love organizing the work and creating the rules and systems. A third type is the entrepreneur, an imaginative and creative type driven to come up with new ideas and solutions. The fourth is the integrator, the person who is socially oriented and always concerned with group dynamics and what other people are thinking.

Individuals may possess one or more of these characteristics, with the rare person possessing all four. While it's no guarantee of success, executive teams should be made up of people who collectively possess all four characteristics, and since it's rare for a CEO to have all four qualities, executive teams, as well as leadership teams across larger organizations, need to be thoughtfully balanced. For example, Adizes says it is common for company founders to be strong Ps and Es, a producer and entrepreneur, yet lack A or I, administrative or integrative capability. If the founder is the only executive, they will create new products and services and produce strong results at the pilot level, but they will have great trouble scaling the effort, as that ability requires organizing a larger group or setting up processes that people can follow (all A skills) and keeping everyone engaged while building a strong culture (I skills). The founder will soon become frustrated and wonder why building functional teams is so hard.[13] For the company to grow, the founder needs executive-level help from someone with a strong A who can create the necessary structures and processes. Also needed is someone who can provide the glue to keep teams together with their strong I skills. The A and the I could be the same person or different people; any combination is possible.

---

[13] Ask me how I know.

	Producer	Administrator	Entrepreneur	Integrator
Time	Now	Past	Future	Today
Output	Results	Rules	Ideas	Culture
Thinking	Concrete	Abstract	Systemic	Relational
Risk Tolerance	High	Low	High	Low
Analysis	Literal	Literal	Metaphorical	Metaphorical
Concern	External	Internal	External	Internal
Skill	Goals	Systems	Models	People
Measurement	Quantity	Quantity	Quality	Quality

FIGURE 7.5 Categories of Thinking Styles.[14]

Consider what happens with unbalanced teams. A group with only Ps are lone wolves, hammering away on the same thing day after day. A team of As will become a mighty fortress of bureaucrats with rules and regulations that make them happy but suffocate everyone else. Teams filled with Es will think up new and exciting ideas, but a lack of production, organization, and teamwork means they are arsonists, just lighting creative fires. Finally, a group of just Is means everyone is constantly checking in about everyone else's feelings and making sure nothing gets disrupted: they are super-followers.

One can see how quickly an organization can become dysfunctional if one thinking style is over- or underrepresented on an executive team. Furthermore, if teams contain strong opposite styles, conflict is likely. It's hard for a lone wolf and a super-follower to see eye to eye on priorities, and arsonists and bureaucrats can quickly get on each other's nerves. While few people are extreme in only one style, many people have a distinct bias toward one or more, and this means people must be trained on how to work with people who would otherwise naturally irritate them. Once people recognize that thinking styles are based in brain wiring differences and that organizations need all the styles to succeed, teamwork becomes much easier. It is surprising how well the PAEI structure explains interpersonal conflict.

[14]Adapted from Adizes, *How to Solve the Mismanagement Crisis.*

Lead Practice 7.6: Invest in Great People

One of the most pernicious cultural constraints on nonprofits is the assumption that good nonprofits cannot afford to pay competitive salaries to employees, and especially executives, because that is taking money away from programs.

Cited in the introduction, it's worth revisiting how Dave Phillips, a multiple Pulitzer Prize–winning *New York Times* journalist, wrote an expose in 2016, "Wounded Warrior Project Spends Lavishly on Itself, Insiders Say."[15] Among the many apparent outrages Phillips ostensibly uncovered was the CEO's $473,000 annual salary, an example of the organization's use of practices "modeled . . . on for-profit corporations, with a focus on data, scalable products, quarterly numbers and branding." The report caused a furor, and the CEO was fired. As it turns out, the article was premised on false information.[16] The organization's service to veterans plunged and has yet to recover to pre-2016 levels, and the affair remains a reminder that demonizing nonprofit executives for high pay is misguided and potentially very harmful.

This is just one example of provocative articles that question nonprofit compensation. Forbes asks the tantalizing question "Should Non-Profit U.S. Food Bank Executives Earn Nearly $1 Million Per Year?"[17] CBS reports that senators are probing the Boys and Girls Club

---

[15]Dave Phillips, "Wounded Warrior Project Spends Lavishly on Itself, Insiders Say," *The New York Times*, January 27, 2016, **https://www.nytimes.com/2016/01/28/us/ wounded-warrior-project-spends-lavishly-on-itself-ex-employees-say.html**.
[16]Doug White, "The First Casualty: A Report Addressing the Allegations Made against the Wounded Warrior Project in January 2016," *The Nonprofit Times*, September 6, 2016, **https://www.thenonprofittimes.com/wp-content/uploads/2016/09/ WWP-Report-by-Doug-White.pdf**.
[17]Adam Andrzejewski, "Should Non-Profit U.S. Food Bank Executives Earn Nearly $1 Million Per Year?" Forbes, January 11, 2020, **https://www.forbes.com/sites/ adamandrzejewski/2020/06/11/should-non-profit-us-food-bank-executives- earn-up-to-11-million-per-year/**.

for similar executive compensation practices.[18] There's an organization called Charity Watch (**charitywatch.org**) that lists "Nonprofit Compensation Packages of $1M or More"[19] as if it were muckraking journalism.

Interestingly, these and other articles and websites ignore that the University of Alabama, a 501(c)3 corporation, pays its most highly compensated employee, its football coach, nearly $12 million a year.[20] No scandal there! Apparently, everyone appreciates that football is competitive and top talent is expensive. But hospitals, universities, and multibillion-dollar aid programs should be subject to charity watch lists, exposés, and shame for investing in top leadership.

Invest in Talent

Thoughtful boards base their compensation schedule against the private market. It is a simple fact that strong compensation is necessary to hire top talent. Getting the right people on the bus is essential to success. Financial projections must be structured in a manner that makes heavy investment in talent. Any criticism that the nonprofit is "paying too much" comes from those trapped by the myth of uniqueness, the cultural constraint discussed in the Introduction that imagines nonprofits live in a world with different rules.

Here is a suggested response to objections around investing in competitive salary for staff: "We aren't building a charity to nibble around the edges of a problem. We are building a social impact enterprise to solve the whole problem, and that starts with aggressive compensation so we can get the right people on the bus. Yes, we are paying 50% or even 100% more than a nonprofit would, but this is a smart decision,

----

[18]Stephen Ohlemacher, "Boys and Girls Club Execs' $1M Pay Probed," CBS News, **https://www.cbsnews.com/news/boys-and-girls-club-execs-1m-pay-probed/**.
[19]"Nonprofit Compensation Packages of $1 Million or More," Charity Watch, **https://www.charitywatch.org/nonprofit-compensation-packages-of-1-million-or-more**.
[20]Matt Johnson, "Highest-Paid College Football Coaches 2023: Nick Saban, Kirby Smart Lead NCAA Salaries," Sportsnaut, **https://sportsnaut.com/highest-paid-college-football-coaches/**.

because we know that investing in top staff returns many multiples in terms of growth and impact. Anyone who has built and scaled a successful business knows this. We are a business, too: we are in the business of solving social problems."

Invest in Culture

Pay is only half the battle. Aggressive compensation will bring top talent in the door, but only organizations making concomitant investments in culture will keep them happy and productive.

It would be a mistake to assume that, given the discipline and analysis necessary to embed all these practices, it's necessary to create an intrusive, even oppressive culture. The opposite is true. Woven through the methodology's practices are traction points for fostering a healthy, supportive culture of high performance, but these must not be taken for granted or considered secondarily. As the lead culture artist, the CEO must be both vocal and continuously active in creating a place where support, collegiality, and high performance is the water in which everyone swims, the air everyone breathes. Examine Figure 7.6 for a very succinct overview of healthy culture and how it differs from dysfunctional environments.

Pathological	Bureaucratic	Generative
Power oriented	Rule oriented	Performance oriented
Low cooperation	Modest cooperation	High cooperation
Messengers shot	Messengers neglected	Messengers trained
Responsibilities shirked	Narrow responsibilities	Risks are shared
Bridging discouraged	Bridging tolerated	Bridging encouraged
Failure → scapegoating	Failure → justice	Failure → inquiry
Novelty crushed	Novelty → problems	Novelty implemented

FIGURE 7.6 Leadership Typology.[21]

[21]R. Westrum, "A Typology of Organizational Cultures," *Quality and Safety in Health Care* (2004);13(Suppl II):ii22–ii27.

It bears repeating that the underpinning of a generative culture is psychological safety. It is the oxygen that enables everyone in the organization to breathe. With it, the organization is able to foster and maintain a generative culture, one that is equipped to recognize, diagnose, solve, and even prevent problems through open inquiry.

A terrific lens of how companies create and shape high-performing culture is in the now-famous Netflix Culture Deck,[22] seen millions of times and copied likely near as many. This deck sets a standard for clear, simple, actionable communication, providing traction points for leaders, managers, and staff to consider the behaviors that work and avoid those that don't.

The most extensive and detailed discussion of building high-performing teams is Neel Doshi and Lindsay McGregor's *Primed to Perform*.[23] Like the Netflix deck, it's written from a for-profit perspective, but it contains a wealth of principles and practices of immediate utility to ambitious organizations, especially the larger ones where culture building is harder to do. One of the book's many powerful tools is an organizational performance metric called ToMo, for Total Motivation, a 200-point index that is built from only six survey questions. It enables an immediate, accurate gauge of employee engagement and motivation and gives a variety of ways to improve morale. *Culture* is a very abstract, difficult concept, but Doshi and McGregor put it in terms that leaders can understand, along with the principles and tools leaders can use to create stronger cultures.

Lead Practice 7.7: Ensure Clear Succession Planning

As this methodology makes clear, the board chair and CEO hold tremendous responsibilities as organizational architects. Ultimately, it is

---

[22]"Netflix Culture—Seeking Excellence," Netflix Jobs, **https://jobs.netflix.com/culture**.
[23]Neel Doshi and Lindsay McGregor, *Primed to Perform: How to Build the Highest Performing Cultures Through the Science of Total Motivation* (New York: Harper Collins, 2015).

up to the board chair to set the performance standards for the board and thus for the rest of the organization, and it is up to the CEO to ensure execution to goal. When these positions change, the entire organization's strategy, operations, governance, growth, and impact can be disrupted or destroyed if there is no succession planning.

Executive coach Glenn Tobe tells the following story of his work with Sony's chair, Nobuyuki Idei: "I asked him, 'Idei-san, what are the most important things on your mind?' He said, 'Tobe-san, I have only one important responsibility—my successor, everything else is details.'"

Despite the importance of succession planning, the prevalence of interim executive directors shows how much more attention is needed to this critical success factor. Organizations must actively seek and train executives to carry forward in the CEO role, even with a new CEO. Succession planning worksheets are very useful for this process.[24] Board chair transitions should be conducted in three phases, with the current chair flanked by a vice chair and an emeritus chair, each of whom can provide advice and continuity for this challenging position. Two years in each role provide for smooth transitions and minimal disruption, and this structure should be articulated in the organization's by-laws.

Additional Resources

See **www.altruistaccelerator.org** for tools.

Tools

- Organization Roles and Responsibilities
- Personality & Style Matrix
- Adaptive Leadership & Change Management Guide
- Board Development Matrix
- Sample Policies and Bylaws
- CEO Compensation Guide
- Advisory Council Template

---

[24]See **https://hr.uw.edu/pod/wp-content/uploads/sites/10/2018/08/Succession-Planning-Toolkit.pdf**.

Conclusion

All the practices in this book work. They wouldn't be included here if they hadn't already had a strong basis in the practice literature and passed extensive testing with many dozens of nonprofit organizations.

While this book lays everything out in as close to a "paint-by numbers" process as possible, each step is difficult, and success is far from guaranteed.

Because each phase and practice are challenging, it is easy to get bogged down or stuck. Fight the urge to have endless meetings by adopting an action-and-experiment mindset: "Let's get our plans to 80%, launch, and then see what the KPIs tell us." Allow at least six months of leading and lagging indicator trend data to provide initial feedback on the strategy. The executive scorecard leads into a fresh round of assessment conversations: Does the evidence indicate that we have all the skills, capabilities, and resources that we need? These discussions can then inform improvements to the business plan, fundraising adjustments, and another round of consultation with partners. Ultimately there are revised, improved efforts at execution, and if all goes well, the data will trend more positively. If not, keep trying.

It's a circular process of continuous improvement. Each year the business plan is refreshed, the financial projection is pushed out another year, and the scorecards and dashboards are tuned up. Building this management system is hard, and the first year will reveal many challenges, but by year two, things will start to accelerate, and as we have seen, by year three, real progress happens—often at a rate of 25% year after year.

Despite the challenge of growth, there are many social sector leaders who are up to the task, eager to discard the myths and misguided practices that have constrained their potential. The social sector is filled with thousands of smart, committed changemakers who are running and working in nonprofit organizations every day today, and there are tens of thousands more volunteering their time and skills on boards. If they can break through the barriers to change and embrace the proven practices presented here, they can unleash a wave of social and environmental progress unlike anything the world has ever seen. What a gift that would be to our children.

The small number of nonprofits that understand and use practices like those described here are already demonstrating the tremendous gains in social impact that happen when myths are set aside and proven entrepreneurial behaviors are embraced. We need a movement where this fraction grows to the point where well-managed, data-driven, high-impact nonprofits are the rule, not the rare exception. I close this book with some ideas for helping make this happen:

- Short of creating fully hybridized curriculums, more universities could immediately improve their graduate curricula in education, social work, and other public sector fields by requiring students to attend classes in finance and planning at their business schools.

- Current support organizations for nonprofits often overwhelm their audiences with too much information of dubious quality in areas such as governance or fundraising. And they leave leaders without clear, actionable guidance for other urgent challenges, such as how to improve staff pay or create data-driven programs. We hope they will consider augmenting the guidance they provide their audiences with the practices described here.

- We need more Dan Pallotta–style activism to fight back against the cultural myths and oppressive stereotypes that discourage nonprofits from taking bold risks and making deep performance investments.

- We need far more rigorous, faster, and more intensive board member training programs that are stripped of nonprofit cultural constraints and effectively prepare leaders for the rigor of entrepreneurial growth and impact.

- Corporations can transition their "spray and pray" employee giving practices to focused, long-term relationships with a small cohort of strategically significant nonprofit partners.

- In the spirit of "be the change you want to see in the world," we have launched a new nonprofit ourselves, the Altruist Nonprofit Accelerator, to provide a 12-week course to help nonprofits adopt this growth and impact methodology, for which this book is the curriculum. See **www.altruistaccelerator.org**.

These are only a few examples of improvements we can make to capture the massive untapped potential for creating sustainable economic growth, advancing social justice, improving educational equity, supporting the vulnerable and marginalized, resuscitating damaged ecosystems, advancing health care and housing, and enriching the cultural and artistic fabric of our communities.

Achieving all of this means a paradoxical reframing of what social impact actually is. Even the most cold-hearted economic analysis shows the profound monetary benefits of this methodology. While social and environmental progress merits increased investment, we must stop treating this space as if it delivered something fundamentally different from any other product or service. Social impact is noble, but it is also prosaic: it doesn't need its own niche language or its own set of rules. These mindsets keep it isolated and ineffective. The myth of uniqueness needs to be confronted wherever it exists and eradicated like the destructive prejudice it is. If we can do that, we will start to make progress toward this future.

We remain optimistic about the future of social impact enterprises. The long arc of the universe does indeed appear to be bending toward justice. The increasing numbers of high-performance SIEs are making it happen. But there is so much more work to be done.

In closing, I received many suggestions in early drafts of this book that there is too much talk of how hard this all is and that there should be more "You can do it!" messages in the text. I have resisted that advice so far because this book is written for people who already believe in themselves. Instead, I saved that message for the end, leaving it for those with the tenacity to finish what they start. For those of you still reading, your tenacity is proven. That's all these practices require. Best of luck with your important work.

Glossary

advancement Social sector term for integrated organizational growth strategy encompassing fundraising, marketing, communications, and relationship management.

affinity Evidence of a prospect's genuine interest in the organization's mission.

backbone organization In a collective impact strategy, a coordinating body, typically a nonprofit, that aligns stakeholder resources and contributions and then oversees, monitors, and reports on execution.

balanced scorecard A performance management tool that presents a concise picture of the most important internal and external performance measures to enable the board and staff to analyze and improve progress toward goals.

BHAG Originated by Jim Collins, a *big hairy audacious goal* is a bold statement of a desired outcome used to engage and focus stakeholders and teams.

cadence of accountability One of the four disciplines of execution; a periodic, regular cycle of review and analysis in which teams consider leading and lagging metrics and discuss how to improve performance.

campaign counsel Social sector term for a specialized nonprofit fundraising consultant who helps organizations conduct a one-time effort to generate funding for a specific project.

capacity The size of a prospect's potential philanthropic contribution; a social sector term for a measurement of an organization's size or service volume.

capacity building Social sector term for efforts to grow an organization's service quality and/or quantity.

case statements Social sector term for a sales brochure for a capital campaign.

change management A systematic approach to organizational transition that (1) develops a shared awareness of new desired goals, strategy, and execution and (2) consistently reinforces the new desired pattern of behavior over time until new activities and norms are embedded and the desired organizational state is achieved.

charitable gift   Legal term for a financial contribution to a nonprofit organization.

charitable investment   Proposed alternative term for *charitable gift* to surface the intention to demonstrate the social impact that the gift made possible—the investment is not a financial return, it is a social return, as in *social return on investment.*

charity   The traditional name for a nonprofit, one that is often associated with cultural norms such as martyrdom, humility, self-abnegation, and use of emotional appeals to solicit funding.

collective impact   A social impact strategy that aligns corporate, government, nonprofit, and philanthropic resources and stakeholders in a given community to set goals and strategies in which each stakeholder contributes and participates; execution is guided by a *backbone organization.*

collective impasse   The term used to describe collective impact efforts that fail because participants cannot agree on goals, strategy, KPIs, finance, and/or how to execute.

confront brutal reality   The process of measuring personal or organizational capability or environmental circumstances without wishful thinking or other cognitive bias; facing the truth of a situation without fear or deflection.

consultative sales   The exchange of a product or service for money, in which the seller's aim is to build trust and engage in open dialogue to determine whether what is being sold genuinely solves the buyer's problem or meets the buyer's true needs; may take months or years for larger transactions.

conversion rate   The percentage of a population that advances from one stage in a sales process to the next.

creative obfuscation   A rhetorical strategy to confuse the listener with complex or abstract concepts; a conversational ploy that disguises an unwillingness to cooperate.

dashboard   A short document that presents major organizational performance measures in a manner that allows for quick analysis, like glancing at the dashboard of a car. May be used interchangeably with the term *scorecard.*

disorganization   The natural state of most corporations regardless of tax status.

donor loyalty   The percentage of nonprofit financial supporters who give a second (and subsequent) gift after making an initial one; a chief measure of a nonprofit's ability to engage with its financial supporters.

donor stewardship   Social sector term for the process of communicating with financial supporters and demonstrating gratitude for support and accountability for results produced because of the support.

draft proposal   A technique to reduce the pressure on charitable investment prospects by offering them opportunity to review an initial version of a document that illustrates the forecasted social return on investment for a given level of financial contribution. Provides an opportunity to surface and resolve objections and break what may be a large decision into smaller, easier to manage pieces. Typically contains a cover letter, explanation of proposed social impact, budget, and a copy of the organization's business plan.

due diligence   A series of investigative and research activities and inquiries conducted by a buyer or investor before making a purchase or investment, all in an effort to confirm the veracity of the seller's statements and discover any hidden risks or liabilities; also a legal term.

embrace the no   In a consultative sales process, recognizing that what is being sold will not meet a genuine need for every buyer, and therefore it is in the best interest of both parties to discover and confirm a lack of fit between buyer and seller rather than try to force the sale or delay an inevitable decline of the offer.

features comparison   A table or matrix that succinctly presents the similarities and/or differences between a product or service and comparable organizations in a given marketplace.

firing bullets before cannonballs   A term from *Good to Great*, which denotes a risk management strategy whereby leaders first confirm the success or viability of a new initiative at small scale before investing significant organizational resources in it.

first who, then what   Another *Good to Great* concept that describes how most successful leaders of companies first prioritize building highly talented teams before thinking about strategy or execution.

get the right people on the bus   Yet another *Good to Great* concept that means making sure the right people are in the right places in an organization before commencing organizational activity.

goldilocks   The sweet spot: not too long, not too short; the right level of detail of analysis; the appropriate level of frequency for cadence of accountability meetings (varies by level of information).

growth mindset   A personal attitude of optimism, abundance, and possibility that welcomes change and growth necessary and positive.

impact capital   Risk or rate-adjusted debt provided to nonprofits and social enterprises to provide them access to capital that the commercial markets will not otherwise provide.

investment & partnership scorecard   A dashboard that provides performance indicators for nonprofit fundraising teams/

investment and partnership   An alternative to typical nonprofit terms for fundraising such as *development* or *advancement*. Embodies and surfaces the ideals of transparency, accountability, and collaboration to create a peer dynamic with prospects instead of a subsidiary relationship that comes with "asking for gifts." Also establishes a fresh approach with investment prospects who may be concerned that they might be harassed or manipulated in making a gift.

jazz hands   The use of colorful words and/or gesticulation to distract a listener with form over substance; the substitution of empty words and phrases for substantive facts and clear accounting of activity or results.

key performance indicator (KPI)   *A* quantitative measure used to evaluate the execution of a strategy over time. If carefully selected, organizations can track their overall progress with a small number of KPIs. KPIs enable all organizational participants, partners, stakeholders and observers to quickly and accurately understand organizational value and progress toward a goal.

lagging indicator   A quantitative measure of the desired results of a strategy.

leading indicator   A quantitative measure of current activities that lead to a desired outcome. If selected well, a lead indicator is the cause of the related lag indicator.

logic model   A social sector method of visualizing strategy, resources, and intended outcomes. A less standardized often idiosyncratic method of planning that is largely unfamiliar to those outside the social sector.

low dose, high frequency   A change management strategy borrowed from health care that replaces long, infrequent meetings or exercises with short, continuous ones that are maintained until they are no longer necessary.

major investor   An individual, corporation, foundation, or agency that has made a large financial contribution, typically at least six figures in size, to a nonprofit; replaces the social sector term *major donor* in an attempt to reset language associated with practices that have eroded trust.

make insiders out of outsiders   The fundraising strategy articulated by the former vice president for advancement at the University of Washington, Connie Kravas, in which prospects are given information typically reserved for staff and board members; the process of acting with full transparency and accountability with stakeholders to build trust and strong, mutually supportive relationships.

marry the goal, date the strategies   The organization remains committed to the goal but flexible on how it achieves the goal, using performance management systems to provide data that evolves the strategy; ensures an adaptive, entrepreneurial mindset necessary for solving hard problems.

mission statement   What an organization does to solve a social problem.

myth of uniqueness, the   The illusion that because nonprofits operate under different rules related to taxation and ownership, they are mysterious and unique organizations unknowable to outsiders; statements that present subjective aspects of nonprofit culture as if they were objective facts or even matters of law; rhetorical devices used as smokescreens to maintain power and control and avoid transparency or accountability.

neurobalanced   The characteristic of management teams with a balance of all four thinking styles according to Ichak Adizes: producer, administrator, entrepreneur, and integrator. Teams with too much or too little of any of these four qualities will become dysfunctional.

nonprofit   A corporation whose purpose is to direct profits to achieve a solution to social and environmental problems.

orbital referral   A rhetorical strategy intended to confuse or distract the audience with philosophical, technical, or other complex inquiries.

overhead myth   The cultural assumption that all nonprofit costs other than direct program services are wasteful and should be minimized.

parsimony   Nominal meaning is an extreme unwillingness to spend money; repurposed here for a management technique that seeks to strip away all information except what is vitally important; a linguistic and documentation strategy to promote focus and clarity; the opposite of *creative obfuscation.*

pitch deck   A 10- to 15-slide presentation that presents the major elements of a business plan in as few words as possible.

planned gifts   Contributions of cash, stocks, or other assets to a nonprofit that are legally structured to provide tax advantages or additional advantages, benefits, or choices to the donor; examples include wills, trusts, pooled income funds, and annuities; planned gifts usually enable larger contributions because of their structure; they typically involve specialized counsel and require legal documentation.

planning framework   A one-page summary of a nonprofit's mission, vision, goals, value proposition, growth and impact strategy, first year initiatives, and KPIs. A preliminary version of a business plan meant to build and deliver consensus among and between board and staff.

power players   People with various character flaws who disrupt teamwork; if allowed to remain in positions of influence, power players may damage a nonprofit's ability to grow and deliver impact.

productive paranoia   From *Great by Choice,* a quality that describes effective leaders who never stop scanning for risks to organizational performance.

program-related investments   A loan to a nonprofit organization; may often be convertible to a grant if the project does not succeed; a form of *impact capital.*

proof points   Concise evidence that a nonprofit can produce significant positive social returns for dollars it receives.

psycholinguistic framework The full set of associations, connotations, and cultural and social connections produced by careful word choice.

qualified Concrete evidence that an investor prospect has both *affinity* for a nonprofit mission and financial *capacity* to make the targeted contribution.

reporting An alternative term for *stewardship* in which the non profit provides clear accounting of the social return on investment to a charitable investor.

social impact enterprise (SIE) A nonprofit social enterprise or other impact-focused organization that uses robust organizational methodology to scale the delivery of products or services to solve a social challenge.

social return on investment (SROI) The proof of a nonprofit's success: (1) exactly who or what they change; (2) what the changes actually are; (3) proof that the changes are actually happening; (4) measures of other major influences; and (5) percentage of the problem they are solving.

strategy The integrated set of choices and behaviors an organization makes to achieve a desired outcome; the deliberate design of presenting a product or service in a manner that optimizes efficiency and effectiveness.

tactic Parts of a strategy; individual steps and actions that, linked together, constitute the whole strategy; specific measurable actions.

theory of change Somewhat similar to *logic model*, an approach that uses charts and visualizations to illustrate social impact. There is very little standardization with this approach, and presentations are often abstract and confusing to outside readers.

three levels of information Categories of organizational decision-making and analysis granularity: (1) organization-wide elements such as goals, strategy, KPIs, and finance; (2) unit-level measures such as fundraising or program-level strategy, operations, technology, and HR; and (3) front-line staff activity, the measures and processes at the most detailed level of activity. Enables group clarity and focus on what is being discussed; also lays the foundation for who does what and why.

value proposition   A concrete, concise, compelling argument for supporting the organization.

venture philanthropy   Philanthropic funders who apply the principles of venture capital to nonprofit growth and impact: large amounts of financial support; participatory engagement at the board and/or executive level; access to an ecosystem of mentors, resources, and networks of influence to enhance and promote growth and impact.

vision statement   What the world looks like when the nonprofit has achieved ultimate victory using clear, concrete, and specific terms.

X to Y by Z   The formula for a robust goal or BHAG that concisely describes exactly what will change by when.

zone of insolvency   A risk flag for board members and executive teams activated when organizations approach the state of bankruptcy; the zone begins when there are fewer than six months of expenses in cash reserves and becomes more urgent and immediate when there are fewer than three months of cash on hand.

About the Author

Donald Summers, founder and CEO of Altruist Partners and founder and CEO of the Altruist Nonprofit Accelerator, holds more than 25 years of experience as a teacher, nonprofit executive, foundation CEO, management consultant, and social entrepreneur. He has directed over 100 nonprofit and social enterprise accelerations from the regional to the global level in the fields of education, human services, health, environmental conservation, sustainability, and public media. Results include nearly $1 billion in new earned and contributed revenue and dramatic gains in organizational performance and program impact directly improving the lives of millions around the world.

In 2006, Summers founded Altruist Partners LLC, a social impact advisory boutique, to help nonprofits and social enterprises solve their biggest strategic, fundraising, and organizational challenges to amplify their growth and impact. Working as player-coaches with clients, the Altruist team resolves growth and performance barriers, develops and executes investment-grade business plans, dramatically increases contributed and earned revenue, and delivers hockey-stick increases in social impact by helping boards and teams execute with focus and discipline.

In 2021, Summers founded a parallel nonprofit arm, the Altruist Nonprofit Accelerator, the world's first social impact accelerator open to global nonprofits in any field of impact. Still in its infancy, the Accelerator is now working with its first cohort of NGOs from Asia, Africa, and South America. It aims to provide unlimited, worldwide access to effective nonprofit growth and impact acceleration practices.

He is a frequent speaker, lecturer, and author, and his articles and research have appeared in the *Academy of Arts and Sciences*, the *Stanford Social Innovation Review*, and the *Chronicle of Higher Education*. He holds an undergraduate degree in English from Middlebury College and a master's degree in education, planning, and social policy from Harvard University.

Index